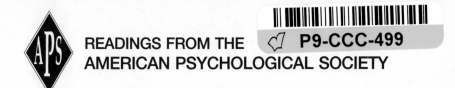

READINGS FROM THE
AMERICAN PSYCHOLOGICAL SOCIETY

P9-CCC-499

Current Directions in

HEALTH PSYCHOLOGY

EDITED BY

Gregory Miller
University of British Columbia

Edith Chen
University of British Columbia

PEARSON

Prentice
Hall

Upper Saddle River, New Jersey 07458

© 2005 by PEARSON EDUCATION, INC.
Upper Saddle River, New Jersey 07458

Current Directions © American Psychological Society
1010 Vermont Avenue, NW
Suite 1100
Washington, D.C. 20005-4907

10 9 8 7 6 5 4 3 2 1

ISBN 0-13-155112-4

Printed in the United States of America

Contents

Readings from
Current Directions in Psychological Science

Psychosocial and Environmental Antecedents of Disease

Health psychology deals with the interconnections between psychology and medicine. A major goal of this field is to understand the extent to which psychosocial and environmental factors contribute to the development and progression of medical conditions. These conditions can range from acute physical symptoms, such as headaches and constipation, to chronic illnesses such as cancer and heart disease, to predicting the length of time a person lives.

This section provides an overview of the psychosocial and environmental characteristics that have been shown to contribute to the onset and course of medical illnesses. Note that these characteristics range across many levels of organization. They can be states or traits of an individual such as stress; features of the social environment such as family structure or work climate; and larger societal-level factors such as income distribution. At the individual level, Cohen demonstrates through a novel and unique research design that both the stressors in an individual's life, as well as the perception of stress, influence one's likelihood of developing the common cold. His research studies involve actually exposing participants to a cold virus and then keeping them in quarantine for several days. This rigorous experimental methodology allows Cohen to be certain that everyone is exposed to the same dose of a virus, and thus an alternative explanation that people who have higher stress are more likely to get exposed to viruses cannot account for his findings.

The Schulz et al. article reveals that individuals who experience a negative emotional state—depression—are prone to higher rates of mortality, particularly from diseases of the heart. While a person who develops heart disease is likely to become somewhat depressed, Schulz et al.'s work shows that these feelings can also worsen the disease, and increase the risk of dying prematurely or having another heart attack. Much of the research in health psychology has focused on the role of negative psychological traits, such as depression and hostility, in health. However, it is also important to study positive psychological states that may help buffer us from detrimental health outcomes. Toward this end, Martin reviews the evidence for humor and laughter as protective factors. Martin describes four potential mechanisms to better health—that laughter may change physiological states, that humor/laughter may change emotional states, that humor/laughter may help make stressful times less stressful, and that humor/laughter may increase one's level of social support. The evidence for laughter as a pathway to health is not as strong as for negative psychological traits; however, this is a recent and emerging field, and more research will soon help to clarify its effects.

1

Next we move from the level of the individual to a broader perspective on the social factors in an individual's life. One important source of social contact is family members. Vitaliano et al.'s article describes what happens when an individual is placed in the role of caring for a family member with a chronic and debilitating illness. What happens in these circumstances? Researchers such as Vitaliano show that caregivers have changes in stress-sensitive biological systems, are more prone to illness and death, and need to take more medications. Outside of family members, the work environment is another major source of social connection for adults. Spector describes how job stress is associated with more illness symptoms and higher blood pressure. He also emphasizes the importance of perceived control at work, and builds the case for a novel theory of workplace conditions. It holds that high levels of demand can be toxic, but only when a person lacks control over his/her decisions and activities.

Finally, we move to the broadest level—societal factors that influence health. These factors include how people of different ethnic backgrounds are treated by others in society, as well as how the socioeconomic status that a person has within society affects health. Contrada et al. describe the processes by which discrimination occurs, including the perception of often ambiguous and subtle cues in the environment, as well as various ways in which people cope with discrimination. Contrada et al. also describe other types of ethnicity-related stressors, such as being concerned with confirming negative stereotypes about one's ethnic group as well as pressure from one's own ethnic group to behave in certain ways. Contrada presents evidence that these types of ethnicity-related stressors are related to health and well-being. Lastly, Chen presents evidence that individuals lower in socioeconomic status (SES) have poorer health across a variety of conditions. Interestingly, these effects are not just due to poverty, since each increase in SES is associated with better health across the whole SES spectrum. Moreover, these effects are robust across numerous diseases in both childhood and adulthood.

Together, these articles provide a glimpse of the evidence linking psychosocial and environmental characteristics to the development and progression of medical illness. They show that this "mind-body" connection arises from multiple sources, ranging from characteristics of an individual, to the structure of work and family life, to broader demographic and socioeconomic factors in society.

Psychological Stress, Immunity, and Upper Respiratory Infections

Sheldon Cohen[1]
Department of Psychology, Carnegie Mellon University, Pittsburgh, Pennsylvania

The belief that when we are under stress we are more susceptible to the common cold, influenza, and other infectious diseases is widely accepted in our culture. It is the topic of numerous contemporary newspaper and magazine articles and has even been addressed in the lyrics of a popular song ("Adelaide's Lament" from *Guys and Dolls*). The wide acceptance of this belief is also supported by data collected from participants in my studies. Sixty percent report that they are more likely to catch a cold during stressful than nonstressful periods of their lives. In this article, I review the scientific evidence that addresses this belief. How could psychological stress influence susceptibility to infectious disease? Is such a relation biologically and psychologically plausible? Is there convincing evidence that psychological stress influences susceptibility to upper respiratory infections?

HOW COULD STRESS INFLUENCE SUSCEPTIBILITY TO INFECTIOUS DISEASE?

Although constantly exposed to bacteria, viruses, fungi, and parasites that can cause infectious disease, we only periodically develop infectious illnesses. This is because our immune system protects us from infectious microorganisms. This defensive function is performed by the white blood cells and a number of accessory cells, which are distributed throughout the organs of the body. Stress is thought to influence susceptibility to infectious disease by compromising the effectiveness of the immune system. Persons with suppressed immune function are less able to fight off infectious agents and hence, given exposure to an agent, more likely to develop an infectious disease.

A simplified view of how stressful events in our lives might alter immunity is presented in Figure 1. When our demands are perceived to exceed our ability to cope, we label ourselves as stressed and experience a negative emotional response (Lazarus & Folkman, 1984). In turn, negative emotional responses could alter immune function through three different pathways (Rabin, Cohen, Ganguli, Lyle, & Cunnick, 1989). Nerve fibers connecting the central nervous system and immune tissue provide one path by which emotional responses may influence immunity. These nerves terminate in immune tissue, where they release chemicals that are thought to suppress the function of immune cells. Stress-induced emotions may also act through their influence on the central nervous system's production and release of hormones such as epinephrine and cortisol. These hormones circulate in the blood and can attach to receptors on immune cells, resulting in the cells' protective functions "turning off." The third mechanism by which stress may affect health derives from the role of behavioral patterns that

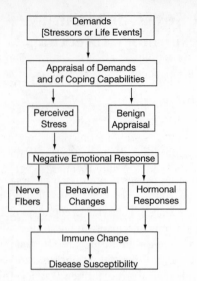

Fig. 1. Pathways through which stressful life events might influence the onset and progression of infectious disease. For simplicity, arrows are drawn in only one direction, from psychological characteristics to disease. This convention does not imply any assumptions about the existence of alternative paths.

reflect attempts to cope with negative emotional responses. For example, persons experiencing psychological stress often engage in unhealthy practices such as smoking and not eating or sleeping properly, and such behavioral changes may suppress the activity of the immune system. They may affect immune responses directly or may influence immune function by altering hormonal responses.

DOES STRESS INFLUENCE IMMUNE FUNCTION?

As just discussed, the key link between psychological stress and susceptibility to infectious agents is thought to be the immune system. There is substantial evidence supporting the role of stress in the regulation of the human immune system. Suppression of immune function has been found among persons taking important examinations (e.g., Kiecolt-Glaser et al., 1984); caring for relatives with chronic diseases (Kiecolt-Glaser, Glaser, et al., 1987); living near the site of a serious nuclear-powerplant accident (McKinnon, Weisse, Reynolds, Bowles, & Baum, 1989); suffering marital conflict (Kiecolt-Glaser, Fisher, et al., 1987); and reporting relatively high levels of unpleasant daily events (Stone et al., 1994), negative moods (Stone, Cox, Valdimarsdottir, Jandorf, & Neale, 1987), or perceived stress (e.g., Jabaaji et al., 1993). Suppression of immune function (called *immunosuppression*) has also been found in response to acute laboratory stressors, including working on challenging cognitive tasks, such as mental arithmetic, and delivering public speeches (e.g., Manuck, Cohen, Rabin, Muldoon, & Bachen, 1991). Clinical depression has also been associated with decreased immune response (Herbert & Cohen, 1993).

DOES STRESS INFLUENCE SUSCEPTIBILITY TO UPPER RESPIRATORY INFECTIONS?

Do studies that demonstrate induced immunosuppression under stressful conditions provide compelling evidence for stress-induced susceptibility to infectious disease? In general, these data are thought to be consistent with, but not definitively supportive of, the hypothesis that stress results in increased susceptibility to disease. The immune response involves a complex cascading series of events. Because studies of stress and immunity are limited to assessing very few markers of immune function in a limited time span, they can provide only a very rough estimate of the body's ability to mount such a defense (Cohen & Williamson, 1991).

Naturalistic Studies of Stress and Upper Respiratory Infection

A more direct approach to addressing the role of psychological stress in susceptibility to infection is examining the correlation between stress and infectious disease in natural settings. Because upper respiratory infections are by far the most prevalent of infectious diseases, the common cold and influenza have been adopted as the primary models for studying how stress might influence susceptibility. A large group of studies has found correlations between psychological stress and self-reported colds and influenza (reviewed in Cohen & Williamson, 1991). This work, however, is generally difficult to interpret. In many cases, third factors such as social class, age, or ethnic background might be responsible directly for increases in both stress and disease. Moreover, because this work is primarily retrospective, being ill may have caused stress rather than vice versa. Another problem is that unverified self-reports of illness are difficult to interpret. Although they may indicate underlying disease pathology, they may also reflect stress-induced biases to view ambiguous physical sensations as symptoms, and to interpret symptoms as indicating the onset of disease (e.g., Cohen et al., 1995).

There are a few investigations that have associated psychological stress and biologically verified (as opposed to self-reported) upper respiratory disease (e.g., Graham, Douglas, & Ryan, 1986; Meyer & Haggerty, 1962). Verification was accomplished by establishing the presence of a responsible bacterium or virus in nasal secretion or of an elevated level of antibody to the infectious agent in blood (serum).[2] In these studies, measures of psychological stress were administered to healthy subjects who were subsequently monitored for up to 12 months for the development of upper respiratory infections. For those reporting infections, nasal secretions or blood samples were used to biologically verify the disease. These studies have found links between psychological stress and the subsequent development of colds and influenza. These results, however, may be attributable to stress-induced increases in exposure to infectious agents, rather than stress-induced immunosuppression. For example, persons under stress often seek out other people, consequently increasing the probability of exposure. The studies also fail to provide evidence about behavioral and biological mechanisms through which stress might influence a person's susceptibility to infection.

Viral-Challenge Studies

In my own work, I have adopted a procedure in which after completing stress questionnaires, volunteers are intentionally exposed to a common cold virus (in nasal drops) and then quarantined and monitored for 5 or more days for the development of disease.[3] Approximately one third of the volunteers exposed to a virus develop a biologically verified clinical cold. The viral-challenge procedure has a number of advantages over naturalistic studies. By experimentally exposing persons to a virus and limiting their contact with other people, I eliminate the possibility that the results are attributable to stress increasing social contact and hence exposure to infectious agents. Moreover, because participants are closely monitored after exposure, it is easier to verify disease onset and to assess the roles of behavioral and biological pathways that might link stress to disease susceptibility. Finally, this methodology allows for a more refined assessment of the body's response to a virus. Specifically, after exposure to a virus, persons can become infected (i.e., their cells replicate the virus) without developing symptoms. In the viral-challenge trials, body fluids used to determine infection are drawn from subjects both with and without upper respiratory symptoms, allowing the identification of subclinical (i.e., with few if any symptoms) as well as clinical infections.

In an attempt to take advantage of the strengths of this methodology, my colleagues and I conducted a viral-challenge study addressing the role of stress in susceptibility to the common cold (Cohen, Tyrrell, & Smith, 1991, 1993). By using a prospective design in which psychological stress is assessed before participants are exposed to a virus, we were able to eliminate the possibility that illness causes stress as an interpretation of our results. Because the primary outcome in viral-challenge studies is categorical (sick or not), large sample sizes are required to maximize study sensitivity. Hence, we accumulated data from 420 healthy volunteers. Collection of these data required more than 40 separate 1-week trials conducted over 4 years. Our main hypothesis was that the higher the level of psychological stress, the higher the risk of developing the upper respiratory illness caused by the virus.

Each participant completed psychological stress questionnaires just prior to being exposed to one of five viruses known to cause common colds. A group of control participants received saline in nasal drops instead of a virus. After 7 days of quarantine, each participant was classified as not infected, infected but not ill, or infected and ill (clinical cold). As expected, none of the participants exposed to saline developed clinical colds, so this control group was not included in subsequent analyses.

The model in Figure 1 suggests that when demands imposed by events in someone's life exceed that person's ability to cope, he or she makes a stress appraisal (perceives stress), and in turn experiences a negative emotional response. In this work, we employed instruments to assess each phase of the stress response: a stressful-life-event scale to measure the cumulative event load, a perceived-stress scale to assess perceptions of overload-induced stress, and a measure of negative emotional response. Figure 2 presents the relations we found between stress (high or low, split at the median response) as assessed by each measure and the probability of developing a clinical cold. For all three stress measures, participants reporting high stress were more likely than those report-

6

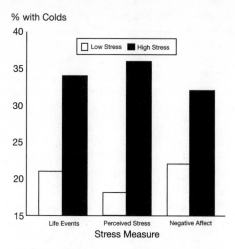

Fig. 2. Percentage of persons developing biologically verified clinical illness as a function of stressful life events, perceived stress, and negative affect. Each participant was exposed to one of five upper respiratory viruses. For each measure, scores were categorized as indicating high or low stress according to whether they were above or below the median score. Adapted from Cohen, Tyrrell, and Smith (1993), with permission of the American Psychological Association.

ing low stress to develop a viral disease. These relations were found consistently for all five viruses. Moreover, these results could not be explained by stress-elicited differences in health practices, including smoking, alcohol consumption, exercise, eating, or sleeping habits. They also could not be explained by stress-induced changes in a series of relatively basic measures of immune status—the numbers of various white blood cell populations or total (nonspecific) antibody levels.[4] A large group of plausible alternative factors that might be correlated with both stress and disease (e.g., age, sex, education, and personality characteristics such as self-esteem and personal control) were also unable to account for the relation between stress and susceptibility. In sum, the results provided strong support for a relation between psychological stress and susceptibility to developing a clinical cold, but did not provide confirming evidence for either a biological or a behavioral pathway responsible for the association.

This study also addressed the validity of the hypothesis that stressful life events influence disease susceptibility by eliciting perceptions of stress and consequent negative emotional responses. However, the data did not totally support this perspective. First, the relation between stressful life events and risk of developing a cold was independent of the relations between perceived stress and colds and between negative affect and colds. That is, more stressful events were associated with greater susceptibility to disease irrespective of whether those events elicited perceptions of stress and negative affect. Second, the association of life events with illness was attributable to different biological processes than the associations of perceived stress and negative affect with illness. Increased risk for developing clinical colds could occur because stress increases the probability of the infectious agent replicating (infection), or because stress increases

7

the production of histamines, bradykinins, or other chemicals that trigger symptoms after infection. In this study, becoming biologically infected was associated with high levels of perceived stress and negative affect, but developing clinical symptoms after infection was associated with high numbers of stressful life events. The fact that these scales have independent relations with clinical illness and that these relations are mediated by different biological processes challenges the assumption that perceptions of stress and negative affect are necessary for stressful life events to influence disease risk. A subsequent viral-challenge study conducted in another laboratory also found that life events and increased susceptibility had a relation independent of perceived stress and negative affect (Stone et al., 1993). As in our data, higher numbers of stressful events were associated with increased symptoms after infection.

A plausible explanation for the direct association between stressful life events and susceptibility is that the effort of coping with events, whether or not successful, results in hormonal responses that modulate immunity (Cohen, Evans, Stokols, & Krantz, 1986). In short, self-perceived negative emotional response may not be the only psychological pathway able to trigger hormonal responses critical to influencing immune function and disease susceptibility.

In sum, there is substantial evidence that both stressful life events and psychological stress (perceptions and negative affect) influence susceptibility to upper respiratory infections. These effects are not a consequence of unhealthy behaviors elicited by stress. We also lack direct evidence that increased susceptibility is attributable to stress-induced immunosuppression. The immune system, however, is terribly complex, and the measures used in human studies may not adequately assess the components most relevant to resisting upper respiratory infections. Finally, contrary to accepted stress and coping theory, the relation between stressful events and susceptibility to infectious disease does not depend on elevated perceptions of stress and negative emotional response.

CONCLUSIONS

The literature linking stress, immunity, and upper respiratory infection is in many ways impressive. First, it provides psychologically and biologically plausible hypotheses for how psychological factors might influence immunity and infectious disease. Second, it provides substantial evidence that psychological factors can influence indicators of immune status and function. Third, it includes consistent and convincing evidence of links between stress and the onset of upper respiratory infections. Where it fails is in identifying the behavioral, hormonal, or immune system pathways that are responsible for the link between stress and disease susceptibility. Only by identifying these pathways will researchers be able to evaluate the extent to which work with upper respiratory viruses provides a generic model that will allow generalization to other infectious agents.

Acknowledgments—Preparation of this article was supported by a Research Scientist Development Award (K02MH00721) and by a grant (MH50429) from the National Institute of Mental Health. I am indebted to Mario Rodriguez and Roberta Klatzky for their helpful comments on an earlier draft.

Notes

1. Address correspondence to Sheldon Cohen, Department of Psychology, Carnegie Mellon University, Pittsburgh, PA 15213.

2. Antibodies are protein molecules that attach themselves to invading microorganisms and mark them for destruction or prevent them from infecting cells. Each antibody recognizes only a single type of microorganism.

3. The diseases caused by these viruses are quite mild common colds. All study participants gave informed consent after receiving both oral and written descriptions of the diseases as well as all possible risks. Participants were examined at the end of the trial, and treatment was available for any complications.

4. A measure of total (nonspecific) antibody assesses the amount of antibody in circulation, but does not provide any information about the amount of antibody that is specific to, and therefore will fight off, a particular virus.

References

Cohen, S., Doyle, W.J., Skoner, D.P., Fireman, P., Gwaltney, J., & Newsom, J. (1995). State and trait negative affect as predictors of objective and subjective symptoms of respiratory viral infections. *Journal of Psychology*, 68, 159–169.

Cohen, S., Evans, G.W., Stokols, D., & Krantz, D.S. (1986). *Behavior, health and environmental stress.* New York: Plenum Press.

Cohen, S., Tyrrell, D.A.J., & Smith, A.P. (1991). Psychological stress and susceptibility to the common cold. *New England Journal of Medicine*, 325, 606–612.

Cohen, S., Tyrrell, D.A.J., & Smith, A.P. (1993). Life events, perceived stress, negative affect and susceptibility to the common cold. *Journal of Personality and Social Psychology*, 64, 131–140.

Cohen, S., & Williamson, G.M. (1991). Stress and infectious disease in humans. *Psychological Bulletin*, 109, 5–24.

Graham, N.M.H., Douglas. R.B., & Ryan, P. (1986). Stress and acute respiratory infection. *American Journal of Epidemiology*, 124, 389–401.

Herbert, T.B., & Cohen, S. (1993). Depression and immunity: A meta-analytic review. *Psychological Bulletin*, 113, 472–486.

Jabaaji, L., Grosheide, P.M., Heiftink, R.A., Duivenvoorden, H.J., Ballieux, R.E., & Vingergoets, A.J.J.M. (1993). Influence of perceived psychological stress and distress on antibody response to low dose rDNA hepatitis B vaccine. *Journal of Psychosomatic Research*, 37, 361–369.

Kiecolt-Glaser, J.K., Fisher, L.D., Ogrocki, P., Stout, J.C., Speicher, C.E., & Glaser, R. (1987). Marital quality, marital disruption, and immune function. *Psychosomatic Medicine*, 49, 13–34.

Kiecolt-Glaser, J.K., Garner, W., Speicher, C.E., Penn, G.M., Holliday, J., & Glaser, R. (1984). Psychosocial modifiers of immunocompetence in medical students. *Psychosomatic Medicine*, 46, 7–14.

Kiecolt-Glaser, J.K., Glaser, R., Shuttleworth, E.C., Dyer, C.S., Ogrocki, P., & Speicher, E. (1987). Chronic stress and immunity in family caregivers of Alzheimer's disease victims. *Psychosomatic Medicine*, 49, 523–535.

Lazarus, R.S., & Folkman, S. (1984). *Stress appraisal and coping.* New York: Springer.

Manuck, S.B., Cohen, S., Rabin, B.S., Muldoon, M., & Bachen, E. (1991). Individual differences in cellular response to stress. *Psychological Science*, 2, 111–115.

McKinnon, W., Weisse, C.S., Reynolds, C.P., Bowles, C.A. & Baum, A. (1989). Chronic stress, leukocyte subpopulations, and humoral response to latent viruses. *Health Psychology*, 8, 389–902.

Meyer, R.J., & Haggerty, R.J. (1962). Streptococcal infections in families. *Pediatrics*, 29, 539–549.

Rabin, B.S., Cohen, S., Ganguli, R., Lyle, D.T., & Cunnick, J.E. (1989). Bidirectional interaction between the central nervous system and immune system. *CRC Critical Reviews in Immunology*, 9, 279–312.

Stone, A.A., Bovbjerg, D.H., Neale, J.M., Napoli, A., Valdimarsdottir, H., Cox, D., Hayden, F.G., & Gwaltney, J.M. (1993). Development of common cold symptoms following experimental rhinovirus infection is related to prior stressful life events. *Behavioral Medicine*, 8, 115–120.

Stone, A.A., Cox, D.S., Valdimarsdottir, H., Jandorf, L., & Neale, J.M. (1987). Evidence that secretory IgA antibody is associated with daily mood. *Journal of Personality and Social Psychology, 52*, 988–993.

Stone, A.A., Neale, J.M., Cox, D.S., Napoli, A., Valdimarsdottir, H., & Kennedy-Moore, E. (1994). Daily events are associated with a secretory immune response to an oral antigen in men. *Health Psychology, 13*, 440–446.

Recommended Reading

Cohen, S., & Herbert, T.B. (1996). Psychological factors and physical disease from the perspective of human psychoneuroimmunology. *Annual Review of Psychology, 47*, 113–142.

Glaser, R., & Kiecolt-Glaser, J. (Eds.). (1994). *Handbook of human stress and immunity.* New York. Academic Press.

Depression and Mortality in the Elderly

Richard Schulz,[1] Lynne M. Martire, Scott R. Beach,
and Michael F. Scheier
*Department of Psychiatry (R.S., L.M.M.) and University Center for
Social and Urban Research (R.S., L.M.M., S.R.B.), University of
Pittsburgh, Pittsburgh, Pennsylvania, and Department of Psychology,
Carnegie Mellon University, Pittsburgh, Pennsylvania (M.F.S.)*

Abstract

It is well known that depression can be a consequence of medical illness and disability, but a growing literature suggests also that depression can cause biological changes linked to morbidity and mortality. Depression is strongly implicated as a contributor to cardiovascular disease and mortality. Using the cascade-to-death model as a conceptual framework, we explore the complex relations among behavior, affect, motivation, and pathophysiology that might account for the association between depression and premature death. Our model suggests that some individuals become entrapped in a downward spiral in which behavior, medical illness, and depressive affect feed on each other to undermine the biological integrity of the organism. In addition to specifying behavioral and biological mechanisms linking depression to mortality, future research needs to more closely examine phenomenological aspects of depression in order to determine what aspects of depression and related constructs such as hopelessness, vital exhaustion, and motivational depletion account for the link between depression and mortality.

Keywords

depression; death; elderly; motivation; hopelessness

Scientists have long been interested in the underlying causes of death, and in the past two centuries have identified a wide array of behavioral and biological factors linked to mortality. For example, scientists now have a good understanding of how a behavior such as smoking undermines the functioning of multiple physiological systems, which in turn leads to disease and, ultimately, death. Much less is known about psychological processes such as depression and hopelessness and their role in causing death, although it is widely believed that they are important contributing factors to mortality. The role of depression in mortality is clearly illustrated in the act of a depressed person who commits suicide; however, this role is less apparent when the primary cause of death is a medical illness. It is suspected that depression may cause or exacerbate medical illness, or interact with other biological vulnerabilities brought about by medical illness.

This article explores the relation between depression and mortality in the elderly. We focus on the elderly because both disease and death are highly prevalent in late life, and symptoms characteristic of depression, although not necessarily clinical depression, are relatively common among individuals of advanced age. Thus, from a scientific perspective, the convergence of depression, illness, and mortality in the elderly provides an ideal platform for studying the relation among these variables.

11

IS DEPRESSION RELATED TO MORTALITY?

Before answering this question, it is useful to describe how investigators test hypotheses concerning the relation between depression and mortality. A frequently used approach in large population studies is to identify a group of individuals, assess their levels of depression, and identify those who die within a fixed follow-up period. The depression-mortality hypothesis predicts that people who are more depressed are more likely to die or will die sooner than individuals who are less depressed. Of course, this simple test of the depression-mortality link is open to a major criticism: People who are ill are more likely both to be depressed (Dew, 1998) and to die, something that has been known for a long time. To address this methodological problem, researchers have typically controlled for the known associates of mortality, including demographic factors (e.g., gender, age), behavioral risk factors (e.g., smoking), biological risk factors (e.g., being overweight), and subclinical and prevalent disease. (Subclinical disease is a condition in which a disease is detected by special tests but does not reveal itself by overt symptoms, e.g., blockage of the coronary artery indicating atherosclerosis but without the presence of chest pain or shortness of breath. Prevalent disease refers to conditions, such as cancer or heart disease, with overt symptoms.)

To the extent that depression is associated with mortality after known causes of death are controlled for, one might conclude that depression is a unique contributor to mortality. For example, in a recent study of 5,201 persons aged 65 and older (Schulz et al., 2000), we showed that those who had high levels of depressive symptoms were 25% more likely to die within 6 years than those who had low levels of depressive symptoms, after we controlled for a large number of sociodemographic, disease, and biological and behavioral risk factors. Even larger effects of depression on mortality have been found in studies examining the relation between depression and cardiovascular disease and mortality. Depression is a risk factor for the onset of ischemic heart disease (i.e., significant blockage of blood flow to the heart) among individuals initially free of disease. In addition, individuals who already have heart disease and are depressed are more likely to die than individuals who have heart disease and are not depressed (Glassman & Shapiro, 1998). Attempts to link depression and other causes of mortality such as cancer have yielded less consistent results, and, more generally, the literature includes numerous studies that have failed to find an association between depression and mortality (Wulsin, Vaillant, & Wells, 1999).

Whether or not a study finds that depression has an effect on mortality depends on a number of factors, including the choice of control variables, the manner in which they are measured, the completeness of follow-up, and whether the sample size is large enough to detect statistically significant differences given the mortality rate in the population studied. In general, the chances of finding that depression is associated with mortality diminish to the extent that studies have small samples with relatively few deaths or include large numbers of control variables, particularly if the control variables include other subjective self-assessments that conceptually overlap with depression. Our own work and recent reviews of this literature suggest that depression substantially increases the risk of death (Glassman & Shapiro, 1998; Musselman, Evans, & Nemeroff, 1998; Wulsin et al., 1999). This effect has been observed in diverse populations, including patients needing psychiatric care, patients in long-term-care facilities, persons who have diverse medical illnesses and are in acute-care hospitals, post–heart attack and cancer patients, and persons who reside in the community and are not medically ill.

HOW DOES DEPRESSION INCREASE THE RISK OF MORTALITY?

Whether or not one agrees with the proposition that depression affects mortality depends to some extent on the plausibility of specific mechanisms that might account for this relation. To address this issue, investigators have searched for linkages between depression and known behavioral and pathophysiological causes of death.

Figure 1 illustrates our cascade model of mortality and shows how four major categories of health-related variables might cause an individual to die. Although variables within each category can directly cause death, less proximal causes (i.e., causes that are typically farther removed from death) such as behavioral risk factors are thought to have their impact on mortality primarily through more proximal downstream causes (i.e., more immediate causes of death) such as biological risk factors, subclinical disease, and, finally, prevalent disease. For example, depression can lead to inactivity, increased alcohol consumption, eating and sleeping problems, and lack of adherence to treatment for medical problems. Each of these factors may directly or indirectly, through other factors downstream, lead to mortality. Similarly, depression has been linked to activation of the hypothalamic-pituitary-adrenal (HPA) axis and compromised immune function, which in turn may predispose individuals to infectious disease, cancer, or the exacerbation of existing medical illness. (The HPA axis is involved in the body's stress response. Neurons within the hypothalamus send a signal to the pituitary gland, which in turn secretes a hormone that causes the adrenal glands to secrete the stress hormone cortisol into the bloodstream.)

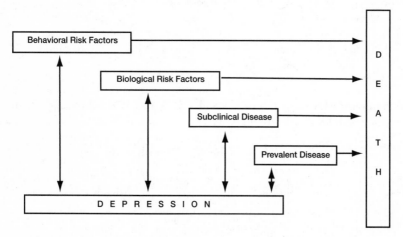

Fig. 1. Depression and the cascade to death.

One of the most robust findings in the literature is the relation between depression and cardiovascular disease and mortality, suggesting that the path physiologies of heart disease and depression are closely intertwined. Compared with no depressed persons, depressed individuals have been found to have both functional and structural changes in the brain that may result in pathophysiological changes such as reduced heart rate variability or ventricular arrhythmias, which are known to be risk factors for cardiovascular disease and mortality (Musselman et al., 1998). It is tempting to conclude that depression can cause cardiovascular disease and mortality, but it is also possible that another factor, perhaps genetic, causes both depression and cardiovascular disease (Lesperance & Frasure-Smith, 1999).

Although our discussion thus far implies a causal direction from depression to behavioral and health mediators to death, Figure 1 also suggests reciprocal causation between the mediators and depression. This is most apparent with subclinical and clinical disease (e.g., cardiovascular disease), which may affect brain chemistry to cause depression or result in depression because of the functional consequences of medical illness (e.g., disability). Thus, our model of depression and mortality is a complex interactive system involving affect, behavior, and physiology with multiple feedback loops. One can easily envision a downward spiral leading to death that is instigated and perpetuated by any one of the mechanisms involved in depression and mortality.

The search for mechanisms of the association between depression and mortality will likely yield both behavioral-affective and biological answers. In addition, researchers in this area have paid little attention to the underlying motivational states that are considered part of the depressive syndrome and may be directly linked to health-related behaviors. For example, analysis of scales used to assess depression in the elderly has shown that the link with mortality is strongest for items reflecting motivational depletion (e.g., "I could not get going," "Everything I did was an effort"; Schulz et al., 2000). It has also been suggested that states such as vital exhaustion, which is characterized by lack of energy, increased irritability, and feelings of demoralization, are key factors contributing to death (Kop, Appels, Mendes de leon, de Swart, & Bar, 1994), as are related constructs such as hopelessness or pessimism (Scheier & Carver, in press). Studying these motivational states and their behavioral, affective, and health-related consequences may help researchers better understand the link between depression and mortality.

WHAT CAN INTERVENTION STUDIES TELL US ABOUT DEPRESSION AND MORTALITY?

A number of studies comparing individuals given an antidepressant (nortriptyline or fluoxetine) or a placebo have shown greater improvement in physical functioning in the active-treatment group compared with the placebo group. Psychotherapy interventions for depression have also been shown to increase people's ratings of their own health. Conversely, successful treatment of many medical illnesses results in the reduction of depressive symptoms. These findings are consistent with those of descriptive studies, but add little new information to this puzzle. One of the limitations of most depression treatment studies is that they are typically not powered to detect changes in medical morbidity or mortality. One exception to this is the ongoing SADHART (Sertraline Antidepressant Heart Randomized Trial) study, a large, multicenter trial in which post–heart attack patients who also have major depression are randomly assigned to treatment groups that receive either the antidepressant sertraline or a placebo. Another study currently under way (Enhancing Recovery in Coronary Heart Disease, or ENRICHD) is comparing rates of heart attack and mortality among depressed post–heart attack patients who receive psychosocial treatment (e.g., counseling and group sessions) and those who receive standard medical care. These studies have the potential to provide important information about the effectiveness and safety of treating post–heart attack patients for depression, as well as about the mechanisms linking depression to cardiovascular disease and mortality.

FUTURE DIRECTIONS

Clearly, researchers are only just beginning to unravel the mystery of why depression might lead to mortality. To better understand the mechanisms that might link depression and mortality, one would want to simultaneously assess depression, behavioral and pathophysiological mediators, and their relation over time. An underlying assumption of the cascade-to-death model is that individuals can become entrapped in a downward spiral in which behavior, medical illness, and depressive affect feed on each other to undermine the biological integrity of the organism. An important clinical implication of this view is that the downward spiral can be broken through multiple treatment approaches. One could treat the depression, the behavioral problems, the medical illness and its functional consequences, or some combination of these factors. Achieving desired effects in any one of these domains will likely have a positive impact on the remaining factors as well. Because depression is often not recognized or treated in the elderly, its diagnosis and treatment should receive high priority among health professionals. The successful treatment of depression not only will improve the quality of life of older persons, but may also enhance their physical health and survival, as well as reduce health care costs and enhance productivity.

Conceptual and empirical work is also needed to help determine what aspect of depression accounts for the depression-mortality link. Depression is a complex syndrome, involving affective, somatic, cognitive, and motivational elements, each of which may have unique relations to the behavioral and biological factors identified in our model. Researchers also need to explore in this context the relation between depression and related constructs such as hopelessness, pessimism, and vital exhaustion, which also have been linked to mortality. Is there a critical underlying feature of these constructs that needs to be identified and assessed with new measurement tools? Possible candidates for this underlying construct might include motivational depletion, giving up on life, or disengagement from life and health-related goals. The stakes for unraveling this mystery are clearly high. But the payoffs may be equally high, when viewed in the context of the enhanced quality and duration of life that would ensue should underlying mechanisms be accurately identified and effective interventions devised to counteract their effects.

Recommended Reading

Schulz, R., Beach, S.R., Ives, D.G., Martire, L.M., Ariyo, A.A., & Kop, W.J. (2000). (See References)

Wulsin, L.R., Vaillant, G.E., & Wells, V.E. (1999). (See References)

Acknowledgments—Preparation of this manuscript was supported in part by grants from the National Institute of Mental Health (R01 MH46015, R01 MH52247, T32 MH19986), National Institute on Aging (AG13305, AG01532), and National Heart, Lung and Blood Institute (P50 HL65112).

Note

1. Address correspondence to Richard Schulz, University Center for Social and Urban Research, 121 University Pl., University of Pittsburgh, Pittsburgh, PA 15260.

References

Dew, M.A. (1998). Psychiatric disorder in the context of physical illness. In B.P. Dohrenwend (Ed.), *Adversity, stress, and psychopathology* (pp. 177–218). New York: Oxford University Press.

Glassman, A.H., & Shapiro, P.A. (1998). Depression and the course of coronary artery disease. *American Journal of Psychiatry, 155*, 4–11.

Kop, W.J., Appels, A.P., Mendes de leon, C.F., de Swart, H.B., & Bar, F.W. (1994). Vital exhaustion predicts new cardiac events after successful coronary angioplasty. *Psychosomatic Medicine, 56*, 281–287.

Lesperance, F., & Frasure-Smith, N. (1999). The seduction of death (Editorial Comment). *Psychosomatic Medicine, 61*, 18–20.

Musselman, D.L., Evans, D.L., & Nemeroff, C.B. (1998). The relationship of depression to cardiovascular disease: Epidemiology, biology, and treatment. *Archives of General Psychiatry, 55*, 580–592.

Scheier, M.F., & Carver, C.S. (in press). Adapting to cancer: The importance of hope and purpose. In A. Baum & B.L. Andersen (Eds.), *Psychosocial interventions for cancer.* Washington, DC: American Psychological Association.

Schulz, R., Beach, S.R., Ives, D.G., Martire, L.M., Ariyo, A.A., & Kop, W.J. (2000). Association between depression and mortality in older adults: The Cardiovascular Health Study. *Archives of Internal Medicine, 160*, 1761–1768.

Wulsin, L.R., Vaillant, G.E., & Wells, V.E. (1999). A systematic review of the mortality of depression. *Psychosomatic Medicine, 61*, 6–17.

Is Laughter the Best Medicine? Humor, Laughter, and Physical Health

Rod A. Martin[1]
Department of Psychology, University of Western Ontario, London, Ontario, Canada

Abstract

This article examines research evidence for the popular idea that humor and laughter have beneficial effects on physical health. Potential theoretical mechanisms for such effects are discussed first. Empirical evidence for beneficial effects of humor and laughter on immunity, pain tolerance, blood pressure, longevity, and illness symptoms is then summarized. Overall, the evidence for health benefits of humor and laughter is less conclusive than commonly believed. Future research in this area needs to be more theoretically driven and methodologically rigorous.

Keywords

humor; laughter; health; immunity; pain

Belief in beneficial effects of humor and laughter on physical health has become increasingly popular in recent years. The media frequently report claims about scientific evidence for health benefits of humor and laughter. Some practitioners have even begun to advocate the use of "therapeutic humor" in the treatment of illness and maintenance of health, and clowns and comedy carts have become familiar sights in many hospitals. The idea that laughter is good for one's health can be traced to biblical times, and was revived periodically by various physicians and philosophers through the centuries. In recent decades, interest in the healing power of laughter was given new impetus by the best-selling account by Cousins (1979) of his recovery from a progressive and painful rheumatoid disease after treating himself with daily bouts of laughter, along with massive doses of vitamin C.

THEORETICAL MECHANISMS

How might humor and laughter influence physical health? There are at least four potential mechanisms, each involving a different aspect of humor, and each suggesting different implications for the application of humor to well-being. First, laughter might produce physiological changes in various systems of the body, which may have beneficial effects on health. Various authors have suggested, for example, that vigorous laughter exercises and relaxes muscles, improves respiration, stimulates circulation, increases the production of pain-killing endorphins, decreases the production of stress-related hormones, and enhances immunity. According to this theoretical model, hearty laughter is crucial in the humor-health connection, whereas humorous perceptions and amusement without laughter would not be expected to confer any health benefits.

Second, humor and laughter might affect health by inducing positive emo-

17

tional states, which may in turn have beneficial effects on health, such as increasing pain tolerance, enhancing immunity, and undoing the cardiovascular consequences of negative emotions (Fredrickson, 2000). Compared with the first model, this model gives humor and laughter a less unique role in health enhancement, as they are only one means of increasing positive emotions, along with love, joy, optimism, and so forth. Furthermore, according to this model, overt laughter may not even be necessary for health benefits to occur, because humor and amusement may induce positive moods even without laughter.

Third, humor might benefit health indirectly by moderating the adverse effects of stress on health. A considerable body of research indicates that stressful life experiences can have adverse effects on various aspects of health, including suppression of the immune system and increased risk of infectious disease and heart disease (O'Leary, 1990). A sense of humor may enable individuals to cope more effectively with stress by allowing them to gain perspective and distance themselves from a stressful situation, enhancing their feelings of mastery and well-being in the face of adversity. Indeed, there is considerable experimental and correlational evidence for stress-moderating effects of humor, at least with regard to the effects of stress on moods such as anxiety and depression (Martin, Kuiper, Olinger, & Dance, 1993; Newman & Stone, 1996). Individuals with a good sense of humor may cope more effectively with stress than other people do, and therefore might also experience fewer of the adverse effects of stress on their physical health. According to this model, the cognitive-perceptual components of humor are more important than mere laughter, and the ability to maintain a humorous outlook during times of stress and adversity is particularly important. Humor and laughter during non-stressful circumstances would be less relevant to health. This view also introduces the possibility that certain styles of humor (e.g., mildly self-deprecating humor) may be more adaptive and health-enhancing than others (e.g., sarcasm).

Finally, humor may indirectly benefit health by increasing one's level of social support. Individuals with a good sense of humor may be more socially competent and attractive than other people, and better able to reduce tensions and conflicts in relationships, which might result in greater intimacy and more numerous and satisfying social relationships. In turn, the greater levels of social support resulting from these relationships may confer stress-buffering and health-enhancing effects (Cohen & Wills, 1985). In this model, the focus is on interpersonal aspects of humor and the social competence with which the individual expresses humor in relationships, rather than on the simple response of laughter or even a generally humorous outlook on life. This model also emphasizes the importance of distinguishing styles of humor that are potentially socially maladaptive from humor that facilitates relationships.

RESEARCH FINDINGS

About 45 published studies have examined the relation between humor or laughter and various aspects of physical health, including immunity, pain tolerance, blood pressure, longevity, and illness symptoms. The main findings of these studies are briefly summarized in this section (for a more detailed review, see Martin, 2001).

Immunity

A number of experimental studies have examined the effects of amusement and laughter on various components of the immune system by taking saliva or blood samples from participants before and after exposing them to humorous stimuli, such as comedy videotapes. The majority of these studies have examined only salivary immunoglobulin A (S-IgA), a component of the immune system that is found in saliva and is involved in the body's defense against upper respiratory infections. A handful of additional studies have measured circulating blood levels of a wide variety of hormones, several kinds of white blood cells, and other components of the immune system.

Most (but not all) of these studies have reported significant changes in at least some components of immunity following exposure to comedy. However, numerous methodological problems with the studies make it difficult to draw firm conclusions. In particular, most of the studies did not include adequate control conditions to control for such factors as normal daily fluctuations in immunity levels, the effects of exposure to an interesting videotape, and possible effects of other positive and negative emotions. Consequently, it is difficult to determine whether the observed changes in immunity were specifically due to laughter, or to amusement and positive emotions generally, or to generalized emotional arousal, or to some other nonspecific variable present in the experimental conditions. In addition, in most of the studies, the researchers did not directly monitor participants' laughter, so it is impossible to determine whether overt laughter (as opposed to mere amusement) is necessary to produce the observed changes in immunity.

A further difficulty is that the findings are rather inconsistent across studies and across immune-system variables, with some studies showing immuno-enhancing effects, others showing immunosuppressive effects, and still others showing no effects with particular components of immunity. The small sample sizes and large numbers of statistical tests performed in many of these studies also raise concerns that the reported findings are no more than would be expected by chance alone. Thus, although the findings are somewhat promising, more well-controlled studies are clearly needed before any firm conclusions may be drawn concerning the effects of humor and laughter on the immune system.

Besides these laboratory experiments, several studies have examined correlations between levels of S-IgA and participants' sense of humor as measured by self-report scales. Although two early studies with small sample sizes found sizable positive correlations between sense-of-humor scores and S-IgA, a number of later studies with larger sample sizes failed to replicate these findings. Dobbin and I (Martin & Dobbin, 1988) also found support for a stress-moderating hypothesis: Individuals with higher scores on a sense-of-humor test were less likely than individuals with lower scores to show a stress-related decrease in immunoglobulins over 1 1/2 months.

Pain Tolerance

A number of studies have examined potential analgesic effects of laughter by testing participants' pain threshold or tolerance before and after exposing them to comedy videotapes. These studies have generally been more carefully controlled and methodologically rigorous than the immunity research. Most of the studies have had several control groups, controlling for such factors as distraction, relaxation, and negative emotion. Overall, these studies provide fairly consistent evidence that exposure to comedy results in increases in pain threshold and tolerance that do not appear to be simply due to distraction. There is also some evidence from field studies that the analgesic effects of humor observed in the laboratory may extend to clinical interventions, but only with mild to moderate levels of pain.

However, because none of these studies have examined correlations between overt laughter and changes in pain tolerance, it is unclear whether the effects are due to laughter in particular or to positive emotions associated with amusement. Moreover, studies that have included negative-emotion control conditions have demonstrated similar increases in pain threshold and tolerance after exposure to videotapes inducing negative emotions such as disgust, horror, or sadness. These findings suggest that the observed analgesic effects may occur with both positive and negative emotional arousal, rather than being specific to laughter or amusement. It is also important to note that, contrary to frequent claims in the media, there is no evidence to date that these changes in pain tolerance are due to laughter-stimulated increases in naturally occurring opium-like substances such as endorphins. Indeed, some studies have shown that levels of endorphins in the blood do not change following exposure to comedy.

Blood Pressure

Although some people have speculated that hearty laughter may lead to a reduction in blood pressure over time, experimental studies indicate that laughter is actually associated with short-term increases in blood pressure and heart rate, but no longer-term effects. However, in a correlational study, Lefcourt, Davidson, Prkachin, and Mills (1997) found sex differences in correlations between sense-of-humor test scores and systolic blood pressure (SBP) during a series of stressful laboratory tasks. Women showed the expected negative correlations between sense of humor and SBP, whereas the correlations for men were in the opposite direction, higher humor being associated with higher SBP. These authors suggested that the findings may be due to differences in the ways in which men and women express humor, with women engaging in more tolerant, self-accepting, and adaptive forms of humor, potentially leading to more beneficial physiological effects.

Longevity

Two studies have examined the hypothesis that individuals with a greater sense of humor will live longer. Rotton (1992) found that the life duration of comedians and humor writers did not differ from that of serious entertainers and authors. Friedman et al. (1993) reported analyses of data from 1,178 male and female participants in the Terman Life-Cycle Study, who have been followed since 1921. A composite measure of cheerfulness was derived from parents' and teachers' ratings of these individuals' sense of humor and optimism at the age of 12. Surprisingly, survival analyses revealed that individuals with higher rated cheerfulness at age 12 had significantly *higher* mortality rates throughout the ensuing decades. The authors suggested that these results might have been due to more cheerful individuals being less concerned about health risks than less cheerful individuals were, and therefore taking less care of themselves. In any case, the existing evidence, though scanty, does not support the hypothesis that a sense of humor increases longevity.

Illness Symptoms

Several researchers have examined simple correlations between tests of sense of humor and overall health, as measured by self-report checklists of physical symptoms. A few of these studies have found significant negative correlations between these variables, indicating that individuals with a greater sense of humor report fewer symptoms of illness and medical problems. Other studies, however, have failed to replicate these findings. Additionally, some studies have found a stress-moderating effect of sense of humor on self-reported illness symptomatology, although these findings have not been replicated in other studies.

It is important to note that self-report measures of illness symptoms are notoriously confounded with negative emotionality or neuroticism, making them somewhat unreliable measures of health (Watson & Pennebaker, 1989). Because sense of humor tends to be negatively related to neuroticism, observed correlations between sense of humor and self-reported illness symptoms may be due to this shared neuroticism component rather than any actual health benefits of humor. Indeed, research indicates that correlations between sense of humor and physical-symptom measures disappear after controlling for neuroticism.

CONCLUSIONS AND FUTURE RESEARCH DIRECTIONS

Overall, the existing empirical evidence concerning health benefits of humor and laughter is less convincing than what is often portrayed in popular-media reports. However, despite these rather equivocal findings, there is reason to pursue further investigations, using more systematic, careful, and rigorous research methods and more sophisticated theoretical formulations. The methodological weaknesses in much of the experimental research, including inadequate controls and generally small sample sizes, often make it difficult to draw conclusions one way or the other. In addition, several of the hypothesized mechanisms discussed earlier have not been adequately tested, and little attention has been given to distinguishing particular styles of humor that may be more healthy than others. Given the longevity and popularity of the idea of health benefits of humor, and the important implications of such an effect if indeed it exists, more careful investigation is warranted.

Each of the four hypothesized mechanisms discussed earlier merits more thorough investigation. Much of the past experimental research involving exposure to comedy videotapes was presumably based on the hypothesis that laughter produces health-enhancing physiological changes in the body. However, most of these studies failed to monitor the actual occurrence of laughter, to distinguish various types of laughter (e.g., genuine vs. feigned), or to examine the relation between duration, frequency, or intensity of laughter and physiological outcomes. Thus, it may be that genuine physiological effects of particular types or degrees of laughter have gone largely undetected because of sloppy methodological procedures. In addition, as noted, more adequate control groups are needed to rule out possible alternative explanations for findings.

The hypothesis that health effects of humor may be mediated by positive emotion has also not received adequate research attention. Laboratory studies with comedy conditions should include control conditions eliciting non-humor-related positive emotions and negative emotions, in addition to emotionally neutral conditions, so that researchers can examine the degree to which any observed effects are specific to humor and laughter, are common to positive emotions generally, or occur with negative as well as positive emotional arousal.

The stress-moderating hypothesis also merits further investigation using more sophisticated approaches. Certain types of humor may be effective in coping with certain types of stress. Recently developed measures that distinguish between potentially beneficial and deleterious uses of humor (Martin, Puhlik-Doris, Larsen, Gray, & Weir, in press) may yield more meaningful results than previous humor scales that tended to blur these distinctions. Alternatively, it may be beneficial to examine individuals intensively over time rather than to compare individuals at one point in time, so that processes of coping and use of humor can be studied.

Finally, the hypothesis that health benefits of humor are mediated by social support has received almost no research attention. It seems intuitively likely that compared with serious individuals, humorous individuals find it easier to attract friends and develop a rich social-support network, and therefore gain the well-established health benefits of social support. However, little research has examined the effects of humor on social support or other aspects of interpersonal relationships.

In conclusion, despite the popularity of the idea that humor and laughter have significant health benefits, the current empirical evidence is generally weak and inconclusive. More carefully conducted and theoretically informed research is needed before one can have any confidence that humor or laughter affects physical health in a positive way.

Recommended Reading

Martin, R.A. (2001). (See References)
Ruch, W. (Ed.). (1998). *The sense of humor: Explorations of a personality characteristic.* Berlin, Germany: Walter de Gruyter.

Note

1. Address correspondence to Rod A. Martin, Department of Psychology, University of Western Ontario, London, Ontario, Canada N6A 5C2; e-mail: ramartin@uwo.ca.

References

Cohen, S., & Wills, T.A. (1985). Stress, social support, and the buffering hypothesis. *Psychological Bulletin, 98,* 310–357.
Cousins, N. (1979). *Anatomy of an illness.* New York: Norton.

Fredrickson, B.L. (2000). Cultivating positive emotions to optimize health and well-being. *Prevention and Treatment, 3,* 1–26.

Friedman, H.S., Tucker, J.S., Tomlinson-Keasey, C., Schwartz, J.E., Wingard, D.L., & Criqui, M.H. (1993). Does childhood personality predict longevity? *Journal of Personality and Social Psychology, 65,* 176–185.

Lefcourt, H.M., Davidson, K., Prkachin, K.M., & Mills, D.E. (1997). Humor as a stress moderator in the prediction of blood pressure obtained during five stressful tasks. *Journal of Research in Personality, 31,* 523–542.

Martin, R.A. (2001). Humor, laughter, and physical health: Methodological issues and research findings. *Psychological Bulletin, 127,* 504–519.

Martin, R.A., & Dobbin, J.P. (1988). Sense of humor, hassles, and immunoglobulin A: Evidence for a stress-moderating effect of humor. *International Journal of Psychiatry in Medicine, 18,* 93–105.

Martin, R.A., Kuiper, N.A., Olinger, L.J., & Dance, K.A. (1993). Humor, coping with stress, self-concept, and psychological well-being. *Humor, 6,* 89–104.

Martin, R.A., Puhlik-Doris, P., Larsen, G., Gray, J., & Weir, K. (in press). Individual differences in uses of humor and their relation to psychological well-being: Development of the Humor Styles Questionnaire. *Journal of Research in Personality.*

Newman, M.G., & Stone, A.A. (1996). Does humor moderate the effects of experimentally-induced stress? *Annals of Behavioral Medicine, 28,* 101–109.

O'Leary, A. (1990). Stress, emotion, and human immune function. *Psychological Bulletin, 108,* 363–382.

Rotton, J. (1992). Trait humor and longevity: Do comics have the last laugh? *Health Psychology, 11,* 262–266.

Watson, D., & Pennebaker, J.W. (1989). Health complaints, stress, and distress: Exploring the central role of negative affectivity. *Psychological Review, 96,* 234–254.

Is Caregiving a Risk Factor for Illness?

Peter P. Vitaliano,[1] Heather M. Young,[2] and Jianping Zhang[3]

[1]Department of Psychiatry and Behavioral Sciences, University of Washington; [2]School of Nursing, Oregon Health and Science University School of Nursing; and [3]Department of Psychology, Indiana University–Purdue University

Abstract

This article focuses on the physical health of persons who provide care to family members and friends with dementia. Such caregivers are under extended chronic stress because of the particular demands that this illness places on them. Caregiver research has made important contributions in two areas of health psychology. First, this research has increased understanding of the impact of chronic illness in families. Second, it has explored the complex relationships between stress and human responses (psychological and physiological) in the context of aging, using caregiving as a prototypic chronic stressor. This article discusses the relationship between distress, health habits, physiological changes, and, ultimately, health risks. There is evidence for greater health risks in caregivers than in noncaregivers. In addition, vulnerabilities and resources influence the relationship between caregiver stressors and health. One of the greatest methodological challenges of research on caregiver health is that the studies occur under natural conditions, so that it is not possible to randomly assign people to be caregivers and then observe changes in their health. Careful designs are required to infer the reasons for health risks.

Keywords

caregiving; dementia; physical health; stress; risk

In this article, we discuss current research on caregiving as a risk factor for physical health problems, theoretical and methodological issues in making inferences from such research, and recommendations for future research. We focus on informal (unpaid) caregivers of persons with dementia. Such caregivers provide the majority of long-term care in the United States, and the market value of this care was estimated to be approximately $196 billion in 1997, dwarfing concurrent national spending on formal home health care ($32 billion) and nursing home care ($83 billion). In the next 20 years, caregivers will be more critical than ever because the prevalence of Alzheimer's disease will increase, as will the prevalence of other chronic diseases. For these reasons, promoting health for caregivers is of potential benefit not only to these individuals, but to society as well.

Address correspondence to Peter P. Vitaliano, Department of Psychiatry and Behavioral Sciences, Box 356560, University of Washington, Seattle, WA 98195-6560.

WHAT DOES CAREGIVING FOR A PERSON WITH DEMENTIA ENTAIL?

Caring for a person with dementia poses specific challenges, including unrelenting psychosocial, physical, and financial demands over an extended period of time (3–15 years), lack of control over the disease, and resulting social isolation. With the progressive intellectual, social, and physical declines associated with dementia, caregivers experience an extended grieving period as they slowly lose a loved one to this illness. Moreover, caregiving can be a full-time job, and many caregivers are themselves older adults with their own chronic health problems or adult children who are balancing competing demands of work and child rearing. Hence, caregiving is conducive to distress, and trying to meet the care recipient's needs can result in perceptions of burden, depressed mood, and the absence of positive experiences.

HOW HAS CAREGIVING BEEN STUDIED?

Caregiving was first recognized as a chronic stressor more than 30 years ago. Early reports were anecdotal, describing the effects of caregiving demands on family members. Research then progressed to examine the psychosocial aspects of caregiving in more detail, and within a few years, investigators were beginning to look at possible effects on self-reported health. An important advance occurred when study designs began to include noncaregiving control groups, so that by comparing groups, researchers could attempt to isolate the effects of caregiving from those of general stressors experienced in the course of daily life. As the research became more sophisticated, investigators began to include more objective measures of health, to augment caregivers' reports of their own health. Finally, prospective designs enabled researchers to examine new health problems that arose during the course of caregiving. Caregiver research has made important contributions in two areas of health psychology. First, this research has increased understanding of the impact of chronic illness in families. Second, it has explored the complex relationships between stress and human responses (psychological and physiological) in the context of aging, using caregiving as a prototypic chronic stressor.

THE CONNECTION BETWEEN DISTRESS AND HEALTH

The unchallenged and implicit assumption of this research has been that the demands of caregiving influence caregivers' distress and health problems. Indeed, much research has shown that in general populations, chronic stress is associated with distress (e.g., depression), sleep problems, risky health habits (e.g., poor diet, sedentary behaviors), and illness progression in persons with existing health problems (Taylor, 1995).

In this regard, there is growing evidence of mind-body connections and the relationship between mental stress and physical responses. Distress and poor health habits elevate levels of stress hormones, thereby stimulating further physiological activity that can lead to negative health outcomes such as hyperglycemia (elevated levels of blood sugar), hyperinsulinemia (elevated levels of blood insulin), higher blood pressure (BP), and poorer immune functioning. If prolonged, these conditions can compromise health (Lovallo, 1997). In particular, physiological indicators of coronary risk and diabetes risk include heightened levels of resting BP, BP reactivity in response to stressors, low levels of high-density (good) cholesterol, high levels of blood fats and sugar, and obesity. Markers thought to reflect poor immune functioning include reduced ability to fight tumor cells, poor antibody production in response to viruses, and slow wound-healing responses.

RESEARCH ON CAREGIVER HEALTH

Schulz, Visintainer, and Williamson (1990) provided one of the first reviews of caregivers' physical and mental health. Most of the 34 studies in their review examined mental health (only 11 examined physical health) and assessed self-reported health rather than using objective measures. Some studies observed that the health of caregivers was similar to that of age- and sex-matched noncaregivers, whereas others found that caregivers rated their health as "poorer" than matched control participants did. Later, Schulz, O'Brien, Bookwala, and Fleissner (1995) reviewed 40 additional studies comparing caregivers with noncaregivers and observed conflicting results regarding self-reported chronic illnesses and medication use.

Given the inconsistent results and the absence of reviews that quantified the degree of added illness risks in caregivers relative to noncaregivers, we (Vitaliano, Zhang, & Scanlan, 2003) performed a meta-analysis of 23 studies, over a 38-year period, that compared 1,594 caregivers of persons with dementia to 1,478 noncaregivers who were similar in their distributions of age and sex. The meta-analytic approach enabled us to combine the results from these studies to estimate quantitative relationships between caregiving and illness risks. Eleven health categories were examined: five categories of self-reported health (global self-reported health, health care use, and reports of symptoms, major and minor illnesses, and medications) and six physiological categories of health. The physiological categories included antibody responses to vaccination and viruses, enumerative cellular immunity (counts of immune-cell markers), functional cellular immunity (ability to fight tumors and viruses), cardiovascular measures (e.g., BP), metabolic measures (e.g., glucose levels, weight), and levels of stress hormones.

The aggregate analysis showed that caregivers reported poorer global health and took more medications for physical problems than noncaregivers did. Furthermore, they had 23% higher levels of stress hormones, and a 15% lower level of antibody responses. These findings are important because prolonged physiological reactions to elevated stress hormones can increase one's risk for hypertension and diabetes. Caregivers may also have reduced resistance to viruses because of poorer antibody production. This may be especially critical to older caregivers, who are already at added risk for influenza because of their age.

PROBLEMS WITH THE RESEARCH ON CAREGIVER HEALTH

Theoretical Models

Research on caregiver health has not made full use of stress models that focus on differences between people. For example, differences in vulnerabilities and resources can modify (i.e., moderate) or increase or decrease (i.e., mediate) the effects of stress. Models that incorporate differences between people should improve researchers' ability to explain health problems that may result from caregiving, make it possible to identify high-risk caregivers, and allow for a better understanding of factors that mediate or moderate the relationship of caregiving with health problems.

We have proposed a model of caregiver health in which stressors and individual differences interact to influence the caregiver's level of distress (e.g., perceived hassles, depression, burden, few positive experiences) and health habits (e.g., amount of exercise, diet, substance abuse), which in turn mediate health outcomes (Vitaliano et al., 2002). Vulnerabilities, which include being a man, having a hostile disposition, and having coexisting medical conditions (e.g., hypertension, heart disease), are typically hard-wired or relatively static characteristics that exist prior to caregiving. Resources, such as coping skills, social supports, and income, are more mutable, and availability of resources is generally predictive of better health. The model predicts that caregivers who are high in vulnerabilities and low in resources will have greater distress and poorer health habits than caregivers with fewer vulnerabilities and more resources (Vitaliano, Russo, Young, Teri, & Maiuro, 1991).

Individual Differences in Research on Caregiver Health

In our meta-analysis, the relationships between caregiving and self-reported health were greater for older than for younger participants. Perhaps this was true because greater age is accompanied by increases in physical illnesses and disabilities, and these may be exacerbated by distress. This analysis also showed that for women, caregiving was related much more strongly to self-reported global health than to a physiological measure combining cardiovascular, metabolic, and stress hormone data; the relationship between caregiving and the physiological measure was minute. In contrast, for men, caregiving was related to both the combined physiological measure and self-reported health. These results are especially meaningful to clinicians, researchers, and policymakers because the analysis was strictly limited to studies that simultaneously compared male caregivers with male noncaregivers and female caregivers with female noncaregivers. Such comparisons are important because they provide some control for basic biological differences and differences in self-report tendencies between men and women. Also, if the difference between caregivers and noncaregivers is greater for men than women, but the caregiver-noncaregiver comparisons for men and women come from different studies (i.e., involving different procedures, labs, and samples), it is difficult to evaluate whether the difference is moderated by sex or by study differences.

The relationships between caregiver status and physiological risk may be particularly strong for persons with coexisting health conditions (Vitaliano et al., 2003). For example, caregivers with cancer histories have lower natural killer activity, a defense against tumors, than do noncaregivers with cancer histories, but natural killer activity does not differ for caregivers and noncaregivers who have not had cancer. Also, hypertensive caregivers have greater BP reactivity (while experiencing a potential stressor, such as discussing their relationship with their spouse) than do hypertensive noncaregivers, but caregiver status is not related to BP reactivity in persons with normal blood pressure. Finally, caregivers with coronary disease have higher values on an estimate of the metabolic syndrome than do noncaregivers with heart disease; however, no difference occurs for caregivers and noncaregivers free of heart disease. The metabolic syndrome is important to health because it involves five physical signs that are predictive of both heart disease and the exacerbation of this disease after it occurs. These signs include obesity, elevated BP, high cholesterol, high levels of glucose, and high levels of insulin.

Given the interactions that occur between caregiving and coexisting health conditions, it is unfortunate that most researchers have either excluded persons with coexisting conditions in their designs or have not analyzed the presence/absence of such conditions as moderators of relationships of caregiver/noncaregiver status with health. These practices may limit studies to those caregivers who are least likely to show health or physiological problems, and prevent researchers from discovering relationships between caregiving and disease progression.

Additional Design Issues

Most studies have compared caregivers with noncaregivers after they have already developed health problems. Such studies do not allow one to determine whether illnesses reported preceded caregiving or vice versa. However, some prospective studies have been done. These studies examined only caregivers and noncaregivers who were initially free of health problems and followed them to assess whether caregivers were more likely than noncaregivers to become ill. Shaw et al. (1997) found that over 1 to 6 years, caregivers who provided the most assistance were more likely to develop at least one new health problem than were either caregivers who provided less assistance or noncaregivers. Schulz and Beach (1999) observed that over an average of 4 years, strained caregivers had a 63% higher death rate than noncaregivers. Finally, we (Vitaliano et al., 2002) observed that over 27 to 30 months, male caregivers had a higher rate of new cases of heart disease (8 out of 19 participants) than male noncaregivers (3 out of 20 participants). Distress was related to caregiver status and the care recipients' cognitive and functional deficits, and was further related to poor health habits; in turn, poor health habits predicted greater physiological risk, via the metabolic syndrome, 15 to 18 months later.

Although these prospective studies allow one to conclude that caregiving preceded the outcomes assessed, they were prospective for illness and mortality only, and not for caregiving. That is, the participants were already caregivers and noncaregivers at the start of these studies, so only retrospective data were potentially available for analyzing the precaregiving lifestyle of the caregivers and the lifestyle of the noncaregivers during a similar earlier period of time. Because caregiver research is based primarily on real-world observations and not experiments, characteristics (poor diet and insufficient exercise) that increase health risks may be present in caregivers prior to caregiving and not be the result of caregiving. Indeed, because these characteristics vary across couples and families, it may be these characteristics, and not caregiving per se, that are responsible for greater health problems in caregivers than in noncaregivers.

In an attempt to control for effects of unknown confounders, researchers typically match age and gender in the caregiver and noncaregiver groups they study. However, biases can occur if other important variables are ignored. Income is one such variable because it is negatively related to health, and persons who become caregivers (especially men) may have lower incomes than persons who are eligible to be caregivers but opt out of caregiving and pay for it instead because they have the income to do so (Vitaliano et al., 2003). Bias can also occur because of assortative mating (the tendency to marry someone like oneself) and mutual influences of spouses on each other. For example, spouses tend to have similar health habits (Davis, Murphy, Neuhaus, Gee, & Quiroga, 2000), and poor health habits and distress may increase one's risk for dementia (Leonard, 2001; Skoog, 1998). Thus, prior to caregiving, caregivers may have greater distress and poorer health habits than noncaregivers. In addition, the same experiences that influence the development of dementia in care recipients may influence the development of other illnesses in caregivers, with genetic predispositions affecting how these shared risk factors are manifested.

Only studies that are doubly prospective, that examine a cohort both before caregiving and before a target illness develops, allow one to examine how changes in caregiver status and illness relate to psychosocial, behavioral, and physiological changes. A doubly prospective study could begin with persons who are not caregivers and not ill and then follow them to determine what happens after some become caregivers and others remain noncaregivers. The first question of interest would be whether those who become caregivers develop health problems at a higher rate than those who remain noncaregivers. In addition, researchers could determine whether such higher incidences in caregivers can be explained by variables such as greater demands, greater distress, and poorer health habits in caregivers than in noncaregivers. Combining caregiver research with ongoing population studies should make doubly prospective studies possible. However, illnesses take time to be detected, and extensive follow-up may be necessary.

MEASUREMENT ISSUES

Research on caregiver health began with an emphasis on self-report measures. However, more recent work has also included direct physiological assessments. Although these studies have been conducted primarily in laboratories, ecological validity can be improved by examining measures taken in natural settings, such as the home, over longer time periods. For example, BPs that are taken in the home while caregivers engage in their usual activities may be greater than BPs taken in clinic or work settings, especially when taken in the presence of the persons being cared for (King, Oka, & Young, 1994).

Another benefit may come from medical records. It may be difficult for caregivers to recall and distinguish their use of health care versus that of the persons for whom they are caring. Therefore, collecting such information from alternate sources might be useful. Medical records may not only provide information on doctors' visits, but may also be repositories of other valuable data, such as lab results, dates and nature of diagnoses, information on treatments and medications, and prognoses. Caregivers may not know such information or may not report it accurately. In using medical records, researchers can develop quality-control checklists to document participants' treatments, symptoms, and diagnoses and to assess the reliability of their records and the quality of their data. We also recommend physical exams, because they can uncover problems undetected in medical records. Some reported health measures may be used more productively than in the past. Instead of simply counting illnesses, for example, researchers should assess which illnesses are most related to caregiving. Medication data could be more useful to researchers if they considered frequencies, dosages, and the health implications of such medications.

IMPORTANT NEXT STEPS

Although the observational nature of caregiver research precludes the definitive inference that caregiving is a risk factor for illness, doubly prospective studies and studies that examine disease progression in caregivers and noncaregivers with and without coexisting conditions should be useful for clarifying potential causes of the added risk caregivers appear to experience. Using theoretical models in research will promote identification of factors amenable to change and development of targeted interventions that might promote overall health for caregivers by improving their health-related behaviors and stress management.

Although the research reviewed here focused on caregivers of persons with dementia, caregivers of persons with cancer, coronary disease, injuries, and mental illnesses are also under stress. The model we have presented could be extended to them, and differences among types of caregiving situations could be explored. By helping caregivers to maintain their health, such studies and interventions should also help care recipients and society. The added health risks for caregivers are provocative because there are more than 5 million caregivers of persons with dementia in the United States and another 4 million care recipients that will be affected if their caregivers become ill. Finally, caregiver's own illnesses are a major reason why caregivers institutionalize their care recipients (Deimling & Poulshock, 1985), and improved caregiver health may delay or avoid many institutionalizations.

Recommended Reading

American Association of Retired Persons. (1988). *National survey of caregivers: Summary of findings.* Washington, DC: Author.

Kasl, S.V. (1983). Pursuing the link between stressful life experiences and disease: A time for reappraisal. In C.L. Cooper (Ed.), *Stress research: Issues for the eighties* (pp. 79–102). New York: John Wiley & Sons.

Mechanic, D. (1967). Invited commentary on self, social environment and stress. In M.H. Appley & R. Trumbull (Eds.), *Psychological stress* (pp. 123–150). New York: Appleton-Century-Crofts.

Rowe, J.W., & Kahn, R.L. (1998). *Successful aging.* New York: Pantheon Books.

Vogel, F., & Motulsky, A.G. (1986). *Human genetics.* New York: Springer-Verlag.

Acknowledgments—This research was supported by the National Institute of Mental Health, Grant RO1 MH57663.

References

Davis, M.A., Murphy, S.P., Neuhaus, J.M., Gee, L., & Quiroga, S. (2000). Living arrangements affect dietary quality for U.S. adults aged 50 years and older: NHANES III 1988–1994. *Journal of Nutrition, 130,* 2256–2263.

Deimling, G.T., & Poulshock, S.W. (1985). The transition from family in-home care to institutional care. *Research on Aging, 7,* 563–576.

King, A.C., Oka, R.K., & Young, D.R. (1994). Ambulatory blood pressure and heart rate responses to the stress of work and caregiving in older women. *Journal of Gerontology, 49,* 239–245.

Leonard, B.E. (2001). Changes in the immune system in depression and dementia: Causal or co-incidental effects? *International Journal of Developmental Neuroscience, 19,* 305–312.

Lovallo, W.R. (1997). *Stress & health.* Thousand Oaks, CA: Sage.

Schulz, R., & Beach, S.R. (1999). Caregiving as a risk factor for mortality: The Caregiver Health Effects Study. *Journal of the American Medical Association, 282,* 2215–2260.

Schulz, R., O'Brien, A.T., Bookwala, J., & Fleissner, K. (1995). Psychiatric and physical morbidity effects of dementia caregiving: Prevalence, correlates, and causes. *The Gerontologist, 35,* 771–791.

Schulz, R., Visintainer, P., & Williamson, G.M. (1990). Psychiatric and physical morbidity effects of caregiving. *Journal of Gerontology: Psychological Sciences, 45,* 181–191.

Shaw, W.S., Patterson, T.L., Semple, S.J., Ho, S., Irwin, M.R., Hauger, R.L., & Grant, I. (1997). Longitudinal analysis of multiple indicators of health decline among spousal caregivers. *Annals of Behavioral Medicine, 19*(1), 101–109.

Skoog, I. (1998). Status of risk factors for vascular dementia. *Neuroepidemiology, 17,* 2–9.

Taylor, S.E. (1995). *Health psychology* (3rd ed.). New York: McGraw Hill.

Vitaliano, P.P., Russo, J., Young, H.M., Teri, L., & Maiuro, R.D. (1991). Predictors of burden in spouse caregivers of individuals with Alzheimer's disease. *Psychology and Aging, 6,* 392–401.

Vitaliano, P.P., Scanlan, J.M., Zhang, J., Savage, M.V., Hirsch, I., & Siegler, I.C. (2002). A path model of chronic stress, the metabolic syndrome, and coronary heart disease. *Psychosomatic Medicine, 64,* 418–435.

Vitaliano, P.P., Zhang, J., & Scanlan, J.M. (2003). Is caregiving hazardous to one's physical health? A meta-analysis. *Psychological Bulletin, 129,* 946–972.

Employee Control and Occupational Stress

Paul E. Spector[1]
Department of Psychology, University of South Florida, Tampa, Florida

Abstract

Occupational stress has been recognized as a major health issue for modern work organizations. Conditions of the workplace have been shown to lead to negative emotional reactions (e.g., anxiety), physical health problems in both the short term (e.g., headache or stomach distress) and the long term (cardiovascular disease), and counterproductive behavior at work. Perceptions of control play an important role in this process, being associated with all of these variables. Evidence is growing that enhanced control at work can be an important element in employees' health and well-being. These relationships can be understood in the context of the control-stress model.

Keywords

occupational stress; control; employee health

Occupational stress has been recognized as one of the most significant workplace health hazards for employees in the United States and other developed countries. Cartwright and Cooper (1997) pointed out that in the short term stress can lead to emotional distress, stomach disorder, headaches, sleeplessness, and loss of energy, and in the long term it can contribute to serious illness and even premature death, most likely due to cardiovascular disease. They argued that occupational stress costs American businesses more than $150 billion per year because of absence, lost productivity, and health costs. Furthermore, occupational stress seems to be endemic to the modern workplace, as national surveys have shown that a large proportion of workers report feeling highly stressed at work (see Sauter et al., 1999).

There are a number of work-place factors, called *job stressors*, that make jobs stressful. Some stressors concern the nature of the job and job tasks. For example, jobs with heavy workloads requiring long periods of attention (e.g., driving a truck) and jobs that are highly repetitive and boring will likely be perceived as stressful. Other stressors concern interpersonal relationships at work, such as conflicts with co-workers or abusive behavior by supervisors. Finally, there are stressors in the organizational context, such as having insufficient resources to do the job (e.g., defective equipment or inadequate supplies), or unfair payment and reward systems.

Research has demonstrated that all of these job stressors are associated with employees' health and well-being. Investigators often ask employees to answer questionnaires about their job stressors and their health and well-being. For example, Schaubroeck and Fink (1998) surveyed 214 employees from a national insurance company about their job stressors, physical health symptoms, and attitudes about the job. As is typically found in such studies, higher levels of stressors (e.g., heavy workload and uncertainty about supervisors' expectations) were associated with physical symptoms, such as headaches, and poor job attitudes. Sometimes job-stress studies include physical measures of the workplace as well. For example, Melamed, Fried, and Froom (2001) conducted a study of 1,507 factory workers in Israel. Researchers visited each workplace and took measurements of the noise level with sound-intensity meters. Experts observed each worker for a day and then provided ratings of how complex each job was. Finally, each participant received a physical examination that included a blood pressure reading. Results showed that noise at work was associated with increased blood pressure, especially when the job was complex and required mental concentration.

CONTROL AND JOB STRESS

One of the most important elements in the occupational-stress process is the perception of control. Control can be over any aspect of work, including location, scheduling, and how tasks are done. Jobs differ tremendously in the amount and type of control they allow employees. At one extreme is machine-paced factory work in which the employee must work at precisely determined times, performing specified tasks at the intervals determined by the machine. The classic "I Love Lucy" comedy sketch in a candy factory illustrates what happens when the employee cannot keep up with the assembly line, and shows Lucy frantically stuffing candy everywhere she can as she falls farther and farther behind. At the other extreme are the jobs of high-level management employees who are given assignments that can be done at any place, at any time, and in almost any manner they see fit.

A Control-Stress Model

Figure 1 provides an overview of how the job-stress process appears to operate (based on Spector, 1998). It begins at the left-hand side with the workplace environment. Throughout the workday, employees experience and perceive conditions and events, most of which are typically benign and are paid little attention. Certain events, however, are perceived and interpreted as somehow threatening to physical or psychological well-being—these are the perceived job stressors. The stressors result in negative emotional reactions, perhaps most commonly anger or anxiety. These emotions then lead to strains, both behaviors

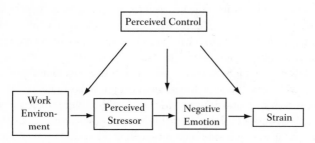

Fig. 1. Control model of occupational stress.

and physical conditions associated with stress. As the figure illustrates, perceived control is an important element at all stages of this process.

Job stressors can include anything that a person finds threatening, but researchers have focused on a very small number involving amount of work and work demands, constraints that interfere with work or prevent employees from getting their work done, interpersonal conflicts among employees, and uncertainty about what employees should be doing. Behavioral strains consist of actions people take to cope with stressors and the associated emotions. They can be constructive acts that successfully deal with stressors, such as finding a way to overcome a shortage of resources, or acts that are destructive to the individual (e.g., alcohol or other drug abuse, heavy smoking) and employer (e.g., not coming to work, purposely doing work incorrectly, starting a fight with a co-worker, stealing). Physical strains are related to both the fatigue of hard work (effort) and the physiology of negative emotion (distress). Both kinds of physical strains can increase physiological arousal, resulting in elevated blood pressure and heart rate, as well as secretion of so-called stress hormones, such as adrenaline, into the blood stream. In the short term, such physiological changes can result in minor physical symptoms, such as headache or upset stomach. Chronic elevation of heart rate and blood pressure can contribute to more serious health conditions, and ultimately heart disease in some individuals.

A great deal of evidence links perceptions of control to several different kinds of strains. For example, a short-term questionnaire study showed that low levels of perceived control were associated with a variety of strains: anxiety, frustration, physical symptoms for the past 30 days (e.g., headache and stomach upset), and doctor visits for the prior 3 months (Spector, Dwyer, & Jex, 1988). These results suggest that perceptions of control may play an important role in emotions and short-term physical well-being.

Subsequent work by other researchers has included longer-term studies that provide even more convincing evidence for a link between control and health. Ganster, Fox, and Dwyer (2001) conducted a 5-year study of job stress and control in a sample of nurses. They found that high control at the beginning of their study predicted lower use of medical services (assessed from health insurance records) over the following 5 years, as well as better mental health. They also measured both objective and perceived workload. Objective workload was indicated by the patient loads each nurse had, whereas a scale that asked the nurses to rate their workload was the subjective measure. Interestingly, control was related to the subjective but not the objective measure, suggesting, as expected, that control is an important factor in people's perceptions of stressors, regardless of the actual level of those stressors.

Bosma, Stansfeld, and Marmot (1998) showed a link between work control and cardiovascular disease in an English study of more than 9,000 civil servants. They assessed perceived job control by use of a survey, and got a parallel measure of job control from the supervisors of their study participants. In a 5-year follow-up, they found that job control predicted subsequent coronary heart disease. This relationship was found with both measures of control. These results suggest that both perceived and objective control are important elements in cardiovascular health.

Control-Demand Model

Perhaps the most influential job-stress theory is Karasek's (1979) job demand-control model, which links perceived control and stressors. The theory suggests that there are two important elements involved in the job-stress process: control and demands (job stressors related to work tasks, such as workload and uncertainty about what should be done). In this model, control buffers the effects of demands, such that high-demand jobs lead to adverse reactions only among employees who have low control. Employees with high control see such demands as challenges to overcome rather than threats. Although Karasek provided some support for the buffering effect, results across studies have been equivocal. As Terry and Jimmieson (1999) discussed, sound tests of this theory are hard to find, and although control has been shown to relate to strain, only some studies have found it acts as a buffer. In part this may be because tests of the theory have not looked at control over specific stressors themselves.

Explanations for the Control-Stress Connection

Figure 1 shows that control is important at several points in the job-stress process. First, when a person perceives control in a situation, he or she will be less likely to perceive workplace conditions and events as job stressors. However, to be effective in reducing perceived stressors, the control must be over the stressful situation itself and not some other aspect of work. For example, it is helpful to have control over work tasks and be free to use a variety of procedures to do the job if there is stress deriving from tasks. In this case, the employee will be able to reduce the stressor by changing how the task is done. However, if the job stressor comes from conflict with the supervisor, having control over tasks will not be helpful. Instead, having control over where or when the work is done would enable the employee to avoid the supervisor and reduce the problem to some extent. Being able to control the conflict itself would be most helpful.

Second, perceived control helps employees minimize emotional reactions to job stressors. One explanation of these first two effects of perceived control is the minimax principle (see Thompson, 1981), which says control allows one to minimize the maximum damage or danger that can occur in a situation. If a person perceives control over the work situation, he or she will believe the magnitude of the stressor can be contained within tolerable limits. The situation will therefore be seen as less stressful, and the emotional response to it will be less extreme. A person with a heavy workload and control over it, for example, will be confident he or she can keep the workload within tolerable limits. Thus, the person's reaction might be the positive feeling of challenge rather than negative emotions and distress.

Finally, control affects a person's choice of coping strategy. Perceived control tends to lead to constructive coping, whereas perceived lack of control is more likely to lead to destructive coping. Individuals who perceive they have control over job stressors are likely to see the situation as a challenge to be overcome and will likely engage in behaviors designed to do just that. Individuals who feel they have lost control may resort to destructive behaviors that may serve merely to make them feel better. Thus, they may strike back at the perceived source of the stressors, which can be co-workers, supervisors, or the organization. Often such behavior is covert or passive, such as avoiding work or performing tasks incorrectly on purpose.

The concepts of primary and secondary control (Rothbaum, Weisz, & Snyder, 1982) can help explain reactions to job stressors. Primary control is direct action taken to affect the environment, whereas secondary control is action that affects one's own reaction to the environment. In general, people are motivated to control and exert mastery over aspects of the environment that affect them. Given a choice, they usually prefer primary control (direct action) to change the environment to suit themselves. However, primary control is not always possible, and in such cases people must rely on secondary control to cope. Thus, they engage in actions that affect their reactions to the environment, and these actions may make them feel better about the situation. Given a job stressor that induces negative emotion, such as anger, an individual may resort to counterproductive work behavior that may help vent that emotion if primary control is unavailable. Unfortunately, such behavior can have detrimental effects on organizations.

CONCLUSIONS AND FUTURE DIRECTIONS

Control has played a prominent role in both research and theory in occupational stress. A large number of studies, a handful of which were mentioned here, have linked perceptions of control to both perceived job stressors and strains. Compared with individuals who perceive they have low control, individuals who perceive they have high control will be less likely to interpret the environment as stressful, will have lower negative emotional responses, and will exhibit less strain. The majority of studies in this area have used cross-sectional (one-time) questionnaires on which employees report their own job stressors, control, and strains. However, a number of studies have used stronger research designs allowing more confident conclusions that control can have causal effects on subsequent strain.

At issue, however, is the exact role of control and the mechanism through which it operates. The popular demand-control model implies that control can ameliorate the negative effect of job stressors on health and well-being. Unfortunately, the evidence for this model has been equivocal, and there have been few strong empirical tests of it. At the current time, it is not clear why only some studies find the effect. Part of the problem may be linked to the methodologies used, which rely almost exclusively on self-reports to measure perceived control. The link between objective control and perceptions of control may be a key element in the process through which health is affected, and studies that assess both the objective environment and perceptions of it are needed.

Another limitation to the literature is that there have been few intervention studies investigating the effects of programs designed to enhance control. Such studies would be useful in helping to show how objective control can affect people's perceptions and well-being. The study of interventions may help explain how and why control relates to job stressors and strains, and how it fits in the stress process. It seems clear that negative emotion is a central variable in this process.

The past two decades have seen an explosion of interest in understanding factors underlying health and well-being in the workplace. Occupational stress has been recognized as a major health issue in the United States and other industrialized nations. There is mounting evidence that perceived control at work is an important element in employees' health and well-being. A better understanding of how the process works can contribute to a healthier and more productive workforce.

Recommended Reading

Cartwright, S., & Cooper, C.L. (1997). (See References)
Perrewé, P.L., & Ganster, D.C. (Eds.). (2001). *Research in occupational stress and well being: Vol. 1. Exploring theoretical mechanisms and perspectives.* New York: JAI Press.
Spector, P.E. (1998). (See References)
Terry, D.J., & Jimmieson, N.L. (1999). (See References)

Note

1. Address correspondence to Paul E. Spector, Department of Psychology, University of South Florida, Tampa, FL 33620; e-mail: spector@chuma.cas.usf.edu.

References

Bosma, H., Stansfeld, S.A., & Marmot, M.G. (1998). Job control, personal characteristics, and heart disease. *Journal of Occupational Health Psychology, 3,* 402–409.
Cartwright, S., & Cooper, C.L. (1997). *Managing workplace stress.* Thousand Oaks, CA: Sage.
Ganster, D.C., Fox, M.L., & Dwyer, D.J. (2001). Explaining employees' health care costs: A prospective examination of stressful job demands, personal control, and physiological reactivity. *Journal of Applied Psychology, 86,* 954–964.
Karasek, R.A. (1979). Job demands, job decision latitude, and mental strain: Implications for job redesign. *Administrative Science Quarterly, 24,* 285–308.
Melamed, S., Fried, Y., & Froom, P. (2001). The interactive effect of chronic exposure to noise and job complexity on changes in blood pressure and job satisfaction: A longitudinal study of industrial employees. *Journal of Occupational Health Psychology, 6,* 182–195.
Rothbaum, F., Weisz, J.R., & Snyder, S.S. (1982). Changing the world and changing the self: A two-process model of perceived control. *Journal of Personality and Social Psychology, 42,* 5–37.
Sauter, S., Murphy, L., Colligan, M., Swanson, N., Hurrell, J., Jr., Scharf, F., Jr., Sinclair, R., Grubb, P., Goldenhar, L., Alteman, T., Johnston, J., Hamilton, A., & Tisdale, J. (1999). *Stress at work.* Cincinnati, OH: National Institute of Occupational Safety and Health.
Schaubroeck, J., & Fink, L.S. (1998). Facilitating and inhibiting effects of job control and social support on stress outcomes and role behavior: A contingency model. *Journal of Organizational Behavior, 19,* 167–195.
Spector, P.E. (1998). A control model of the job stress process. In C.L. Cooper (Ed.), *Theories of organizational stress* (pp. 153–169). London: Oxford University Press.
Spector, P.E., Dwyer, D.J., & Jex, S.M. (1988). The relationship of job stressors to affective, health, and performance outcomes: A comparison of multiple data sources. *Journal of Applied Psychology, 73,* 11–19.
Terry, D.J., & Jimmieson, N.L. (1999). Work control and employee well-being: A decade review. In C.L. Cooper & I.T. Robertson (Eds.), *International review of industrial and organizational psychology 1999* (pp. 95–148). Chichester, England: John Wiley.
Thompson, S.C. (1981). Will it hurt less if I can control it? A complex answer to a simple question. *Psychological Bulletin, 90,* 89–101.

Ethnicity-Related Sources of Stress and Their Effects on Well-Being

Richard J. Contrada,[1] Richard D. Ashmore, Melvin L. Gary, Elliot Coups, Jill D. Egeth, Andrea Sewell, Kevin Ewell, Tanya M. Goyal, and Valerie Chasse

Department of Psychology, Rutgers—The State University of New Jersey, Piscataway, New Jersey (R.J.C., R.D.A., M.L.G., E.C., J.D.E., A.S., K.E., T.M.G.), and Social Sciences Area, Warren County Community College of New Jersey, Washington, New Jersey (V.C.)

Abstract

Early research on ethnicity focused on the stereotyped thinking, prejudiced attitudes, and discriminatory actions of Euro-Americans. Minority-group members were viewed largely as passive targets of these negative reactions, with low self-esteem studied as the main psychological outcome. By contrast, recent research has increasingly made explicit use of stress theory in emphasizing the perspectives and experiences of minority-group members. Several ethnicity-related stressors have been identified, and it has been found that individuals cope with these threats in an active, purposeful manner. In this article, we focus on ethnicity-related stress stemming from discrimination, from stereotypes, and from conformity pressure arising from one's own ethnic group. We discuss theory and review research in which examination of ethnicity-related outcomes has extended beyond self-esteem to include psychological and physical well-being.

Keywords

ethnicity; stress; coping; discrimination; stereotypes; well-being

Racial and ethnic categories, such as "white," "black," "Asian," and "Hispanic," reflect complex sets of sociocultural and historical factors (Williams, Spencer, & Jackson, 1999). The meaning and impact of these factors at an individual psychological level are not well understood. Of the many aspects of ethnicity[2] that appear to influence psychological processes, several may be conceptualized as psychological stressors, that is, as perceived threats to physical or psychological well-being. A number of qualitatively distinct ethnicity-related stressors have recently been subject to intensified investigation; we discuss three of them in this review.

ETHNIC DISCRIMINATION

Ethnic discrimination involves unfair treatment that a person attributes to his or her ethnicity. We discuss discrimination at some length because it has been given increased attention recently in journalistic accounts and in analyses involving systematic coding of the content of interviews with victims of discrimination. Discrimination also has been recognized in recent quantitative research and in theoretical analyses as a psychological stressor and a possible risk factor for physical illness. These efforts have sparked new interest in the topic and identified some major issues. They represent a shift away from an emphasis on determinants of discriminatory behavior toward a focus on the perception and experience of discrimination by minority-group members. In another shift, by contrast with earlier accounts that emphasized major, often institutional, forms of discrimination (e.g., hiring practices), more recent accounts have highlighted subtle forms of discrimination that are embedded in everyday life (e.g., being followed in a store as a suspected shoplifter).

There have been several efforts to delineate the various forms of ethnic discrimination. For example, in a recent study (Contrada et al., in press), we identified five: (a) *verbal rejection*: insults, ethnic slurs; (b) *avoidance*: shunning; (c) *disvaluation*: actions that express negative evaluations; (d) *inequality-exclusion*: denial of equal treatment or access; and (e) *threat-aggression*: actual or threatened harm. This set of distinctions accords well with Allport's (1954) suggestion that the behavioral expression of prejudice may be described in terms of a continuum of increasing intensity.

Explicit conceptualization of discrimination as a psychological stressor has guided several recent theoretical analyses. This work suggests that members of ethnic minority groups form expectations regarding the likelihood that discrimination will be encountered in certain settings, decide whether to approach or avoid situations in which it is anticipated, and prepare for its occurrence (Swim, Cohen, & Hyers, 1998). Thus, the ever-present possibility of discrimination itself constitutes a stressor, requiring vigilance and other proactive coping responses.

Minority-group members also must judge whether specific events constitute discrimination. Feldman Barrett and Swim (1998) have conceptualized this process in terms of signal detection theory. This theory was developed as a way to distinguish between noticing a stimulus and responding to it once it is noticed, using the concepts of *sensitivity* and *response bias*. In the present context, sensitivity involves the ability to detect the presence or absence of cues indicating discrimination. It is determined, in part, by properties of discriminatory events or conditions. Acts of discrimination are often ambiguous because they can be subtle or involve treatment that is of borderline acceptability ("The waiter seemed to be ignoring me . . . "), the ethnicity-related motives that define them as discriminatory (" . . . because I am black . . . ") are often unobservable, and the behavior in question may be subject to alternative explanations (" . . . though the restaurant was extremely busy"). Sensitivity also may reflect attributes of the person, such as general knowledge, previous experience, and social awareness. Response bias involves the tendency either to underestimate or to overestimate the occurrence of discrimination. It is influenced by general beliefs about the probability that individuals are prejudiced, and by the goals a person has (e.g., self-protection) when judging whether discrimination has occurred.

When subjected to possible discriminatory behavior, members of ethnic minorities may be motivated to protect themselves against unfair treatment, but they also may wish to avoid false alarms (i.e., perceiving discrimination when it did not in fact occur). False alarms can disrupt social relations, cause members of ethnic minority groups to be identified as "thin-skinned," and undermine life satisfaction. One important task now being pursued by researchers is identifying conditions that favor minimizing false alarms, and those that favor being careful not to miss detecting acts of discrimination when they do occur (Feldman Barrett & Swim, 1998). There is accumulating evidence that when the situation is even just slightly ambiguous, members of ethnic minority groups may minimize the personal experience of discrimination. For example, they may attribute negative outcomes (e.g., unfavorable evaluations) to personal factors (e.g., the quality of their performance), which apparently serves to enhance their perception of personal control (Ruggiero & Taylor, 1997).

Coping with discrimination also requires decisions based on a complex set of factors (Swim et al., 1998). Different responses to perceived discrimination may serve different goals, some aimed at dealing with the initiating social situation, and some focusing on its emotional impact. Assertive reactions, such as the highly visible, confrontational communication of displeasure, may be directed at terminating the offensive behavior or at retaliation. Less assertive responses, such as trying to placate the perpetrator, may be aimed at self-protection or preservation of social relationships. Cognitive coping responses, such as reinterpreting the event as benign or as not ethnicity related, may preserve a positive, if illusory, view of the social consequences of one's ethnicity. Because discrimination can cause members of ethnic minority groups to feel badly about themselves personally, or about their group as a whole (Crocker, Major, & Steele, 1998), certain coping responses may be self- or identity-focused. They may, for example, involve either reduction or enhancement of psychological identification with one's ethnic group (Deaux & Ethier, 1998). Deciding whether and how to respond to discrimination appears to involve cost-benefit considerations, similar to those involved in the perception of discrimination, that have only recently begun to receive systematic attention (Swim et al., 1998).

STEREOTYPE THREAT AND STEREOTYPE-CONFIRMATION CONCERN

Stereotype threat has been defined, in part, as the condition of being at risk of appearing to confirm a negative stereotype about a group to which one belongs (Steele, 1997). Stereotype threat has been examined as a social psychological state created by situational cues in susceptible individuals. Much of this work has investigated stereotype threat associated with the American cultural beliefs that African Americans are low in intellectual ability and that women are not skilled in mathematics and physical sciences. One way stereotype threat is induced in this research is by instructing participants that their scores on tests that they are about to take will be diagnostic of their intellectual ability. Results have suggested that induction of stereotype threat activates relevant stereotypes in the thinking of participants, increases anxiety, and impairs test performance. In the long term, these experiences may promote *disidentification*, which, in this context, is a coping response of psychological disengagement from academic activity (Osborne, 1995). Thus, threat created by very subtle cues associated with ethnic stereotypes may have a negative impact with severe long-term implications.

Stereotype-confirmation concern arises from the relatively enduring or recurring experience of stereotype threat (Contrada et al., in press). It refers to a dimension defined at one extreme by chronic apprehension about appearing to confirm an ethnic stereotype, and at the other extreme by the absence of such concern. Stereotype-confirmation concern reflects both environmental factors (e.g., other people's ethnicity-related attitudes and behaviors) and personal attributes (e.g., one's ethnicity, the sensitivity and response bias constructs described earlier). Members of all ethnic groups are susceptible to stereotype-confirmation concern, and for each group, there are multiple stereotypes that may create such concern. For example, college undergraduates of diverse ethnicities have reported stereotype-confirmation concern with respect to a wide range of behaviors that might be linked to ethnic stereotypes (e.g., eating certain foods, dressing or speaking a certain way; Contrada et al., in press). Reports of stereotype-confirmation concern have been found to be only moderately correlated with reports of ethnic discrimination. Therefore, although not as widely recognized as ethnic discrimination, stereotype-confirmation concern appears to represent a distinct dimension of ethnicity-related stress.

OWN-GROUP CONFORMITY PRESSURE

Members of an ethnic group often have expectations about what is appropriate behavior for that group. For example, some African Americans who excel academically are accused by their peers of "acting white" (Fordham & Ogbu, 1986). This appears to be just one facet of a wider and more general form of stress originating in one's own ethnic group—what is called *own-group conformity pressure*.

Own-group conformity pressure is defined as the experience of being pressured or constrained by one's ethnic group's expectations specifying appropriate or inappropriate behavior for the group. This experience may be shaped by both internal and external factors, the former including one's ethnicity and perception of in-group norms and expectations, and the latter including explicit, overt sanctions for violating ethnic-group norms, as well as more subtle reminders about "how 'we' are supposed to behave." As with stereotype-confirmation concern, own-group conformity pressure is relatively enduring or recurring, and is potentially applicable to persons of all ethnic groups. Among ethnically diverse college students, reports of own-group conformity pressure relate to personal style and interests (e.g., pressure to dress a certain way, listen to particular music) and social relations (e.g., pressure to date or interact with members of one's own group only; Contrada et al., in press). Reports of own-group conformity pressure in these students are only moderately correlated with reports of ethnic discrimination and stereotype-confirmation concern. Thus, ethnicity-related stressors can arise from members of other ethnic groups, from societal stereotypes, and from members of one's own ethnic group, and these three categories of stressors are all relatively independent.

ETHNICITY-RELATED STRESSORS AND WELL-BEING

Until recently, research examining the impact of ethnicity-related stressors focused on the possibility that internalizing the pejorative stereotypes and prejudiced attitudes of the dominant majority might have a negative impact on the self-concepts of members of ethnic minority groups. However, the evidence does not suggest that being a member of an ethnic group that is devalued by the dominant majority leads inevitably, or even usually, to lower self-regard. For example, it has been found that African Americans do not score lower than whites on self-esteem measures (Crocker et al., 1998).

Regarding psychological outcomes other than self-esteem, there is evidence that members of certain minority groups experience higher rates of depressive symptoms than Euro-Americans (Crocker et al., 1998). However, simple comparisons of ethnic groups may reflect numerous causal determinants, including socioeconomic status and sociocultural norms, in addition to ethnicity-related stressors (Anderson & Armstead, 1995). The contributions of these factors to ethnic-group differences in well-being have yet to be teased apart. Nonetheless, several studies that have examined ethnic discrimination directly have reported that it is associated with negative psychological health outcomes (Williams et al., 1999).

A small but growing body of research has implicated ethnicity-related stressors as a determinant of physical health outcomes. Much of this work has focused on discrimination experienced by African Americans, whose rates of physical disease and mortality significantly exceed those of Euro-Americans (Williams et al., 1999). Some studies have focused directly on disease outcomes. For example, Krieger and Sidney (1996) found that higher blood pressure among African Americans, compared with whites, could be partially explained when blacks' experience of discrimination and their coping responses to such treatment were taken into account. Other work has examined physiological and behavioral factors that may increase risk of disease. Regarding the former, Armstead, Lawler, Gorden, Cross, and Gibbons (1989) demonstrated that when blacks viewed videotaped vignettes of situations involving discrimination, they showed cardiovascular responses thought to contribute to the development of cardiovascular disorders. In an example of research addressing cigarette smoking, a major behavioral risk factor for disease, it was found that African Americans with high scores on a measure of discrimination experienced in everyday life were significantly more likely to be smokers than those with low scores (Landrine & Klonoff, 1996).

CONCLUSION

Research on ethnic discrimination, stereotype threat and stereotype-confirmation concern, and own-group conformity pressure illustrates an emerging new perspective based on the premise that members of ethnic minority groups are not passive victims of prejudice and discrimination, but rather are active agents in making sense of and coping with multiple and distinct ethnicity-related threats. Among the many unresolved questions raised by this proposition are those pertaining to the features of social situations that give rise to ethnicity-related stress, and to the psychological factors that influence detection of these stressors and shape ensuing coping activities. Equally important is the need to isolate the effects of ethnicity-related stressors from the effects of other correlates of ethnic-group membership that may influence psychological and physical well-being, and to identify aspects of ethnic-group membership that may buffer the impact of these stressors. The concept of ethnicity-related stress provides new directions for investigating just some of the many psychological ramifications of ethnic-group membership.

Recommended Reading

Cose, E. (1993). *The rage of a privileged class*. New York: HarperCollins.
Crocker, J., Major, B., & Steele, C. (1998). (See References)
Feagin, J.R., & Sikes, M.P. (1994). *Living with racism: The black middle-class experience.* Boston: Beacon Press.
Phinney, J.S. (1996). When we talk about American ethnic groups, what do we mean? *American Psychologist, 51*, 918–928.
Steele, C.M. (1997). (See References)

Notes

1. Address correspondence to Richard J. Contrada, Department of Psychology, Rutgers University, 53 Avenue E, Piscataway, NJ 08854-8040; e-mail: contrada@rci.rutgers.edu.

2. We use the term ethnicity to refer both to broad groupings of individuals based on culture of origin and to those social groupings conventionally referred to in terms of "race," without presupposing that these groupings reflect a single, fixed quality or essence, biological or otherwise.

References

Allport, G.W. (1954). *The nature of prejudice*. Garden City, NY: Doubleday.
Anderson, N.B., & Armstead, C.A. (1995). Toward understanding the association of socioeconomic status and health: A new challenge for the biopsychosocial approach. *Psychosomatic Medicine, 57*, 213–225.
Armstead, C.A., Lawler, K.A., Gorden, G., Cross, J., & Gibbons, J. (1989). Relationship of racial stressors to blood pressure responses and anger expression in Black college students. *Health Psychology, 8*, 541–556.
Contrada, R.J., Ashmore, R.D., Gary, M.L., Coups, E., Egeth, J.D., Sewell, A., Ewell, K., Goyal, T., & Chasse, V. (in press). Measures of ethnicity-related stress: Psychometric properties, ethnic group differences, and associations with psychological and physical well-being. *Journal of Applied Social Psychology.*
Crocker, J., Major, B., & Steele, C. (1998). Social stigma. In D.T. Gilbert, S.T. Fiske, & G. Lindzey (Eds.), *The handbook of social psychology* (4th ed., Vol. 2, pp. 504–553). Boston: McGraw-Hill.
Deaux, K., & Ethier, K.A. (1998). Negotiating social identity. In J.K. Swim & C. Stangor (Eds.), *Prejudice: The target's perspective* (pp. 301–323). New York: Academic Press.
Feldman Barrett, L., & Swim, J.K. (1998). Appraisals of prejudice and discrimination. In J.K. Swim & C. Stangor (Eds.), *Prejudice: The target's perspective* (pp. 11–36). New York: Academic Press.
Fordham, S., & Ogbu, J.U. (1986). Black students' school success: Coping with the "burden of acting White." *Urban Review, 18*, 176–206.
Krieger, N., & Sidney, S. (1996). Racial discrimination and blood pressure: The CARDIA study of young Black and White adults. *American Journal of Public Health, 86*, 1370–1378.
Landrine, H., & Klonoff, E.A. (1996). The Schedule of Racist Events: A measure of racial discrimination and a study of its negative physical and mental health consequences. *Journal of Black Psychology, 22*, 144–168.
Osborne, J.W. (1995). Academics, self-esteem, and race: A look at the underlying assumptions of the discrimination hypothesis. *Personality and Social Psychology Bulletin, 21*, 449–455.
Ruggiero, K.M., & Taylor, D.M. (1997). Why minority group members perceive or do not perceive the discrimination that confronts them: The role of self-esteem and perceived control. *Journal of Personality and Social Psychology, 72*, 373–389.

Steele, C.M. (1997). A threat in the air: How stereotypes shape intellectual identity and performance. *American Psychologist, 52,* 613–629.

Swim, J.K., Cohen, L.L., & Hyers, L.L. (1998). Experiencing everyday prejudice and discrimination. In J.K. Swim & C. Stangor (Eds.), *Prejudice: The target's perspective* (pp. 38–61). New York: Academic Press.

Williams, D.R., Spencer, M.S., & Jackson, J.S. (1999). Race, stress, and physical health: The role of group identity. In R.J. Contrada & R.D. Ashmore (Eds.), *Self, social identity, and physical health: Interdisciplinary explorations* (pp. 71–100). New York: Oxford University Press.

Why Socioeconomic Status Affects the Health of Children: A Psychosocial Perspective

Edith Chen

University of British Columbia, Vancouver, British Columbia, Canada

Abstract

This article provides an overview of research on socioeconomic status (SES) and physical health in childhood. SES has a gradient relationship with children's health, such that for each incremental increase in SES, there is a comparable benefit in children's health. In this article, I discuss psychosocial mechanisms underlying this association and argue that it is important to utilize knowledge about how the relationship between SES and health changes with age to inform a developmentally plausible search for mediators of this relationship. Furthermore, SES at different points in a child's lifetime may have different effects on health. I advocate an interdisciplinary approach to searching for mediators that would allow researchers to understand how characteristics of society, the neighborhood, the family, and the individual child are involved in the processes linking SES and children's health.

Keywords

socioeconomic status; children's health; psychosocial

One of the most striking and profound findings in epidemiology is that individuals lower in socioeconomic status (SES) have poorer health than individuals higher in SES. This relationship holds true whether health is measured as the prevalence rate of illness, the severity of illness, or the likelihood of mortality, and it is true for most types of diseases, as well as for many risk factors for diseases. This finding has been reported for many countries, including those with and those without universal health care. And it has been demonstrated across the life span, from childhood to older adulthood (Adler et al., 1994; Anderson & Armstead, 1995; Chen, Matthews, & Boyce, 2002).

One of the most intriguing aspects of the relationship between SES and health is that it exists as a gradient. That is, it is not just that poor people have poorer health than rich people. Rather, each step increase in SES is accompanied by incremental benefits in health. This gradient makes the search for underlying mechanisms a challenge for researchers. Obvious mechanisms, such as inadequate nutrition, housing, or health insurance, cannot explain why upper-middle-class individuals have slightly poorer health than upper-class individuals. In this article, I discuss psychosocial explanations for the SES-health relationship, with an emphasis on children's health. I focus here on physical health; however, other researchers have explored these issues for children's mental health and well-being (see Leventhal & Brooks-Gunn and McLoyd under Recommended Reading).

Address correspondence to Edith Chen, University of British Columbia, Department of Psychology, 2136 West Mall, Vancouver, B.C. V6T 1Z4, Canada.

45

POSSIBLE PSYCHOSOCIAL PATHWAYS

Researchers have suggested many explanations for the effect of SES on health. For example, the effect may be due to genetic influences, environmental exposures to toxins, quality of medical care, and psychological-behavioral factors, just to name a few possibilities (Anderson & Armstead, 1995). Here I provide a brief overview of some of the primary psychological-behavioral factors. Research in this area has focused on individual characteristics that fall into four main categories: stress, psychological distress, personality factors, and health behaviors (Adler et al., 1994; Anderson & Armstead, 1995).

With respect to stress, lower-SES children and adults experience more negative life events (stressors) than higher-SES individuals; in addition, they perceive greater negative impact from any given event (stress appraisal). In turn, a large body of literature has linked stress to a wide variety of negative biological and health outcomes in both children and adults. Evidence has documented that stress is one plausible mediator linking SES to health (Cohen, Kaplan, & Salonen, 1999). Thus, one theory is that as one moves down in SES, the amount of stress one experiences increases, which in turn takes a physiological toll on the body, putting one at greater risk for a variety of diseases.

A second possibility is that psychological distress plays a role. Because of the social environments in which they grow up, lower-SES individuals may be more prone to experiencing negative emotional states than higher-SES individuals are, and if the experience of negative emotions has biological consequences, this could also lead to poorer health. Previous research has found support for the notion that lower-SES individuals are more likely to experience negative emotions such as depression and anxiety, and that these negative emotions are linked to illnesses, such as cardiovascular disease, as well as to mortality rates (Gallo & Matthews, 2003).

A third hypothesis is that lower-SES individuals are likely to possess personality traits that are detrimental to health. That is, lower SES individuals may be more likely than higher-SES individuals to possess certain dispositional traits that are adaptive in the social environments in which they live, but have negative health consequences. For example, living in a dangerous neighborhood may make lower-SES individuals likely to mistrust others and to hold cynical attitudes toward others. Thus, one might expect lower-SES individuals to be more hostile and less optimistic about their future than higher-SES individuals are. In turn, such personality traits have been found to place individuals at increased risk for illnesses (Adler et al., 1994).

Finally, compared with individuals of higher SES, those of lower SES may be less likely to engage in healthy behaviors, such as exercising, eating a healthy diet, and not smoking. In part, this may be because of available resources. For example, the availability of healthy products in grocery stores varies by the SES of neighborhoods (Williams & Collins, 2001); people with reduced access to healthy products in their neighborhood grocery stores will have increased difficulty maintaining a healthy diet. Lower-SES neighborhoods also are more dangerous than higher-SES neighborhoods, and less likely to have public parks and venues for exercise (Williams & Collins, 2001); thus, decreases in SES increase the barriers to engaging in regular exercise.

These factors are promising possibilities for clarifying the psychosocial reasons why decreases in SES are associated with decreases in health. However, most of these factors focus on the individual. In trying to understand the health of children, it is particularly important to consider the role of factors in the family and the larger environment. In addition, given the vast social, cognitive, emotional, and biological differences between young children and older adolescents, it is important to consider whether the relevance of the various factors depends on the individual's age.

DEVELOPMENTAL TRAJECTORIES

Exploring the strength of the SES-health relationship during different periods of childhood may provide insight into pathways linking SES with health. My colleagues and I have argued that the relationship between SES and health may be stronger in certain periods of childhood than others. In trying to understand why this is so, one should consider developmental factors that are important during each period of childhood.

Previously, we proposed three models of how the relationship between SES and health may change across childhood (Chen et al., 2002). The childhood-limited model states that relationships between SES and health are strongest in early childhood, and weaken with age. This suggests that factors that are particularly important during early childhood may play a role in explaining health outcomes. For example, the quality of child care, attachment to parents, and housing conditions may be important factors during this period. Research has shown, for example, that injuries are strongly correlated with SES early in childhood, but not during adolescence (West, 1997). It may be the case that unsafe housing conditions are most relevant to young children, who do not have the ability to recognize and avoid danger in their homes, but that as children age and improve in cognitive abilities, they more easily recognize and avoid dangers at home, so the strength of the relationship between SES and injury decreases.

The adolescent-emergent model states that relationships between SES and health are weak early in life, but strengthen with age. According to this model, factors that become important during adolescence, such as peer influence or certain personality characteristics, may play a role in the SES-health relationship. For example, physical activity is more strongly correlated with SES during adolescence than earlier in childhood (Chen et al., 2002). One explanation may be that earlier in life, health behaviors are shaped strongly by parents as role models, but as a child ages, peers begin to exert influence on his or her health behaviors. The combination of parent plus peer influence may lead to stronger relationships between SES and health behaviors during adolescence than earlier in childhood.

Finally, the persistence model states that relationships between SES and health are similar throughout childhood and adolescence. In such cases, factors that would not be expected to change with children's age may be important. For example, the correlation between severity of asthma and SES is similar across childhood and adolescence (Chen et al., 2002). One possible explanation for this correlation is that asthma severity is in part determined by a family's trust in their health care provider. Compared with higher-SES families, lower-SES families may have greater mistrust of the medical community, which in turn may lead to poorer adherence to instructions and advice regarding medications and behaviors for managing asthma. If this psychosocial factor does not change significantly as a child ages, then one would expect to see the relationship between SES and asthma severity follow a persistence model.

LONGITUDINAL RELATIONSHIPS

In addition to considering the relationship between SES and health at different points during childhood, it is important to understand how SES may change over children's lives, and what impact these changes have on children's health. Family SES can fluctuate dramatically from year to year, and a child's history of SES may affect health differently than current SES does. For example, current SES may affect the quality of health care a family has access to, as well as how they are treated in medical settings. In contrast, history of SES may play a role in the development of health problems.

For example, SES effects may accumulate over time. Previous research has shown that amount of time spent in low SES is an important predictor of adult mortality rates (McDonough, Duncan, Williams, & House, 1997), young adults' self-reported health (Power, Manor, & Matthews, 1999), and cognitive development and behavioral problems in children (Duncan, Brooks-Gunn, & Klebanov, 1994). These findings suggest that it takes time for SES to have effects on health.

Some researchers have suggested that there may be critical periods in childhood when SES has its biggest effect. For example, early childhood experiences may program a pattern of biological and behavioral responses that has prolonged effects across the life span. Research has demonstrated that SES early in life is a predictor of adult health behaviors (Lynch, Kaplan, & Salonen, 1997), and that early childhood environments predict adult cardiovascular disease (Barker, 1992). In addition, these relationships persist even after accounting for the effect of adult SES. These findings suggest that it may be important to understand the characteristics of a child's environment during critical windows in order to understand health consequences later in life.

LEVELS OF EXPLANATIONS

Explanations for how SES affects children's health are not likely to be limited to pathways involving individual psychological characteristics. For example, there could be SES differences in societal-level factors, neighborhood-levels factors, and family factors that also contribute to health disparities in children.

Societal factors could include social policies, such as ones that affect how access to and quality of health care vary across SES. Also, some researchers have argued that different societies have different levels of trust and cohesion among community members, and of investment in the community (social capital). Those communities that have low levels of social capital may have access to fewer public goods (such as community-organized group transportation) and find day-to-day life more stressful (e.g., difficulty getting to health care clinics) than those that have high levels of social capital. The communities of lower-SES families are likely to have lower levels of social capital than the communities of higher-SES families, and, in turn, social capital has been found to mediate the relationship between SES and health (Kawachi, Kennedy, Lochner, & Prothrow-Stith, 1997).

At the neighborhood level, there are several factors that may contribute to the SES-health relationship. A neighborhood that is dangerous creates barriers to engaging in positive health behaviors such as participating in sports or exercising. Lower-SES neighborhoods also are characterized by more toxic environments (greater pollution, more lead paint, etc.) than higher-SES neighborhoods. Finally, neighborhoods vary in terms of their degree of segregation. Neighborhoods that are segregated tend to receive less investment in public services than integrated neighborhoods do. More segregated neighborhoods tend to be lower in SES and to have higher mortality rates (Williams & Collins, 2001).

In addition, when studying children's health, it is important to consider the role of the family. Factors at this level include the quality of relationships within the family, such as whether they are characterized by conflict and aggression, as well as the degree of supportiveness in the home. Researchers have documented that families with high levels of conflict and with cold, unsupportive relationships are more likely than other families to have children who experience health problems throughout life, and have dysregulated biological systems (Repetti, Taylor, & Seeman, 2002).

At the individual level, as I have already described, factors such as stress, psychological distress, personality traits, and health behaviors are likely to play a role. In addition, certain psychological factors may buffer low-SES individuals from poor health outcomes. For example, one study found that individuals who were low in SES but believed they had a high degree of control over their lives had health profiles that were more similar to those of high-SES individuals than to those of low-SES individuals who did not believe that they had control over their lives (Lachman & Weaver, 1998).

CONCLUSIONS

Research has documented an intriguing gradient relationship between SES and children's health. Future research that addresses two main themes is needed. First, the field will achieve a more integrated understanding of the mechanisms behind the SES-health relationship by utilizing interdisciplinary collaborations to determine the extent to which societal-level variables (e.g., social capital), neighborhood-level variables (e.g., residential segregation), family-level variables (e.g., relationship quality), and individual-child factors (e.g., stress) contribute to this relationship. Methods from epidemiology, sociology, psychology, and medicine, among other disciplines, could be used not only to develop state-of-the-art assessments of factors at each of these levels, but also to determine how factors at one level interact with factors at another level to influence health. For example, thus far, studies have rarely examined the extent to which the neighborhood environment affects an individual child's personality development, or, conversely, the extent to which the personality of an individual child or adult contributes to the characteristics of a whole neighborhood; neither have many studies investigated how individual and neighborhood factors synergistically combine to affect health. Studies that take a broad view and consider factors at multiple levels would provide researchers and the public with greater knowledge about important contributors to health, and help society learn to effectively implement health-enhancing interventions.

The second important theme for future research is to more extensively explore dynamic effects of SES on physical health. It is important to understand whether each type of health outcome is more strongly shaped by early childhood SES, fluctuations in SES, or current SES. An understanding such as this would be critical for determining the timing of health interventions. That is, interventions should be targeted toward early childhood if SES early in life turns out to be critical; in contrast, if cumulative SES turns out to be important, intervention at any stage in life (to reduce the total amount of time spent in low SES) would be beneficial. Such effective targeting of health interventions could help tremendously in maximizing the long-term health of society.

Recommended Reading

Adler, N.E., Boyce, W.T., Chesney, M.A., Folkman, S., & Syme, S.L. (1993). Socioeconomic inequalities in health: No easy solution. *Journal of the American Medical Association, 269,* 3140–3145.

Chen, E., Matthews, K.A., & Boyce, W.T. (2002). (See References)

Duncan, G.J., & Brooks-Gunn, J. (1997). *Consequences of growing up poor.* New York: Russell Sage Foundation.

Leventhal, T., & Brooks-Gunn, J. (2000). The neighborhoods they live in: The effects of neighborhood residence on child and adolescent outcomes. *Psychological Bulletin, 126,* 309–337.

McLoyd, V.C. (1998). Socioeconomic disadvantage and child development. *American Psychologist, 53,* 185–204.

Acknowledgments—I thank Gregory Miller for his helpful comments on this manuscript.

References

Adler, N.E., Boyce, T., Chesney, M.A., Cohen, S., Folkman, S., Kahn, R.L., & Syme, S.L. (1994). Socioeconomic status and health: The challenge of the gradient. *American Psychologist, 49,* 15–24.

Anderson, N.B., & Armstead, C.A. (1995). Toward understanding the association of socioeconomic status and health: A new challenge for the biopsychosocial approach. *Psychosomatic Medicine, 57,* 213–225.

Barker, D.J.P. (1992). *Fetal and infant origins of adult disease.* London: British Medical Journal.

Chen, E., Matthews, K.A., & Boyce, W.T. (2002). Socioeconomic differences in children's health: How and why do these relationships change with age? *Psychological Bulletin, 128,* 295–329.

Cohen, S., Kaplan, G.A., & Salonen, J.T. (1999). The role of psychological characteristics in the relation between socioeconomic status and perceived health. *Journal of Applied Social Psychology, 29,* 445–468.

Duncan, G., Brooks-Gunn, J., & Klebanov, P. (1994). Economic deprivation and early childhood development. *Child Development, 65,* 296–318.

Gallo, L.C., & Matthews, K.A. (2003). Understanding the association between socioeconomic status and physical health: Do negative emotions play a role? *Psychological Bulletin, 129,* 10–51.

Kawachi, I., Kennedy, B.P., Lochner, K., & Prothrow-Stith, D. (1997). Social capital, income inequality, and mortality. *American Journal of Public Health, 87,* 1491–1498.

Lachman, M.E., & Weaver, S.L. (1998). The sense of control as a moderator of social class differences in health and well-being. *Journal of Personality and Social Psychology, 74,* 763–773.

Lynch, J.W., Kaplan, G.A., & Salonen, J.T. (1997). Why do poor people behave poorly? Variation in adult health behaviors and psychosocial characteristics by stages of the socioeconomic lifecourse. *Social Science and Medicine, 44,* 809–819.

McDonough, P., Duncan, G.J., Williams, D., & House, J. (1997). Income dynamics and adult mortality in the United States, 1972 through 1989. *American Journal of Public Health, 87,* 1476–1483.

Power, C., Manor, O., & Matthews, S. (1999). The duration and timing of exposure: Effects of socioeconomic environment on adult health. *American Journal of Public Health, 89,* 1059–1065.

Repetti, R.L., Taylor, S.E., & Seeman, T. (2002). Risky families: Family social environments and the mental and physical health of offspring. *Psychological Bulletin, 128,* 330–366.

West, P. (1997). Health inequalities in the early years: Is there equalisation in youth? *Social Science and Medicine, 44,* 833–858.

Williams, D.R., & Collins, C. (2001). Racial residential segregation: A fundamental cause of racial disparities in health. *Public Health Reports, 116,* 404–416.

Critical Thinking Questions

1. Factors that influence health range across many levels of organization. How might factors at different levels influence each other? How might these factors in turn influence health? Sketch a model that links together variables at the individual, social, and societal levels and their effects on health.

2. How would you expect each of the factors (stress, depression , ethnicity, etc.) discussed in this section to operate across the lifespan? That is, what might the effects of each variable be during childhood, adulthood, and among the elderly?

3. Chen's article discusses how the SES gradient is linear in nature. That is, for each small increase in social status, there is a corresponding benefit in terms of health. While it's easy to generate hypotheses explaining why poor individuals have worse health than wealthy individuals, it's much more challenging to account for disparities at the upper end of the gradient. What are some mechanisms that can explain this pattern? Among well-educated and highly paid individuals, why would small differences in social status continue to confer health benefits?

4. Imagine that you're an industrial psychologist advising companies about how to improve employee satisfaction and productivity. Based on Spector's theory about control in the workplace, what kinds of assessments and interventions might you implement?

5. Nearly all of the studies described in these articles have correlational designs. As a result, we cannot infer causal relationships from them. Psychosocial characteristics could be "causing" disease to develop more rapidly, but they also could be a result of the disease itself, or some third factor could be influencing both processes. How would you design a study that determines with certainty whether psychosocial factors such as stress and depression influence the development and progression of disease? Obviously, inducing these states in human subjects would be unethical and impractical. What are your other options?

How Do Psychosocial and Environmental Characteristics Get Inside the Body to Influence Health?

Section 1 provided an overview of the psychosocial and environmental characteristics that are known to contribute to the development and progression of medical illness. However, the field of health psychology would be remiss if it stopped at that level, and did not try to explain how these characteristics influence the disease processes. That is, what specific biological systems are affected by psychosocial and environmental factors? What are plausible models for explaining how one goes from a psychological state to a disease outcome? To begin to explain these links, we need to understand biological systems that are influenced by psychosocial and environmental factors, and at the same time are involved in disease pathogenesis.

To begin, Kemeny provides a nice overview of three major systems—the autonomic nervous system, the hypothalamic-pituitary-adrenal axis, and the immune system—that have been linked to stress. In addition, Kemeny emphasizes an important point for health psychologists: that psychological states do not produce uniform effects on biological systems. For example, although negative emotions are thought to be bad for health, there are many different types of negative emotions (e.g., depression, anxiety), and each may have different physiological consequences. Kemeny provides evidence that different psychological states can have different hallmark physiological profiles, a concept known as specificity.

Next, we turn to articles that examine the mechanisms linking specific psychosocial and environmental characteristics with disease outcomes. Adler and Conner-Snibbe discuss possible mechanisms for the effects of low SES on physical health that you read about in Section 1. Their review highlights the importance of considering environmental (e.g., exposure to toxins), psychological (e.g., negative affect), and behavioral (e.g., diet) factors on biological systems and subsequent health. To best understand health outcomes, it is important to not just focus on one type of mediator (e.g., psychological), but rather to consider a broad variety of influences on health. Uchino et al. take on another major characteristic studied in health psychology—the role of social support. They document that social support has effects on the major biological systems, including cardiovascular, neuroendocrine, and immune function, and suggest that these effects could work through similar psychological and behavioral pathways as Adler suggests. Moreover, Uchino et al. argue that there are many different types of social support—for example, one can get advice (informational support) or one can get emotional support during times of stress. It is important for researchers to study the conditions under which different types of support are beneficial or harmful.

Overmier and Murison review animal studies that document the effects of psychological states such as stress on the development of peptic ulcers. Animal models of research are important to health psychology because they allow researchers to conduct more tightly controlled experiments that are often not feasible and/or ethical in human subjects. For example, researchers have exposed animals to chronic stressors such as shock, and by doing so have been able to convincingly demonstrate that stress leads to the development of ulcers. This work also has revealed that the stress responses can be modulated—for example, allowing animals to predict when the stressor will occur or to control the stressor will reduce the likelihood of ulcer. Importantly, Overmier and Murison discuss the notion that stress is not the sole cause of ulcers, but rather that it modifies other processes, such as animal's ability to fight off the bacteria that cause disease. Thus, it is critical for researchers to understand how psychosocial characteristics interact with microbial organisms and biological systems involved in defense.

The last two articles discuss the specific roles of the immune system and genes in the relationship between social/environmental factors and disease. Ader emphasizes how the immune system is not autonomous, but is affected by other biological systems, as well as behavior. Ader demonstrates how the immune system can be modified by external stimuli—for example, animals can be conditioned to exhibit an immune response when they are exposed to a stimulus that has nothing to do with the immune system (e.g., a sweet liquid), if that stimulus has previously been paired with a drug that affects the immune system. Gottlieb discusses how genes and environment affect behavior, and dispels the myth that genes work unidirectionally to influence behavior. Instead, Gottlieb presents evidence that genes themselves are affected by environmental stimuli. This implies that we should not be thinking that genes are determining our destiny, but rather of genes and environment as working together and influencing each other to shape human behavior. This will likely be one of the most important next frontiers in research on mechanisms in health psychology—determining how psychosocial and environmental characteristics influence the turning on and off of genes.

The Psychobiology of Stress

Margaret E. Kemeny[1]
Department of Psychiatry, University of California, San Francisco, San Francisco, California

Abstract

Stressful life experience can have significant effects on a variety of physiological systems, including the autonomic nervous system, the hypothalamic-pituitary-adrenal axis, and the immune system. These relationships can be bidirectional; for example, immune cell products can act on the brain, altering mood and cognition, potentially contributing to depression. Although acute physiological alterations may be adaptive in the short term, chronic or repeated provocation can result in damage to health. The central dogma in the field of stress research assumes a stereotyped physiological response to all stressors (the generality model). However, increasing evidence suggests that specific stressful conditions and the specific way an organism appraises these conditions can elicit qualitatively distinct emotional and physiological responses (the integrated specificity model). For example, appraisals of threat (vs. challenge), uncontrollability, and negative social evaluation have been shown to provoke specific psychobiological responses. Emotional responses appear to have specific neural substrates, which can result in differentiated alterations in peripheral physiological systems, so that it is incorrect to presume a uniform stress response.

Keywords

stress; endocrine; autonomic; immune; physiology; emotion; cognitive

The term stress is used in the scientific literature in a vague and inconsistent way and is rarely defined. The term may refer to a stimulus, a response to a stimulus, or the physiological consequences of that response. Given this inconsistency, in this review I avoid using the term stress (except when discussing the field of stress research) and instead differentiate the various components of stress. *Stressors*, or stressful life experiences, are defined as circumstances that threaten a major goal, including the maintenance of one's physical integrity (physical stressors) or one's psychological well-being (psychological stressors; Lazarus & Folkman, 1984). *Distress* is a negative psychological response to such threats and can include a variety of affective and cognitive states, such as anxiety, sadness, frustration, the sense of being overwhelmed, or helplessness. Researchers have proposed a number of stressor taxonomies, most of which differentiate threats to basic physiological needs or physical integrity, social connectedness, sense of self, and resources. A number of properties of stressful circumstances can influence the severity of the psychological and physiological response. These properties include the stressor's controllability (whether responses can affect outcomes of the stressor), ambiguity, level of demand placed on the individual, novelty, and duration.

PHYSIOLOGICAL EFFECTS OF EXPOSURE TO STRESSFUL LIFE EXPERIENCE

Extensive research in humans and other animals has demonstrated powerful effects of exposure to stressors on a variety of physiological systems. These specific changes are believed to have evolved to support the behaviors that allow the organism to deal with the threat (e.g., to fight or flee). In order for the organism to respond efficiently, physiological systems that are needed to deal with threats are mobilized and physiological systems that are not needed are suppressed. For example, when responding to a threat, the body increases available concentrations of glucose (an energy source) to ready the organism for physical activity; at the same time, the body inhibits processes that promote growth and reproduction. Although the body is adapted to respond with little ill effect to this acute mobilization, chronic or repeated activation of systems that deal with threat can have adverse long-term physiological and health effects (McEwen, 1998; Sapolsky, 1992). A wide array of physiological systems have been shown to change in response to stressors; in this section, I summarize the effects on the three most carefully studied systems (Fig. 1).

Impact on the Autonomic Nervous System

Since Walter Cannon's work on the fight-or-flight response in the 1930s, researchers have been interested in the effects of stressful experience on the

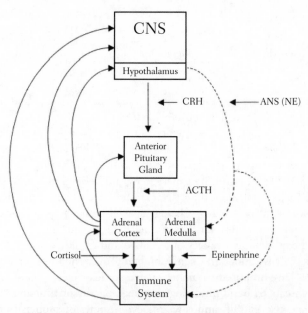

Fig. 1. Schematic representation of interrelationships among the central nervous system (CNS), the hypothalamic-pituitary-adrenal axis, the autonomic nervous system (ANS), and the immune system. Dashed lines indicate ANS neural pathways, and solid lines indicate hormonal pathways. ACTH = adrenocorticotropic hormone; CRH = corticotropin-releasing hormone; NE = norepinephrine.

sympathetic adrenomedullary system (the system is so named because the sympathetic nervous system and adrenal medulla are its key components; see Fig. 1). Cannon correctly proposed that exposure to emergency situations results in the release of the hormone epinephrine from the adrenal medulla (the core of the adrenal gland, located above the kidney). This effect was shown to be accomplished by the activity of the autonomic nervous system (ANS). The ANS has two components: the *parasympathetic nervous system*, which controls involuntary resting functions (activation of this system promotes digestion and slows heart rate, e.g.), and the *sympathetic nervous system*, which comes into play in threatening situations and results in increases in involuntary processes (e.g., heart rate and respiration) that are required to respond to physical threats. Fibers of the sympathetic nervous system release the neurotransmitter norepinephrine at various organ sites, including the adrenal medulla, causing the release of epinephrine (also known as adrenaline) into the bloodstream. Research has demonstrated that exposure to a variety of stressors can activate this system, as manifested by increased output of norepinephrine and epinephrine, as well as increases in autonomic indicators of sympathetic arousal (e.g., increased heart rate). This extremely rapid response system can be activated within seconds and results in the "adrenaline rush" that occurs after an encounter with an unexpected threat.

Impact on the Hypothalamic-Pituitary-Adrenal Axis

A large body of literature suggests that exposure to a variety of acute psychological stressors (e.g., giving a speech, doing difficult cognitive tasks), for relatively short durations, can cause an increase in the levels of the hormone cortisol in the blood, saliva, and urine. This increase is due to activation of the hypothalamic-pituitary-adrenal (HPA) axis (see Fig. 1). Neural pathways link perception of a stressful stimulus to an integrated response in the hypothalamus, which results in the release of corticotropin-releasing hormone. This hormone stimulates the anterior part of the pituitary gland to release adrenocorticotropic hormone, which then travels through the blood stream to the adrenal glands and causes the adrenal cortex (the outer layer of the adrenal gland) to release cortisol (in rodents this hormone is called corticosterone). The activation of this entire system occurs over minutes rather than seconds (as in the case of the ANS). The peak cortisol response occurs 20 to 40 min from the onset of acute stressors. Recovery, or the return to baseline levels, occurs 40 to 60 min following the end of the stressor on average (Dickerson & Kemeny, 2002).

Impact on the Immune System

Exposure to stressful experiences can diminish a variety of immune functions. For example, stressful life experiences, such as bereavement, job loss, and even taking exams, can reduce circulating levels of classes of immunological cells called lymphocytes; inhibit various lymphocyte functions, such as the ability to proliferate when exposed to a foreign substance; and slow integrated immune responses, such as wound healing (Ader, Felten, & Cohen, 2001). Individuals' autonomic reactivity to stressors correlates with the degree to which their immune system is affected by acute laboratory stressors. Extensive evidence that autonomic nerve fibers innervate (enter into) immune organs and alter the function of immune cells residing there supports the link between the ANS and the immune system. In addition, some of the immunological effects of stressors are due to the potent suppressive effects of cortisol on immunological cells. Cortisol can inhibit the production of certain cytokines (chemical mediators released by immune cells to regulate the activities of other immune cells) and suppress a variety of immune functions.

Exposure to stressors can also enhance certain immune processes, for example, those closely related to inflammation. Inflammation is an orchestrated response to exposure to a pathogen that creates local and systemic changes conducive to destroying it (e.g., increases in core body temperature). However, chronic, inappropriate inflammation is at the root of a host of diseases, including certain autoimmune diseases such as rheumatoid arthritis, and may play a role in others, such as cardiovascular disease. There is a great deal of current interest in factors that promote inappropriate inflammation outside the normal context of infection. Exposure to some psychological stressors can increase circulating levels of cytokines that promote inflammation, perhaps because stressful experience can reduce the sensitivity of immune cells to the inhibitory effects of cortisol (Miller, Cohen, & Ritchey, 2002).

Not only can the brain and peripheral neural systems (systems that extend from the brain to the body—e.g., the ANS and HPA axis) affect the immune system, but the immune system can affect the brain and one's psychological state. In rodents, certain cytokines can act on the central nervous system, resulting in behavioral changes that resemble sickness (e.g., increases in body temperature, reduction in exploratory behavior) but also appear to mimic depression (e.g., alterations in learning and memory, anorexia, inability to experience pleasure, reductions in social behavior, alterations in sleep, behavioral slowing). Emerging data indicate that these cytokines can induce negative mood and alter cognition in humans as well. These effects may explain affective and cognitive changes that have been observed to be associated with inflammatory conditions. They may also explain some depressive symptoms associated with stressful conditions (Maier & Watkins, 1998).

Health Implications

Activation of these physiological systems during exposure to a stressor is adaptive in the short run under certain circumstances but can become maladaptive if the systems are repeatedly or chronically activated or if they fail to shut down when the threat no longer exists. McEwen (1998) has coined the term *allostatic load* to refer to the cumulative toll of chronic overactivation of the physiological systems that are designed to respond to environmental perturbations. For example, evidence suggests that chronic exposure to stressors or distress (as in posttraumatic stress disorder and chronic depression) can cause atrophy in a part of the brain called the hippocampus, resulting in memory loss. Chronic exposure to stressful circumstances has also been shown to increase vulnerability to upper respiratory infections in individuals exposed to a virus. Researchers have observed effects on other health outcomes as well, but complete models of stress and health that document all the mediating mechanisms from the central nervous system to the pathophysiological processes that control disease are not yet available (Kemeny, 2003).

GENERALITY VERSUS SPECIFICITY IN THE PHYSIOLOGICAL RESPONSE TO STRESSORS

The central dogma of most stress research today is that stressors have a uniform effect on the physiological processes I have just described. Hans Selye shaped the thinking of generations of researchers when he argued that the physiological response to stressful circumstances is nonspecific, meaning that all stressors, physical and psychological, are capable of eliciting the triad of physiological changes he observed in his rodent research: shrinking of the thymus (a central immune organ), enlargement of the adrenal gland (which produces corticosterone), and ulceration of the gastrointestinal tract. Very little research has directly tested this *generality model* by determining whether or not differences in stressful conditions are associated with distinctive physiological effects in humans. Modern versions of the generality model propose that if stressors lead to the experience of distress (or perceived stress), then a stereotyped set of physiological changes will be elicited in the systems I have described. These models also emphasize the important role of a variety of psychological and environmental factors that can moderate the relationships among stressor exposure, distress, and physiological activation (see Fig. 2). However, these newer versions are essentially generality models because all of the factors are considered relevant to the extent that they buffer against or exacerbate the experience of distress, without considering that different kinds of distress (e.g., different emotional responses) might have distinctive physiological correlates. According to these models, distress has a uniform relationship to physiology.

There is, however, increasing evidence for specificity in the relationship between stressors and physiology. Weiner (1992) advocated an integrated specificity model of stressor physiology, arguing that "organisms meet . . . challenges and dangers by integrated behavioral, physiological patterns of response that are appropriate to the task" (p. 33). According to this model, both behavior and physiology are parts of an integrated response to address a specific environmental condition (see Fig. 3), and specific conditions or environmental signals

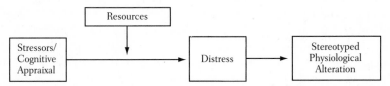

Fig. 2. The generality model of stress. This model proposes that exposure to stressors and the cognitive appraisals of those events can lead to distress. The nature of this relationship depends on the resources available to deal with the stressors (e.g., coping skills, social support, personality factors, genetics, environmental resources). Elevations in distress cause a stereotyped physiological alteration in stress-responsive systems. Bidirectional relationships between many components of the model are assumed but are not indicated here.

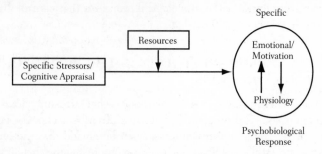

Fig. 3. The integrated specificity model of stress. This model proposes that exposure to specific stressful conditions and cognitive appraisals of those conditions shape the specific nature of an integrated psychobiological response (including emotion-motivation and physiology) to promote adaptive responses to the threat. For example, threats that are appraised as uncontrollable may lead to an integrated psychobiological response that includes disengagement from the goal that is threatened by the stressor (manifested in withdrawal, inactivity, and reduced effort), related affective states (e.g., depression), and physiological changes that support disengagement. Threats appraised as controllable may lead to an integrated response involving engagement with the threat and physiological responses supporting active coping processes. As in the generality model, resources available to deal with the stressors can moderate this relationship.

elicit a patterned array of hormonal and neural changes that are designed to ready the organism to deal with the specific nature of the threat. In animals, specific neural and peripheral changes occur in concert with behaviors such as fighting, fleeing, defending, submitting, exerting dominance, and hunting prey, among others. Distinctive behaviors (fight, flight, and defeat) have also been elicited by activating specific regions of the brain with excitatory amino acids.

COGNITIVE APPRAISALS SHAPE PHYSIOLOGICAL RESPONSES

Cognitive appraisal processes can profoundly shape the specific nature of the physiological response to stressful circumstances and play a central role in the integrated specificity model. Cognitive appraisal is the process of categorizing a situation in terms of its significance for well-being (Lazarus & Folkman, 1984). Primary appraisal relates to perceptions of goal threat, whereas secondary appraisal relates to perceptions of resources available to meet the demands of the circumstance (e.g., intellectual, social, or financial resources). Three categories of cognitive appraisals have been shown to elicit distinctive affective and physiological responses.

Threat Versus Challenge

According to Blascovich and Tomaka (1996), the experience of threat results when the demands in a given situation are perceived to outweigh the resources. When resources are perceived to approximate or exceed demands, however, the individual experiences a challenge response. These two motivational states are associated with distinctive ANS alterations. In situations that require active responses to obtain a goal, challenge is associated with increases in sympathetic arousal (increased cardiac performance) coupled with reduced or unchanged peripheral resistance (resistance to blood flow). These changes parallel those observed with metabolically demanding aerobic exercise. Threat, in contrast, although also associated with sympathetic arousal involving increased cardiac performance, is associated with *increased* peripheral resistance, leading to increased blood pressure. Thus, different cognitive appraisals can result in distinctive patterns of ANS reactivity with potentially distinguishable implications for health. The issue here is not degree of activation of the sympathetic nervous system, but rather distinctive qualities of activation depending on the specific nature of the cognitive appraisal process.

Perceived Control

Animal and human research demonstrates that uncontrollable circumstances, or those perceived as uncontrollable, are more likely to activate key stressor-relevant systems than are circumstances that the organism perceives to be controllable. For example, when rodents with and without control over exposure to identical stressors are compared, those with control show a reduced cortisol response. A meta-analysis (a statistical analysis that summarizes findings across studies) has demonstrated that humans who are exposed to stressors in an acute laboratory context are significantly more likely to experience HPA activation if the stressors are uncontrollable than if they are controllable (Dickerson & Kemeny, 2002). Threats that are appraised as controllable but in fact are uncontrollable have been shown to elicit less severe physiological alterations (e.g., in the immune system) than those appraised as uncontrollable.

Social Cognition

The social world has a powerful effect on stress-relevant physiological systems (Cacioppo, 1994). For example, social isolation has a very significant effect on health, which is likely mediated by the physiological systems described here. Other social processes can regulate physiological systems as well. For example, place in a dominance hierarchy has a significant effect on physiological systems. Subordinate animals, who have low social status, demonstrate a more activated HPA axis, higher levels of cytokines that promote inflammation, and other physiological changes compared with their dominant counterparts. A meta-analytic review has demonstrated that demanding performance tasks elicit HPA activation when one's social status or social self-esteem is threatened by performance failures, but these effects are greatly diminished when this social-status threat is not present (Dickerson & Kemeny, 2002). Cognitive appraisals of social status and social self-esteem appear to play an important role in these effects (Dickerson, Gruenewald, & Kemeny, in press).

CONCLUSIONS

The research findings on cognitive appraisal and physiological systems lead to two important conclusions. First, depending on the nature of the eliciting conditions, different patterns of physiological response can occur. Second, when cognitive appraisals of conditions are manipulated, distinctive physiological effects can be observed within the same context. Therefore, the way the individual thinks about the situation may override the impact of the specific nature of the conditions themselves.

In the integrated specificity model of stressful experience, stressful conditions and appraisals of them elicit integrated psychobiological responses (including emotion and physiology) that are tied to the nature of the threat experienced. A number of researchers have found that different neural and autonomic pathways are activated during different emotional experiences. Thus, specific emotions, in all likelihood, play a central role in the nature of the physiological response to stressful conditions. A more intensive evaluation of the role of distinct emotions would be an important contribution to future stress research. It is most likely that distinctions will be observed when researchers evaluate patterns of physiological change across systems, rather than relying on single response systems (e.g., cortisol level), and when emotional behavior is assessed in conjunction with self-report data.

Recommended Reading

Dickerson, S.S., & Kemeny, M.E. (2002). (See References)
Kemeny, M.E., & Gruenewald, T.L. (2000). Affect, cognition, the immune system and health. In E.A. Mayer & C. Saper (Eds.), *The biological basis for mind body interactions* (pp. 291–308). Amsterdam: Elsevier Science.
Lazarus, R.S., & Folkman, S. (1984). (See References)
Sapolsky, R.M. (1992). (See References)
Weiner, H. (1992). (See References)

Acknowledgments—This article is dedicated to the memory of Herbert Weiner, a pioneer in the field of stress research, who profoundly shaped the thinking of the generations of stress researchers he trained.

Note

1. Address correspondence to Margaret E. Kemeny, Health Psychology Program, Department of Psychiatry, Laurel Heights Campus, University of California, 3333 California St., Suite 465, San Francisco, CA 94143.

References

Ader, R., Felten, D.L., & Cohen, N. (2001). *Psychoneuroimmunology* (3rd ed.). New York: Academic Press.
Blascovich, J., & Tomaka, J. (1996). The biopsychosocial model of arousal regulation. *Advances in Experimental Social Psychology, 28*, 1–51.
Cacioppo, J.T. (1994). Social neuroscience: Autonomic, neuroendocrine, and immune responses to stress. *Psychophysiology, 31*, 113–128.
Dickerson, S.S., Gruenewald, T.L., & Kemeny, M.E. (in press). When the social self is threatened: Shame, physiology and health. *Journal of Personality.*
Dickerson, S.S., & Kemeny, M.E. (2002). *Acute stressors and cortisol responses: A theoretical integration and synthesis of laboratory research.* Manuscript submitted for publication.
Kemeny, M.E. (2003). An interdisciplinary research model to investigate psychosocial cofactors in disease: Application to HIV-1 pathogenesis. *Brain, Behavior & Immunity, 17*, 562–572.
Lazarus, R.S., & Folkman, S. (1984). *Stress, appraisal, and coping.* New York: Springer.

Maier, S.F., & Watkins, L.R. (1998). Cytokines for psychologists: Implications of bidirectional immune-to-brain communication for understanding behavior, mood, and cognition. *Psychological Review, 105*, 83–107.

McEwen, B.S. (1998). Protective and damaging effects of stress mediators. *New England Journal of Medicine, 338*, 171–179.

Miller, G.E., Cohen, S., & Ritchey, A.K. (2002). Chronic psychological stress and the regulation of pro-inflammatory cytokines: A glucocorticoid resistance model. *Health Psychology, 21*, 531–541.

Sapolsky, R.M. (1992). Neuroendocrinology of the stress-response. In J.B. Becker, S.M. Breedlove, & D. Crews (Eds.), *Behavioral endocrinology* (pp. 287–324). Cambridge, MA: MIT Press.

Weiner, H. (1992). *Perturbing the organism: The biology of stressful experience.* Chicago: University of Chicago Press.

The Role of Psychosocial Processes in Explaining the Gradient Between Socioeconomic Status and Health

Nancy E. Adler[1] and Alana Conner Snibbe

Health Psychology Program, Department of Psychiatry, University of California, San Francisco, San Francisco, California

Abstract

The gradient between socioeconomic status (SES) and health is well established: Many measures of health show that health increases as SES increases. However, the mechanisms underlying this association are not well understood. Behavioral, cognitive, and affective tendencies that develop in response to the greater psychosocial stress encountered in low-SES environments may partially mediate the impact of SES on health. Although these tendencies might be helpful for coping in the short term, over time they may contribute to the development of allostatic load, which increases vulnerability to disease. Debate remains regarding the direction of causation between SES and health, the impact of income inequality, the interaction of SES with race-ethnicity and gender, and the effects of SES over the life course.

Keywords

socioeconomic status; health; psychosocial mediators; race-ethnicity; stress

Researchers in many fields are increasingly interested in the relationship between socioeconomic status (SES) and health. In 1993, *The New England Journal of Medicine* published several articles documenting marked differences in death rates among individuals at different income and educational levels. The journal's editor, Marcia Angell, observed that "in study after study, socioeconomic status emerges as one of the most important influences in morbidity and mortality" (Angell, 1993, p. 126). She further commented that SES is a "most mysterious" determinant, acting on health not directly, but rather through indirect mechanisms.

Shortly after this series of articles, Adler et al. (1994) challenged psychologists to help unravel this mystery. They noted that the SES-health relationship was not simply a function of poverty and could not be explained by lack of access to health care. Presenting evidence of a graded relationship between SES and health, which appears even in populations with universal access to care, they argued that psychosocial processes could play a mediational role. In this article, we describe the SES-health gradient, review what has been discovered about psychosocial mediators, and discuss current controversies and questions.

THE RELATIONSHIP BETWEEN SES AND HEALTH

SES is a reflection of social position, and is traditionally measured by income, education, and occupation. Each dimension of SES reflects different resources (e.g., education confers knowledge, credentials, and social networks; income provides access to better housing, nutrition, and health care). Though often used interchangeably, these measures are only moderately intercorrelated. Nevertheless, they show similar relationships to health—a graded association such that across the full range of SES, higher SES is associated with better health. Thus, it is not just that individuals in poverty have higher morbidity and mortality rates than those above the poverty line; the middle-class also has worse health than the wealthy. Similarly, people who have not completed high school have higher mortality rates than do high school graduates, who, in turn, have higher mortality rates than do college graduates. The Whitehall Study of health among British civil servants provides a clear demonstration of this SES-health gradient. The initial study found that 10-year survival increased with occupational grade; the highest-grade civil servants had significantly lower mortality than did the next-highest, "executive grade" civil servants, who had lower mortality than did clerical employees, and so on. These effects remained 25 years later, even after many participants had retired (Marmot & Shipley, 1996).

Although income shows a graded association with mortality, the effect is greatest at the lowest income levels, especially for infant mortality. Thus, the effect of additional income on health is greatest for the poorest groups. At the same time, because SES effects continue along the entire income spectrum, and because most people are in the middle of the distribution, most health disparities associated with SES occur among the middle classes. The SES-health gradient is seen for many diseases, but is strongest for cardiovascular disease, arthritis, diabetes, chronic respiratory diseases, and cervical cancer, as well as for the psychiatric disorders of schizophrenia, substance abuse, and anxiety.

POSSIBLE MECHANISMS

No single mechanism accounts for the SES-health gradient. Figure 1 presents a simplified model of pathways through which SES may affect health. This model does not include all pathways, nor does it depict feedback loops and interactions among domains.

Each of the boxes between SES and health in Figure 1 represents a different level of analysis. Within each level, as SES declines, demands increase and resources for dealing with these demands decrease. Consequently, across multiple life domains, individuals with lower SES are exposed to more stress than are individuals with higher SES. Moreover, at any given level of stress, they experience a larger psychological response to that stress. Over time, this combination of stress and stress reactivity diminishes individuals' reserve capacity for responding to environmental challenges, and may make them more vulnerable to disease (Gallo & Matthews, 2003).

Environments

SES is associated with the physical and social environments in which individuals work and live (Fig. 1, Box B). Those individuals with fewer socioeconomic resources generally inhabit environments with higher levels of toxins, pathogens, and noise, and have jobs that subject them to more physical risks (Box D). They

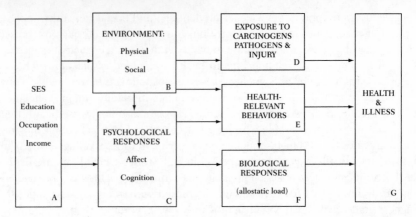

Fig. 1. Simplified model of pathways from socioeconomic status (SES) to health. Modified from Adler and Ostrove (1999).

encounter more social conflict, crowding, and crime, while experiencing less social support. They also have decreased access to means for restoring and maintaining health, including recreation facilities, health care, and healthy foods.

Psychological Tendencies

Physical and social environments shape cognitive and affective tendencies (Fig. 1, Box C). In this section, we present evidence regarding those tendencies that are associated with both SES and health outcomes. Where possible, we discuss studies that have shown specifically that cognitive and affective tendencies play a role in the relationship between SES and health. However, because SES, psychological tendencies, and biological or health outcomes have seldom all been examined within any one sample, such evidence is limited.

Extensive data attest to the centrality of perceived personal control and mastery in the SES-health gradient. Because lower-SES contexts afford fewer opportunities for control, it is not surprising that individuals at lower levels of SES report less mastery and control than do higher-SES individuals. Perceived control is also related to health outcomes, and may influence the relationship between SES and health. For example, Lachman and Weaver (1998) found that low-SES individuals with high levels of perceived control have health outcomes similar to those of high-SES individuals. Control in the work environment appears to be particularly important to health. In the Whitehall sample of civil servants, for example, perceived control at work accounted for more than half of the association between SES and health (Marmot, Bosma, Hemingway, Brunner, & Stansfeld, 1997).

Lower-SES environments may also diminish optimism and foster hopelessness and hostility, which are closely linked to the affective states of depression and anger. Negative cognitions and affective states increase as SES decreases (see Gallo & Matthews, 2003). Hopelessness and depression predict a myriad of health outcomes, including heart attacks and cardiac death, and account for some of the relationship between SES and health (Fiscella & Franks, 1997).

Hostility and anger are likewise potent predictors of mortality and morbidity, and among some groups they mediate the relationship between SES and cardiovascular functioning (Gump, Matthews, & Räikkönen, 1999). Finally, optimism-pessimism predicts such health outcomes as recovery from coronary bypass surgery and onset of AIDS in HIV-positive men.

A specific cognition related to SES is subjective social standing. People are often keenly aware of their own SES standing vis-à-vis others' SES, and of negative stereotypes about their group. Recent studies suggest that individuals' evaluations of where they stand on a "social ladder"—anchored at the top by those having the most income and education and the best jobs, and at the bottom by those having the least resources and worst jobs—are strongly associated with a variety of health indicators, including self-rated health, waist-to-hip ratio, and heart rate (e.g., Adler, Epel, Castellazzo, & Ickovics, 2000). Scores on measures of subjective social standing are correlated with indicators of psychological distress, such as depression and negative affect, but show independent associations with health outcomes. Current research is uncovering what determines individuals' subjective status.

Behavior

Those health-relevant behaviors that contribute the most to morbidity and mortality—smoking, sedentary lifestyle, high-fat diet—also increase as SES decreases (Fig. 1, Box E). Similarly, adherence to prescribed treatments for medical conditions varies by SES. Thus, for example, although diabetics' control over their blood sugar is better the more educated they are, this association disappears in analyses that statistically control for adherence to the treatment regimen (Goldman & Smith, 2002). Differences in health-relevant behaviors across SES levels may reflect the extent to which environments differentially constrain or encourage those behaviors. Environmental constraints operate in conjunction with SES-related cognitive and affective tendencies, such as hostility and depression, to affect people's health-relevant behavior. Although behavior contributes substantially to morbidity and premature mortality, it does not wholly explain the SES-health gradient. Health-related behaviors account for less than half of the association between SES and health (Lantz et al., 2001).

Biological Responses

Exposure to acute and chronic stressors, including those associated with lower SES, elicits a cascade of cognitive, affective, and biological responses. These responses are often functional in the short run, but over time may damage systems that regulate the body's stress response. A useful concept for understanding how these responses cause disease is allostatic load (McEwen, 1998), which is the cumulative wear and tear caused by repeated adaptations. Even relatively small changes in the direction of dysregulation or poorer functioning can increase disease risk if they occur across multiple systems. A person's allostatic load is measured by summing the number of indicators on which he or she is in the highest-risk quartile. These indicators include systolic and diastolic blood pressure, waist-to-hip ratio, HDL and LDL cholesterol, blood glycosylated hemoglobin (the percentage of hemoglobin that is chemically bound to glucose, an indicator of glucose levels over the past 2–3 months), and the hormones cortisol, DHEA (dehydroepiandrosterone), epinephrine, and norepinephrine. Allostatic load may serve as a common biological pathway leading from SES to multiple health outcomes (Fig. 1, Box F). In a sample of healthy elderly adults, for example, allostatic load scores at the start of the study were higher as SES level decreased, and these scores predicted physical and cognitive decline, cardiac events, and mortality up to 7 years later (Karlamangla, Singer, McEwen, Rowe, & Seeman, 2002).

CONTROVERSIES AND QUESTIONS

As psychologists, we have focused on stress as a key mechanism underlying the SES-health gradient, emphasizing individual psychosocial and physiological processes. Researchers from other disciplines, such as sociology, economics, and social epidemiology, place relatively more emphasis on the direct effects of material, historical, and ecological factors on health. Research on income inequality highlights the diverse approaches of these disciplines. Income inequality, a measure of the distribution of income in a given area, is related to mortality rates even in analyses controlling for income. Thus, in two geographic areas with the same mean income, the one in which income is more unequally distributed will likely have a higher mortality rate. Psychologically inclined researchers attribute this association to psychosocial features, such as heightened social anxiety and diminished social trust in communities where income is more unequally distributed. However, other scholars attribute the phenomenon to material features of the environments, arguing that high income inequality results in underinvestment in infrastructure. Still others question whether the finding is due to methodological artifacts, such as the confounding of income inequality with racial composition. Despite ongoing disagreements, the issue of income inequality's effects on mortality has become a crossroads for fruitful interdisciplinary dialogue, underscoring the importance of considering both contextual and individual factors.

At the level of individual SES, there are also questions about the confounding of race-ethnicity with SES. In the United States, because of patterns of discrimination and social disadvantage, many ethnic minorities are overrepresented at lower SES levels. For some diseases and disorders, racial-ethnic differences in prevalence disappear in analyses controlling for SES. However, for others, significant differences remain. These findings suggest that although a substantial portion of the racial-ethnic differences in health is due to social disadvantages associated with low SES, unique effects specific to race-ethnicity also exist, reflecting experiences of discrimination, residential segregation, negative stereotypes, and other circumstances. As a result, measures of SES may have different meanings and implications within different populations and groups. Further work on the joint and independent contributions of SES and race-ethnicity to health is needed.

The meaning of traditional SES measures may also differ by gender. Women's social class has often been determined by their husbands' status, and some studies have found that the husband's occupational status is a better predictor of a woman's health than her own occupational status. These findings illustrate the importance of considering such issues as gender discrimination and relative power in relationships, and the intersection of gender with other demographic variables.

Another growing area of research concerns SES effects across the life span. The SES-health gradient is strongest at birth (i.e., infant mortality) and in mid to late adulthood. Most research on SES and health has focused on adults' current SES. Yet several studies suggest that childhood SES and the length of time spent living in low-SES conditions are also important predictors of adult health outcomes. An unresolved issue is the extent to which childhood SES has an impact primarily as a contributor to adult SES or sets psychological and physiological tendencies that independently affect adult health.

A related issue is the extent to which health affects SES. There is some evidence for the hypothesis that individuals in poorer health "drift" down the SES hierarchy. However, the reverse impact, of SES on health, appears to be greater. This is especially true for educational attainment, which predicts health many years after education is completed. Innovative studies capitalizing on random events that affect SES and studies showing that individuals' health is affected by their spouses' SES provide evidence of causality running from SES to health. Nonetheless, mapping the dynamic relationship between SES and health remains a research challenge.

CONCLUSIONS

Over the past decade, research on the socioeconomic determinants of health has increased exponentially, and researchers are now examining more closely the mechanisms by which SES "gets into the body." Research on psychosocial pathways points to the importance of differential exposure to stress. As SES decreases, individuals are exposed to more demands and have fewer resources with which to address them. Responses to such stress—at the psychological, behavioral, and biological levels—may be adaptive in the short run, but can damage health over time. For example, at the psychological level, threatening environments may foster a degree of distrust that may be functional in protecting individuals against victimization. Such distrust may generalize, however, and individuals may respond to ambiguous events in a distrustful way, heightening physiological arousal and further undermining social trust (Chen & Matthews, 2001). Thus, increased biological risk may derive not just from greater environmental exposure to stressors, but also from greater psychological reactivity to the environment. Similarly, biological responses to stress are functional in that they mobilize energy for a "fight or flight" response, but the cumulative effects of repeated adaptations may increase vulnerability to disease.

A number of controversies and questions about the association between SES and health remain. On the scientific side, these involve establishing the direction of causal influences between SES and health, the relative roles of material and psychosocial conditions, how SES operates in conjunction with race-ethnicity and gender, and whether biological responses to stress constitute a common pathway for a range of diseases. On the policy side, there is debate about the utility of addressing the mediating pathways at the individual level, as opposed to trying to modify SES itself. Although it may be possible to buffer the effects of lower status by helping individuals develop better ways of coping with the stresses that low SES generates, policies that improve education, employment, and income could have broader effects.

Recommended Reading

Adler, N.E., Boyce, W.T., Chesney, M., Cohen, S., Folkman, S., Kahn, R., & Syme, S.L. (1994). (See References)

Adler, N.E., Marmot, M., McEwen, B., & Stewart, J. (Eds.). (1999). *Socioeconomic status and health in industrialized nations: Social, psychological, and biological pathways.* New York: New York Academy of Sciences.

Gallo, L.C., & Matthews, K.A. (2003). (See References)

McEwen, B. (2002). *The end of stress as we know it.* Washington, DC: Joseph Henry Press.

Acknowledgments—Preparation of the article was supported by the John D. and Catherine T. MacArthur Foundation Research Network on SES and Health and by the National Institute of Mental Health (training grant). We would like to thank Judith Stewart and Marilyn Vella for their help.

Note

1. Address correspondence to Nancy E. Adler, University of California, San Francisco, 3333 California St., Suite 465, San Francisco, CA 94143-0848; e-mail: nadler@itsa.ucsf.edu.

References

Adler, N.E., Boyce, W.T., Chesney, M., Cohen, S., Folkman, S., Kahn, R., & Syme, S.L. (1994). Socioeconomic status and health: The challenge of the gradient. *American Psychologist, 49,* 15–24.

Adler, N.E., Epel, E.S., Castellazzo, G., & Ickovics, J.R. (2000). Relationship of subjective and objective social status with psychological and physiological functioning: Preliminary data in healthy white women. *Health Psychology, 19,* 586–592.

Adler, N.E., & Ostrove, J.M. (1999). SES and health: What we know and what we don't. In N.E. Adler, M. Marmot, B. McEwen, & J. Stewart (Eds.), *Socioeconomic status and health in industrialized nations: Social, psychological, and biological pathways* (pp. 3–15). New York: New York Academy of Sciences.

Angell, M. (1993). Privilege and health: What is the connection? *New England Journal of Medicine, 329,* 126–127.

Chen, E., & Matthews, K.A. (2001). Cognitive appraisal biases: An approach to understanding the relation between socioeconomic status and cardiovascular reactivity in children. *Annals of Behavioral Medicine, 23,* 101–111.

Fiscella, K., & Franks, P. (1997). Does psychological distress contribute to racial and socioeconomic disparities in mortality? *Social Science and Medicine, 45,* 1805–1809.

Gallo, L.C., & Matthews, K.A. (2003). Understanding the association between socioeconomic status and physical health: Do negative emotions play a role? *Psychological Bulletin, 129,* 10–51.

Goldman, D.P., & Smith, J.P. (2002). Can patient self-management help explain the SES health gradient? *Proceedings of the National Academy of Sciences, USA, 99,* 10929–10934.

Gump, B.B., Matthews, K.A., & Räikkönen, K. (1999). Modeling relationships among socioeconomic status, hostility, cardiovascular reactivity, and left ventricular mass in African American and White children. *Health Psychology, 18,* 140–150.

Karlamangla, A.S., Singer, B.H., McEwen, B.S., Rowe, J.W., & Seeman, T.E. (2002). Allostatic load as a predictor of functional decline: MacArthur studies of successful aging. *Journal of Clinical Epidemiology, 55*, 696–710.

Lachman, M.E., & Weaver, S.L. (1998). The sense of control as a moderator of social class differences in health and well-being. *Journal of Personality and Social Psychology, 74*, 763–773.

Lantz, P.M., Lynch, J.W., House, J.S., Lepkowski, J.M., Mero, R.P., Musick, M.A., & Williams, D.R. (2001). Socioeconomic disparities in health change in a longitudinal study of US adults: The role of health-risk behaviors. *Social Science and Medicine, 53*, 29–40.

Marmot, M.G., Bosma, H., Hemingway, H., Brunner, E., & Stansfeld, S. (1997). Contribution of job control and other risk factors to social variations in coronary heart disease incidence. *Lancet, 350*, 235–239.

Marmot, M.G., & Shipley, M.J. (1996). Do socioeconomic differences in mortality persist after retirement? 25-year follow up of civil servants from the first Whitehall study. *British Medical Journal, 313*, 1177–1180.

McEwen, B.S. (1998). Protective and damaging effects of stress mediators. *New England Journal of Medicine, 338*, 171–179.

Social Support, Physiological Processes, and Health

Bert N. Uchino,[1] Darcy Uno, and Julianne Holt-Lunstad

Department of Psychology and Health Psychology Program, University of Utah, Salt Lake City, Utah

Abstract

Social relationships serve important functions in people's everyday lives. Epidemiological research indicates that supportive relationships may also significantly protect individuals from various causes of mortality, including cardiovascular disease. An important issue is how social support influences such long-term health outcomes. In this article, we review evidence indicating that social support may influence mortality via changes in the cardiovascular, endocrine, and immune systems. These data suggest that it may be worthwhile to incorporate social-support interventions in the prevention and treatment of physical health problems.

Keywords

social support; cardiovascular function; immune function; health

Relationships with others form a ubiquitous part of people's everyday lives. In the classic analysis by Durkheim (1897/1951), suicide rates were higher among individuals who were less socially integrated than among those who had many social ties. The loneliness and despair that characterize a lack of social connections may be responsible for such unfortunate outcomes. Less obvious, however, is the possibility that individuals with poor relationships may also be more at risk for physical illnesses, such as cardiovascular disease, cancer, or infectious diseases. Is there evidence that such an association exists? If so, how is it that social relationships influence such disease processes?

The answer to the first question is relatively well documented. A review of large prospective studies comparing groups with differing degrees of social integration found that less socially integrated individuals had higher mortality rates from all causes, including cardiovascular mortality (House, Landis, & Umberson, 1988). In fact, the evidence linking social relationships to mortality was comparable to the evidence linking standard risk factors such as smoking and physical activity to mortality. What is less known is the answer to the second question, that is, how social relationships influence such long-term health outcomes. In this article, we review the evidence linking positive aspects of social relationships (i.e., social support) to physiological processes. These associations are helping us to understand how relationships may influence physical health outcomes such as cardiovascular disease.

HOW MIGHT RELATIONSHIPS INFLUENCE PHYSICAL HEALTH OUTCOMES?

Relationships serve important functions. For instance, most people can recall times when others made a difference in their lives by giving good advice (informational support); helping them feel better about themselves (emotional support); directly providing aid, such as money (tangible support); or just "hanging out" with them (belonging support). The actual or perceived availability of these helpful behaviors by others is broadly defined as social support.

Figure 1 depicts a simplified model of how social support might influence physical health outcomes (see Cohen, 1988, for a detailed model). The major pathway depicted in the top portion of the figure suggests that social support may be beneficial because it protects individuals from the deleterious behavioral and physiological consequences of stress. In theory, social support may decrease how stressful an individual finds an event to be. For instance, a person who has supportive ties may experience less job stress because close others provide helpful information or reaffirm other aspects of that person's life (e.g., familial role). The decreased stress appraisal may in turn influence psychological processes such as negative mood states, feelings of personal control, and self-esteem. These psychological processes are thought to influence the cardiovascular, endocrine, and immune systems, with implications for relevant disease outcomes (Kiecolt-Glaser & Glaser, 1995). For instance, over the long term, alterations in cardiovascular function (e.g., heart rate) may influence cardiovascular disorders such as high blood pressure, whereas a decrease in immune function may have implications for cancer and infectious diseases. However, even when individuals are not encountering stressful life events, it is possible that social support may affect physiological processes by directly influencing the psychological processes of self-esteem, feelings of personal control, and negative mood states. For instance, simply being in the company of close friends may elevate one's mood.

An additional pathway by which social support may be linked to physical health outcomes is through the modification of health behaviors, such as smoking, exercise, and diet (Umberson, 1987), that in turn influence relevant physiological processes (e.g., exercise decreases blood pressure). There are several ways in which social support may influence health behaviors. First, higher levels of stress have been linked to poorer health behaviors (Kiecolt-Glaser & Glaser, 1995). Social support may facilitate better health behaviors because it decreases the amount of stress that an individual experiences. Second, social support may

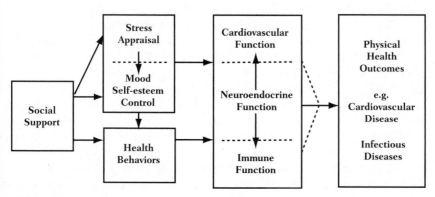

Fig. 1. Simplified model of how social support may influence physical health outcomes. Dotted lines within the boxes separate distinct pathways within the various systems.

directly motivate individuals to engage in more healthy practices. For instance, close family members may place pressures on an individual to exercise or stop smoking. It is also possible that having adequate social support communicates the fact that one is loved, and this may lead to better health behaviors by increasing the motivation to care for oneself.

IS SOCIAL SUPPORT RELATED TO PHYSIOLOGICAL PROCESSES?

The model shown in Figure 1 indicates that social support ultimately influences health outcomes via relevant biological pathways. In a recent review, we examined the evidence linking social support to physiological processes that might influence disease risk (Uchino, Cacioppo, & Kiecolt-Glaser, 1996). In particular, we focused on the cardiovascular, endocrine, and immune systems as potential pathways by which social support might influence health.

Most of the studies we examined investigated the association between social support and cardiovascular function. There were more than 50 such studies, and most focused on blood pressure. Blood pressure is an important variable because over time, elevations in blood pressure can be a risk factor for cardiovascular diseases. In fact, there is increasing concern about the potential risk of elevated blood pressure even below the range that is normally considered hypertensive (MacMahon et al., 1990). Overall, we found in our review of studies that individuals with high levels of social support had lower blood pressure than individuals with lower levels of social support.

It is noteworthy that there was also evidence linking social support to better blood pressure regulation in hypertensive patients. Most of these studies were interventions that utilized the patient's spouse as a source of support to help the patient control his or her blood pressure. These intervention studies provide direct evidence for the health relevance of social support and suggest that recruiting familial sources of support may be a particularly effective (and cost-effective) intervention strategy.

Finally, recent studies suggest that social support can reduce the magnitude of cardiovascular changes during stressful circumstances, a finding consistent with the model in Figure 1. For instance, Gerin, Pieper, Levy, and Pickering (1992) compared physiological reactivity of subjects who participated in a debate task when a supportive person (an individual who agreed with the participant) was or was not present. The presence of the supportive person was associated with lower blood pressure and heart rate changes during the task. The ability of social support to reduce cardiovascular changes during stress is important because it has been hypothesized that heightened physiological reactivity to stress may increase the risk for the development of cardiovascular disorders (Manuck, 1994). The finding of lowered cardiovascular reactivity when social support is available may also have implications for individuals who have existing cardiovascular disease, as heightened cardiovascular changes when psychological stressors are experienced can induce a temporary imbalance of oxygen supply and demand in the heart (Krantz et al., 1991). This imbalance can lead to potentially dangerous cardiac conditions in such at-risk populations.

In our review of the literature, we also examined 19 studies that tested the possibility that social support may be related to aspects of immune function. An association between social support and immunity would be important because the immune system is responsible for the body's defense against infectious and malignant (cancerous) diseases. In general, the available studies suggest that social support is related to a stronger immune response. For instance, natural killer cells are an important line of defense against virus-infected and some tumor cells. In our review, several studies found that individuals with high levels of social support had stronger natural killer cell responses (i.e., ability to kill susceptible tumor cells) than individuals with lower levels of social support.

The associations between social support and immune function are consistent with the results of a recent study by Cohen, Doyle, Skoner, Rabin, and Gwaltney (1997), who examined whether social support predicted susceptibility to the common-cold virus. In this study, consenting participants were directly exposed to common-cold viruses (i.e., via nasal drops) and quarantined for 5 days. Individuals who had more diverse social networks (i.e., relationships in a variety of domains, such as work, home, and church) were less likely to develop clinical colds than individuals with less diverse networks. The authors discussed the possibility that having a diverse social network may be particularly beneficial as support may be obtained from a variety of sources.

It is important to note that many of the studies that found an association between social support and immune function were conducted with older adult populations. Aging is associated with decreased immunity, and infectious diseases are a major source of morbidity and mortality in older adults. Thus, the lowered immune function in older individuals with low social support may be a finding with particular health relevance.

One important way in which social support may influence the immune system is via the release of endocrine hormones. Environmental factors such as stress can lead to the release of hormones (i.e., catecholamines and cortisol) that in turn influence the immune system. This is possible because many cells of the immune system have hormone receptors that can augment or inhibit the cells' function when activated by specific endocrine hormones. Unfortunately, there is not much research examining if social support is related to endocrine function. However, preliminary evidence from the MacArthur studies of successful aging suggests that higher levels of social support may be linked to lower levels of catecholamines and cortisol in men (Seeman, Berkman, Blazer, & Rowe, 1994). These data are consistent with the research linking social support to alterations in the cardiovascular system because endocrine hormones such as catecholamines directly influence cardiovascular function.

CONCLUSIONS

The available evidence is consistent with the possibility that social support may influence physical health outcomes via relevant physiological processes. What is less clear in this literature is exactly how these changes occur. As shown in Figure 1, there are a number of potential pathways, including changes in negative mood states or health behaviors, but direct evidence bearing on the validity of these pathways is presently lacking. A few studies we reviewed did look for a health-behavior pathway, along with psychological pathways involving depression and perceived stress. Although preliminary, these studies found that these factors could not account for the association between social support and physiological function. Unfortunately, many of these studies utilized cross-sectional designs that provide a less sensitive test of the pathways linking social support to physiological function than do longitudinal designs. This point underscores the importance of conducting longitudinal studies that examine how these dynamic processes involving social support, physiology, and actual health outcomes unfold over time.

An additional issue that warrants further attention is the conditions under which social relationships are most beneficial. Not all close relationships are uniformly positive (consider, e.g., marital conflict). This is an important consideration because negative interactions can interfere with effective social support. In addition, having many supportive friends and family could be beneficial, but it may also entail obligations to be a support provider. At least in some circumstances, being a support provider can be a significant source of stress (e.g., the demands of caregiving activities). These issues highlight the importance of investigating how the relative balance of positive and negative aspects of close relationships influences physiological function and subsequent health outcomes.

Overall, however, we believe that the research reviewed has significant implications for present notions of health and well-being. Would it be possible to utilize this research in combination with standard medical approaches in preventing and treating physical disease? Several interventions suggest the promise of such an approach. Spiegel, Bloom, Kraemer, and Gottheil (1989) found that breast cancer patients randomly assigned to a support group lived almost twice as long as patients simply given routine oncological care. There is also indirect evidence of beneficial effects from general psychosocial interventions that include social-support intervention (Linden, Stossel, & Maurice, 1996). For instance, Fawzy et al. (1993) evaluated the effects of a 6-week structured group intervention that provided education, problem-solving skills, stress management, and social support to cancer patients. A 6-year follow-up revealed that only 9% of individuals in the structured group intervention had died, compared with 29% of individuals in the no-intervention condition. These studies suggest the potential promise of future interventions aimed at utilizing social relationships to promote positive health outcomes.

Recommended Reading

Berkman, L.F. (1995). The role of social relations in health promotion. *Psychosomatic Medicine, 57*, 245–254.
House, J.S., Landis, K.R., & Umberson, D. (1988). (See References)
Kiecolt-Glaser, J.K., & Glaser, R. (1995). (See References)
Uchino, B.N., Cacioppo, J.T., & Kiecolt-Glaser, K.G. (1996). (See References)
Wills, T.A. (1997). Social support and health. In A. Baum, S. Newman, J. Weinman, R. West, & C. McManus (Eds.), *Cambridge handbook of psychology, health, and medicine* (pp. 168–171). New York: Cambridge University Press.

Acknowledgments—Preparation of this article was generously supported by National Institute on Aging Grant No. 1 R55 AG13968 and National Institute of Mental Health Grant No. 1 RO1MH58690. We would like to thank our supportive spouses, Heather M. Llenos, Sean Fujioka, and Nathan Lunstad, for their helpful suggestions on this manuscript. This article is dedicated to the memory of Sean K. Okumura.

Note

1. Address correspondence to Bert N. Uchino, Department of Psychology, 390 S. 1530 E., Room 502, University of Utah, Salt Lake City, UT 84112; e-mail: uchino@psych.utah.edu.

References

Cohen, S. (1988). Psychosocial models of the role of social support in the etiology of physical disease. *Health Psychology*, 7, 269–297.

Cohen, S., Doyle, W.J., Skoner, D.P., Rabin, B.S., & Gwaltney, J.M. (1997). Social ties and susceptibility to the common cold. *Journal of the American Medical Association*, 277, 1940–1944.

Durkheim, E. (1951). *Suicide* (J.A. Spaulding & G. Simpson, Trans.). New York: Free Press. (Original work published 1897)

Fawzy, F.I., Fawzy, N.W., Hyun, C.S., Gutherie, D., Fahey, J.L., & Morton, D. (1993). Malignant melanoma: Effects of an early structured psychiatric intervention, coping, and affective state on recurrence and survival six years later. *Archives of General Psychiatry*, 50, 681–689.

Gerin, W., Pieper, C., Levy, R., & Pickering, T.G. (1992). Social support in social interactions: A moderator of cardiovascular reactivity. *Psychosomatic Medicine*, 54, 324–336.

House, J.S., Landis, K.R., & Umberson, D. (1988). Social relationships and health. *Science*, 241, 540–545.

Kiecolt-Glaser, J.K., & Glaser, R. (1995). Psychoneuroimmunology and health consequences: Data and shared mechanisms. *Psychosomatic Medicine*, 57, 269–274.

Krantz, D.S., Helmers, K.F., Bairey, N., Nebel, L.E., Hedges, S.M., & Rozanski, A. (1991). Cardiovascular reactivity and mental stress-induced myocardial ischemia in patients with coronary artery disease. *Psychosomatic Medicine*, 53, 1–12.

Linden, W., Stossel, C., & Maurice, J. (1996). Psychosocial interventions for patients with coronary artery disease. *Archives of Internal Medicine*, 156, 745–752.

MacMahon, S., Peto, R., Cutler, J., Collins, R., Sorlie, P., Neaton, J., Abbott, R., Godwin, J., Dyer, A., & Stamler, J. (1990). Blood pressure, stroke, and coronary heart disease. Part 1, prolonged differences in blood pressure: Prospective observational studies corrected for the regression dilution bias. *Lancet*, 335, 765–774.

Manuck, S.B. (1994). Cardiovascular reactivity in cardiovascular disease: "Once more unto the breach." *International Journal of Behavioral Medicine*, 1, 4–31.

Seeman, T.E., Berkman, L.F., Blazer, D., & Rowe, J.W. (1994). Social ties and support and neuroendocrine function: The MacArthur studies of successful aging. *Annals of Behavioral Medicine*, 16, 95–106.

Spiegel, D., Bloom, J.R., Kraemer, H.C., & Gottheil, E. (1989). Effect of psychosocial treatment on survival of patients with metastatic breast cancer. *Lancet*, 334, 888–891.

Uchino, B.N., Cacioppo, J.T., & Kiecolt-Glaser, K.G. (1996). The relationships between social support and physiological processes: A review with emphasis on underlying mechanisms and implications for health. *Psychological Bulletin*, 119, 488–531.

Umberson, D. (1987). Family status and health behaviors: Social control as a dimension of social integration. *Journal of Health and Social Behavior*, 28, 306–319.

Animal Models Reveal the "Psych" in the Psychosomatics of Peptic Ulcers

J. Bruce Overmier and Robert Murison[1]

Psychology Department, University of Minnesota, Minneapolis, Minnesota (J.B.O.), and Department of Biological & Medical Psychology, University of Bergen, Bergen, Norway (R.M.)

Ulcers have been regarded for many decades as the prototypical psychosomatic disease in which psychological strain ("stress") leads to serious erosion and perforation of the stomach wall ("ulcers"). Yet limited empirical evidence for stress as a causal factor in ulcers (until recently) and recent claims that they may be caused by bacterial infection have cast doubts on the psychosomatic view of ulcers. In this article, we examine evidence for the continued validity of the psychosomatic view of ulcers.

HISTORICAL CONTEXT

Selye (1936) introduced the concept of "stress," including among its sources both biological and psychological factors and among its consequences peptic ulcers in both the stomach (gastrulas) and the entrance to the small intestine (duodenum). Selye believed ulcers are caused by many factors and characterized them as "pluricausal." Both the psychological and the biological causes have remained a mystery to this day, despite continued study by physicians, physiologists, and psychologists.

The idea that psychological factors might cause physiological disease was not new with Selye. Indeed, the term "psychosomatic," always much criticized, can be traced to the 19th century. Mesmer, Charcot, Janet, and Freud exploited "psychological treatments" for physical symptoms. In U.S. popular culture, peptic ulcer became a prototype for psychosomatic disease. Wolf and Wolff (1947) directly observed the functioning of the stomach in a patient called Tom; they observed that the stomach responds to psychological challenges. These classic observations confirmed that psychological factors can influence the gastrointestinal processes important in the induction of ulcers.

Chronic indigestion and ulcers are common today. Medications to treat these are the world's bestselling drugs (e.g., Pepcid-AC, Tagamet, Zantac, Maalox, Rolaids, and Tums). They are among the top 10 nonfood items sold in supermarkets and outsell products for the common cold (CNN, 1997). Only disposable diapers are of comparable popularity! These anti-ulcer products sell well because, in addition to being common, peptic ulcers have proved resistant to cure.

In the 1950s, physiologists such as Brodie and Bonfils followed Selye's lead and used animal models to demonstrate that physical stress such as total immobilization, often combined with exposure to cold temperatures, reliably caused gastric ulcers (Glavin, Paré, Sandbak, Brake & Murison, 1994). Using animal models allowed medical researchers to explore the degree to which a variety of factors that operate inside the stomach (*proximal* factors), such as acid secretion and stomach contractions, contribute to the production of ulcers. It was soon recognized that the processes within the stomach are controlled by the central nervous system (CNS) through several different neurotransmitters and hormones, as well as the activity of the vagus nerve to the stomach. Release of these transmitters and hormones was proved to be stress dependent. Even genetic factors were explored. Psychology, however, was missing from this physiological analysis.

In the 1950s, experimental psychologists, too, sought to create an animal model of this psychosomatic disease, hoping that understanding some of the experiential and psychological causes (*distal* factors) could facilitate its cure. These researchers sought a task in which chronic psychological stressors could directly induce peptic ulcers.

The classic example—and one that was consistent with the popular culture of the time—was the *executive monkey*. Pairs of animals were jointly administered a succession of noxious shocks that could be prevented if one of the monkeys pressed a lever. The monkey whose responses prevented the shocks was designated the "executive" monkey. The other, yoked monkey could respond, but its actions had no effect on the shocks; that is, for it the shocks were uncontrollable. The executive was responsible for managing the fate of both monkeys, and it worked to prevent the shocks. After 4 weeks on this regime, the executive monkey—and only it—would become seriously ill and manifest gross and sometimes fatal gastric ulcers (Brady, Porter, Conrad, & Mason, 1958). This effect was viewed as attributable to the responsibility of and work burdens on the executive, and it was seen as an analogue to the boardroom executive manager ("The Man in the Gray Flannel Suit") who suffered peptic ulcers. This research caught the imagination of both the public and scientists, and work cycles and other variables were studied. In the long term, the model proved unreliable in its effect (but see Barbaree & Harding, 1973). Which monkey became ill may have been a product of the initial individual emotionality that had determined which animal was selected as the executive (Natelson, 1977). Nonetheless, the heuristic value of the executive-monkey model was undeniable.

Thus, the search was on for psychological models of stress that could cause ulcers. For example, some researchers argued that "conflict" was a powerful source of psychological stress. Therefore, Sawrey (e.g., Sawrey, Conger, & Turrell, 1956) carried out a series of experiments in which rats lived continuously for weeks in a situation that induced approach-avoidance conflict. To get to food, they had to endure brief, mild electric shocks. The experimental group that was in conflict did develop more stomach ulcers than a control group that received the same number of shocks independently of going to the food. Developmental experiences such as early weaning and social factors such as separations from the mother appeared to increase vulnerability to the ulcers induced by chronic conflict (Ader, 1962).[2] However, the animals commonly reduced their food consumption during the conflict, resulting in weight loss that approached 40% (Weisz, 1957). That is, the conflicted animals were virtually in self-starvation, and the ulcers occurred exclusively in the upper, nonactive portion of the stomach rather than the lower, glandular portion that is affected by emotions.

This observation indicated that the ulcers were probably artifacts of the starvation rather than the consequence of psychological conflict. Thus, the conflict model soon disappeared from the research scene.

By the 1970s, Seligman (1968) reported that rats chronically exposed to extended periods of uncontrollable, unpredictable shocks of the type tending to result in behavioral helplessness also developed gastric ulcers. This *learned helplessness* was considered to be a potential factor in psychosomatic illness. In this case, again, the shocked animals ate less than the nonshocked animals, making self-starvation the potential causal factor.

Concurrently, a new chronic method for ulcer induction emerged: the *activity-stress* model (Paré, 1976), This model built on the observation that animals that must eat their daily ration in 1 hr each day will increase their activity between meals if they are free to do so. The increase in activity can be quite dramatic and continues for several days. Within 3 weeks, these animals become ill, manifesting severe gastric ulceration. Ulcers do not occur in animals on the same feeding schedule but limited in their activity or in animals of similar activity but able to eat an equivalent amount whenever they want. Interest in this model has been sustained by the analogy between it and anorexia nervosa (Lett, Grant, Neville, Davis, & Koh, 1997), a disease in which young women dramatically limit their food intake and engage in high levels of physical activity.

But also in the 1970s, a different research strategy emerged. Investigators demonstrated that psychologically important variations in experiences modulated the ulcer-inducing effects of a severe, acute stress. For example, Weiss (1971) partially restrained rats and exposed them to an extended series of unpredictable and uncontrollable electric shocks over a 24-hr period. These rats showed substantial gastric ulcerations in the emotional, glandular portion of the stomach. Using a novel paradigm that matched animals on treatment elements such as numbers and durations of shocks, he found that many fewer ulcers developed in rats that could either predict or control the shocks. Furthermore, the effects of predictability and controllability were additive. Predictability and controllability are the bases for two basic forms of learning, classical conditioning and instrumental training, respectively, that are important ways of coping with the environment. Thus, it seems possible that it was these learning processes per se that provided the mechanism for the reduction in stress-induced ulcers; if so, then the psychological demonstrably influenced the physiological. Other important modulators of amount of ulceration included the opportunity to engage in natural coping behaviors such as gnawing or to attack a conspecific (Guile & McCutcheon, 1980; Weiss, Pohorecky, Salman, & Gruenthal, 1976).

IS A PSYCHOSOMATIC VIEW STILL JUSTIFIED?

The 1980s brought about a dramatic change in the medical world's view of peptic ulcer. Early reports about intestinal bacteria in animals (Rosoff & Goldman, 1968) led an Australian physician, B.J. Marshall, to observe that ulcer patients showed signs of an associated infection by a bacterium, now known as *Helicobacter pylori*. Moreover, when the infection per se was treated with antibiotics, peptic ulcer cures were commonly obtained. Suddenly, ulcers were seen as the direct result of a bacterial infection of the stomach and intestine by *H. pylori*. Kill the bug, cure the ulcer—or so it is commonly claimed!

Although there can be little doubt that *H. pylori* can be a factor in peptic ulcer in humans, a careful review of the data by Weiner (1996) made it clear that the bacterial infection is only one of a complex of possible causal factors. He pointed to several inconsistencies in the data. Although 70% to 90% of ulcer patients show signs of *H. pylori* infection, so do up to 80% of control patients who do not suffer from ulcers. Antibiotic eradication of *H. pylori* heals peptic ulcer in only about 80% of infected patients. Moreover, 75% of patients with the duodenal type of ulcers respond favorably to placebo without any disappearance of the *H. pylori* infection. Finally, then, there is the 10% to 30% of ulcer patients who do not have *H. pylori* infection at all.

These facts do not deny that *H. pylori* can injure the stomach wall or that antibiotic therapy has proved to be a useful adjunct to medical treatment of peptic ulcers. But *H. pylori* is not independently a sufficient cause. Something else is modulating the vulnerability of the glandular stomach wall. That something else is likely to be psychological stress. Indeed, because ulcers appear in patients without any *H. pylori* infection, combinations of other factors can also be causal. Thus, *H. pylori* is best characterized as a cause only in the sense of what logicians have called an *INUS* cause: an *I*nsufficient but *N*ecessary component of an *U*nnecessary but *S*ufficient complex (Mackie, 1965).

PREDISPOSING, PRECIPITATING, AND SUSTAINING

As Selye made clear at the outset, peptic ulcer is multiply caused. Weiner (1996) has provided the most sensible appreciation of the complexity of inducing ulcers—or any psychosomatic disorder. He noted that causal factors can be classified as (a) predisposing to vulnerability, (b) precipitating the ulcers, or (c) sustaining the ulcers once manifest. The factors in each of these classes may be biological or psychological In one sense, this latter distinction is artificial in that all psychological processes are themselves biological and mediated through the CNS, but it usefully segregates more distally anchored psychological events from more proximal physiological processes. Weiner illustrated his analysis by reference to Ader's work showing that the social experiences of an infant may predispose to vulnerability in the adult.

Weiner's view has guided our own research in this area, in which we use a known ulcer-inducing physical challenge (Kitagawa, Fujiwara, & Osumi, 1979) that harkens back to the psychobiology of Richter's work (1957) on sudden death and behavioral despair. To induce ulcers, we suspend a moderately restrained and hungry rat in a bath of room-temperature water for about 1 hr. This treatment induces about 15 mm of gastric erosions along the folds of the glandular portion of the stomach. This "physical" ulcer-inducing challenge may well have psychological components because the challenge itself causes ulcers only in a fully conscious animal (Murison & Overmier, 1993b).[3] It is this ulcer induction that we seek to modulate. In the following paragraphs, we briefly review modulation at the predisposing, precipitating, and sustaining phases of the psychosomatic process.

We have explored primarily how past experiences and psychologically important variations in those past experiences make the animal more vulnerable to this
challenge. A number of past experiences that by themselves do not induce ulcers
have now been shown to increase vulnerability to ulcers when animals are later
challenged with the restraint in water. Prior exposure to a series of uncontrollable, unpredictable footshocks that can induce learned helplessness certainly
increases later vulnerability; this helplessness-related increase in vulnerability is
detected even though days or even months separate the footshock experience
from the challenge (Overmier & Murison, 1991). This increase in vulnerability
caused by a history of intermittent shocks is dependent on the activity of natural morphinelike substances (opioids) in the brain (Overmier & Murison, 1994).
That similar ulcer-predisposing effects of a single long shock are not dependent
on these opioids indicates that there are other important mediating pathways.
However, the adrenocortical stress hormone commonly thought to be causal
(e.g., Murphy, Wideman, & Brown, 1979) is in fact likely protective (Murison,
Overmier, Hellhammer, & Carmona, 1989).

The helplessness-induced increase in vulnerability itself can be modulated.
Providing signals that warn of each impending shock reduces vulnerability to the
later physical challenge. Or, giving the rats control over the shocks by allowing
them to escape also prevents increases in vulnerability (Murison & Isaksen,
1982). Even signals that occur at the end of uncontrolled shocks—just when
escape responses would—also partially prevent increases in vulnerability (Overmier, Murison, Skogland, & Ursin, 1985). That is, signals for safety mimic the
ameliorative effect of escape.

There can also be direct modulation of the process of precipitation of ulcers
in the challenged animals. One can reinstate elements from past fearful experiences—such as conditioned stimuli for danger—during the physical ulcer
induction itself, thus increasing the precipitation of the ulcers. Additionally, if
the ulcer induction is carried out in the same environment as prior exposure to
helplessness-inducing shock treatment, the degree of increase in gastric vulnerability is greater than if the induction is carried out in a novel context (Murison & Overmier, 1990).

Further, manipulations after ulcer induction can modulate the severity of
manifest pathology. One such treatment is simply providing a period of relief
after the physical challenge! In fact, a period of rest after induction of ulcers
results in more severe ulcers than continued exposure to ulcer-inducing challenge itself (Desiderato, MacKinnon, & Hissom, 1974; Overmier, Murison, &
Ursin, 1986). The reasons for this outcome are unknown but may have to do
with the dynamics of rebound from the stress. Finally, if danger signals are presented intermittently during the post-ulcer-induction period, the degree of ulceration is greater than if the animals simply rest during this time (Overmier,
Murison, Ursin, & Skoglund, 1987). These rest and danger-signal factors interact in complex ways that are not yet understood (Murison & Overmier, 1986).

In summary, contemporary research shows that psychologically important
variations in experiences prior to, concurrent with, and after biophysical manipulations that directly induce gastric ulcers can modulate the severity of the ulcer
pathology. Psychological factors do participate in predisposing to, precipitating,

and sustaining these model peptic ulcers, thus confirming the psychological as well as biological nature of the phenomenon.

FROM PRESENT TO FUTURE

The recent animal model experiments on psychological modulation of vulnerability to physically induced gastric ulceration are best seen as illustrating that peptic ulcer is psychosomatic rather than being a simple disease. Such animal models, by the very nature of the complex systems involved, will also lead to the illumination of as-yet unknown relations between psychology and biology—yielding insights into new mechanisms (Hofer & Meyers, 1997). This psychosomatic view of ulcers and other health problems is regaining acceptance (Stam, Akkermans, & Wiegant, 1997).

Psychology cannot ignore the new medical findings of a powerful bacterial cofactor if the psychosomatic approach is to remain fully relevant. Psychological stress treatments, such as learned helplessness and variations on it, also have important effects in suppressing the immune system (Murison & Overmier, 1993a). The human body mounts an immune reaction to *H. pylori* (Mezey & Palkovits, 1992) that likely can be compromised by psychological stress. Future human and animal models of psychosomatic factors in peptic ulcer will necessarily be psycho-neuro-immunological. The picture is complex, but future research on peptic ulcer will certainly include psychologists as well as physiologists, immunologists, and physicians.

Notes

1. Address correspondence to Bruce Overmier, Psychology Department/Elliott Hall, University of Minnesota, 75 E River Rd., Minneapolis, MN 55455; e-mail: psyjbo@tc.utnn.edu.

2. It turns out that the cause of this increased vulnerability is not really deprivation of social interactions at all but rather an impaired regulation of body temperature due to early nutritional problems (Ackerman, Hofer, & Weiner, 1978).

3. That these ulcers can be produced by the induction treatment by itself and in such a short time means that these ulcers are not directly caused by one of the *H. pylori* or related bacteria (e.g., *Campylobacter*). Indeed, it is not at all clear that rats spontaneously harbor these ulcerative bacteria, although other animals do (e.g., ferrets; Fox & Lee, 1989).

Recommended Reading

Glavin, G.B., Murison, R., Overmier, J.B., Paré, W.P., Bakke, H.K., Henke, P.G., & Hernandez, D.E. (1991). The neurobiology of stress ulcers. *Brain Research Reviews, 16,* 301–343.

Sapolsky, R.M. (1994). *Why zebras don't get ulcers.* San Francisco: W.H. Freeman.

Weiner, H. (1992). *Perturbing the organism: The biology of stressful experience.* Chicago: University of Chicago Press.

Wolf, S. (1981). The psyche and the stomach: A historical vignette. *Gastroenterology, 80,* 605–614.

References

Ackerman, S.H., Hofer, M.A., & Weiner, H. (1978). Early maternal separation increases ulcer risk in rats by producing a latent thermoregulatory disturbance. *Science, 201*, 373–376.

Ader, R. (1962). Social factors affecting emotionality and resistance to disease in animals; III. Early weaning and susceptibility to gastric ulcers in the rat. *Journal of Comparative and Physiological Psychology, 55*, 600–602.

Barbaree, H.E., & Harding, R.K. (1973). Free operant avoidance behavior and gastric ulceration in rats. *Physiology & Behavior, 11*, 269–271.

Brady, J.V., Porter, R.W., Conrad, D.G., & Mason, J.W. (1958). Avoidance behavior and the development of gastroduodenal ulcers. *Journal of the Experimental Analysis of Behavior, 1*, 69–71.

CNN. (1997, June 5). *The Evening News*. Atlanta, GA: Cable News Network.

Desiderato, P., MacKinnon, J.R., & Hissom, H. (1974). Development of gastric ulcers in rats following stress termination. *Journal of Comparative and Physiological Psychology, 87*, 208–214.

Fox, J.G., & Lee, A. (1989). Gastric campylobacter-like organisms: Their role in gastric disease of laboratory animals. *Laboratory Animal Science, 39*, 543–553.

Glavin, G.B., Paré, W.P., Sandbak, T., Bakke, H.K., & Murison, R. (1994). Restraint stress in biomedical research: An update. *Neuroscience and Biobehavioral Reviews, 18*, 223–249.

Guile, M.N., & McCutcheon, N.B. (1980). Prepared responses and gastric lesions in rats. *Physiological Psychology, 8*, 480–482.

Hofer, M.A., & Meyers, M.M. (1997). Editorial. *Psychosomatic Medicine, 58*, 521–523.

Kitagawa, H., Fujiwara, M., & Osumi, Y. (1979).Effects of water-immersion stress on gastric secretion and mucosal blood flow in rats. *Gastroenterology, 77*, 298–302.

Lett, B.T., Grant, V.L., Neville, L.I., Davis, M.J., & Koh, M.T. (1997). Chlordiazepoxide counteracts activity-induced suppression of eating in rats. *Experimental and Clinical Psychopharmacology, 5*, 24–27.

Mackie, J.L. (1965). Causes and conditions. *American Philosophical Quarterly, 2*, 245–264.

Mezey, E., & Palkovits, M. (1992). Localization of targets for anti-ulcer drugs in cells of the immune system. *Science, 258*, 1662–1665.

Murison, R., & Isaksen, E. (1982). Gastric ulceration and adrenocortical activity after inescapable and escapable preshock in rats. *Scandinavian Journal of Psychology*, Supp. 1, 133–137.

Murison, R., & Overmier, J.B. (1986). Interactions amongst factors which influence severity of gastric ulcerations in rats. *Physiology & Behavior, 36*, 1093–1097.

Murison, R., & Overmier, J.B. (1990). Proactive actions of psychological stress on gastric ulceration in rats–Real psychobiology. *Annals of the New York Academy of Sciences, 597*, 191–200.

Murison, R., & Overmier, J.B. (1993a). Parallelism among stress effects on ulcer, immunosuppression, and analgesia: Commonality of mechanisms? *Journal of Physiology* (Paris), *87*, 253–259.

Murison, R., & Overmier, J.B. (1993b). Some psychosomatic causal factors of restraint-in-water stress ulcers. *Physiology & Behavior, 53*, 577–581.

Murison, R., Overmier, J.B., Hellhammer, D.H., & Carmona, M. (1989). Hypothalamo-pituitary-adrenal manipulations and stress ulcerations in rats. *Psychoneuroendocrinology, 14*, 331–338.

Murphy, H.M., Wideman, C.H., & Brown, C.S. (1979). Plasma corticosterone level and ulcer formation in rats with hippocampal lesions. *Neuroendocrinology, 28*, 123–130.

Natelson, B.H. (1977). The executive monkey revisited. In F.P. Brooks & P.W. Evers (Eds.), *Nerves and the gut*. (pp. 503–515). Thorofare, NJ: CB Slack.

Overmier, J.B., & Murison, R. (1991). Juvenile and adult footshock stress modulate later adult gastric psychophysiological reactions to restraint stresses in rats. *Behavioral Neuroscience, 105*, 246–252.

Overmier, J.B., & Murison, R. (1994). Differing mechanisms for proactive effects of intermittent and single shock on gastric ulceration. *Physiology & Behavior, 56*, 913–919.

Overmier, J.B., Murison, R., Skoglund, E.J., & Ursin, H. (1985). Safety signals can mimic responses in reducing the ulcerogenic effects of shock. *Physiological Psychology, 13*, 243–247.

Overmier, J.B., Murison, R., & Ursin, H. (1986). The ulcerogenic effect of a rest period after exposure to water-restraint stress. *Behavioral Neuroscience, 46*, 372–382.

Overmier, J.B., Murison, R., Ursin, H., & Skoglund, E.J. (1987). Quality of post-stressor rest influences the ulcerative process. *Behavioral Neuroscience, 101*, 246–253.

Paré, W.P. (1976). The activity-stress ulcer: Frequency and chronicity. *Physiology & Behavior, 16,* 699–704.

Richter, C.P. (1957). On the phenomenon of sudden death in animals and men. *Psychosomatic Medicine, 19,* 191–198.

Rosoff, C.B., & Goldman, H. (1968). Effect of the intestinal bacterial flora on acute gastric stress ulceration. *Gastroenterology, 55,* 212–222.

Sawrey, W.L., Conger, J.J., & Turrell, E.S. (1956). An experimental investigation of the role of psychological factors in the production of gastric ulcers in rats. *Journal of Comparative and Physiological Psychology, 49,* 457–461.

Seligman, M.E.P. (1968). Chronic fear produced by unpredictable shock. *Journal of Comparative and Physiological Psychology, 66,* 402–411.

Selye, H. (1936). A syndrome produced by diverse nocuous agents. *Nature, 148,* 84–85.

Stam, R., Akkermans, L.M.A., & Wiegant, V.M. (1997). Trauma and the gut: Interactions between stressful experience and intestinal function. *Gut, 40,* 704–709.

Weiner, H. (1996). Use of animal models in peptic ulcer disease. *Psychosomatic Medicine, 58,* 524–545.

Weiss, J.M. (1971). Effects of coping behavior in different warning signal conditions on stress pathology in rats. *Journal of Comparative and Physiological Psychology, 77,* 1–13.

Weiss, J.M., Pohorecky, L.A., Salman, S., & Gruenthal, M. (1976). Attenuation of gastric lesions by psychological aspects of aggression in rats. *Journal of Comparative and Physiological Psychology, 90,* 252–259.

Weisz, J.D. (1957). The etiology of experimental gastric ulceration. *Psychosomatic Medicine, 19,* 61–73.

Wolf, S., & Wolff, H.G. (1947). *Human gastric function: An experimental study of a man and his stomach.* New York: Oxford University Press.

Psychoneuroimmunology

Robert Ader[1]

Center for Psychoneuroimmunology Research, Department of Psychiatry, University of Rochester School of Medicine and Dentistry, Rochester, New York

Abstract

Psychoneuroimmunology is the study of the relationships among behavioral, neural and endocrine, and immune processes. Bidirectional pathways connect the brain and the immune system and provide the foundation for neural, endocrine, and behavioral effects on immunity. Examples of such effects are conditioned and stress-induced changes in immune function and in susceptibility to immunologically mediated diseases. These data indicate that researchers should no longer study the immune system as if it functioned independently of other systems in the body. Changes in immune function are hypothesized to mediate the effects of psychological factors on the development of some diseases, and research strategies for studying the clinical significance of behaviorally induced changes in immune function are suggested.

Keywords

conditioning; immunity; stress

Once upon a time, the immune system was considered an autonomous agency of defense. Research conducted over the past 25 years, however, has provided incontrovertible evidence that the immune system is influenced by the brain and that behavior, the nervous system, and the endocrine system are influenced by the immune system. Psychoneuroimmunology, a new hybrid subspecialty at the intersection of psychology, immunology, and the neurosciences, studies these interactions (Ader, 1981b).

The immune system's defense of the organism against foreign, "nonself" material (antigens) is carried out by white blood cells, primarily T and B lymphocytes, that respond in various ways to the presence of antigens and retain a "memory" of encounters with them. Different immune processes can be distinguished by the particular cells that mount the body's defense. Antibody-mediated immunity refers to the production of antibodies by B cells derived from bone marrow; cell-mediated immunity refers to the actions of a variety of T cells derived from the thymus gland. Typically, immune defenses involve interactions among T and B cells and other specialized white blood cells (e.g., macrophages) and substances (cytokines) secreted by activated T cells. Not all immunity is based on the body's recognition of a previously encountered antigen, however. Natural killer (NK) cells, implicated in protection against the spread of cancer cells and the recognition of and defense against viruses, are a type of lymphocyte capable of reacting against some antigens without having had prior experience with them. A readily accessible overview of immune system functions is provided at the following Web site: rex.nci.nih.gov/PATIENTS/INFO_TEACHER/bookshelf/NIH_immune.

BACKGROUND

Interactions between the brain and the immune system were first observed in the laboratory in the 1920s, when scientists found that immune reactions could be conditioned (Ader, 1981a). In the 1950s, there was a short-lived interest in the immunological effects of lesions and electrical stimulation of the brain. At the same time, research was initiated to study the effects of stressful life experiences on susceptibility to experimentally induced infectious diseases. Interest in this research was rejuvenated when, beginning in the 1970s, several independent lines of research provided verifiable evidence of interactions between the brain and the immune system.

We now know that the brain communicates with the immune system via the nervous system and neuroendocrine secretions from the pituitary. Lymphoid organs are innervated with nerve fibers that release a variety of chemical substances that influence immune responses. Lymphocytes bear receptors for a variety of hormones and are thereby responsive to these neural and endocrine signals. The best known of these signals are reflected in the anti-inflammatory and generally immunosuppressive effects of adrenocortical steroids (hormones released by the adrenal gland).

Lymphocytes activated by antigens are also capable of producing hormones and other chemical substances that the brain can detect. Thus, activation of the immune system is accompanied by changes in the nervous system and endocrine activity. Cytokines released by activated immune cells provide still another pathway through which the immune system communicates with the central nervous system (CNS). Although the precise site (or sites) at which cytokines act within the brain has not been identified, cytokines cause changes in the activity of the brain, in the endocrine system, and in behavior.

At the neural and endocrine levels, then, there is abundant evidence of interactions between the brain and the immune system. At the behavioral level, the most notable evidence of interactions between the CNS and immune system is the effects of conditioning and stressful life experiences on immune function. Another important line of research (not elaborated here) concerns the effects of immune processes on emotional states and other behaviors such as activity, sleep, and appetite.

BEHAVIORAL INFLUENCES ON IMMUNE FUNCTION

Pavlovian conditioning of alterations of immune function provides the most dramatic illustration of a functional relationship between the brain and the immune system. In a prototypical study using a paradigm referred to as taste-aversion conditioning, animals consumed a novel saccharin solution, the conditioned stimulus (CS), shortly before they were injected with an immunosuppressive drug, the unconditioned stimulus (UCS). When all animals were subsequently injected with antigen, conditioned animals that were reexposed to the CS alone showed an aversion to it and an attenuated antibody response compared with conditioned animals that were not reexposed to the CS and nonconditioned animals that were exposed to saccharin (Ader & Cohen, 1975).

87

Studies have since documented the acquisition and extinction of conditioned nonspecific responses such as NK cell activity and various antibody- and cell-mediated immune responses (Ader & Cohen, 2001). Conditioning is not limited to changes associated with taste-aversion learning, and there is no consistent relationship between conditioned changes in behavior and conditioned changes in immune responses. Also, conditioned immunosuppressive responses cannot be ascribed to stress-induced or conditioned elevations of adrenal hormones. More recently, the conditioned enhancement, as opposed to suppression, of immune responses has been observed using antigens rather than pharmacologic agents as UCSs.

Data on conditioning in humans are limited. The anticipatory (conditioned) nausea that frequently precedes cancer chemotherapy is associated with anticipatory suppression of the capacity of lymphocytes to respond to foreign stimuli, and multiple sclerosis patients being treated with an immunosuppressive drug show a conditioned decrease in total white blood cell count in response to a sham treatment. Healthy subjects show enhanced NK cell activity when reexposed to a distinctive flavor previously paired with injections of adrenaline. In another study, it was shown that repeated injections of saline (which do not elicit an immune response) could attenuate the response to a subsequent injection of antigen. Conversely, however, repeated injections of antigen may not precipitate a reaction to a subsequent injection of saline.

Psychosocial factors, including stressful life experiences, are capable of influencing the onset or severity of a variety of immune disorders and infectious diseases. Such factors are also capable of influencing immune function. The death of a spouse, other "losses" (e.g., divorce), and other chronic stressors (e.g., caregiving for a chronically ill person)—and even less traumatic events such as school examinations—elicit distress and associated declines in immune function, including a depressed response to a viral antigen.

Clinical depression tends to be associated with some immunologically mediated diseases, and this fact has focused attention on the immunological effects of depression. Depressed patients show a decline in several measures of immunity, elevated antibody levels to herpes viruses, and a diminished ability to mount a specific cell-mediated response to varicella zoster virus, which is responsible for shingles (Herbert & Cohen, 1993). In none of these instances, however, has it been demonstrated that changes in immune function specifically cause the health effects of depression or other affective responses to stress.

Evidence documenting stress-induced alterations in immunity comes mostly from animal research. Early life experiences such as disruption of an animal's interactions with its mother, the social environment, exposure to predators, odors emitted by stressed conspecifics, and physical restraint or other noxious conditions induce neuroendocrine changes and modulate both antibody- and cell-mediated immunity. In general, stress suppresses immune function, but the direction, magnitude, and duration of the effects depend on the antigen, the nature of the stressful experience, and the temporal relationship between the stressful experience and the encounter with antigen. The effects of stress also depend on a variety of host factors, such as species, age, and gender.

The neural and endocrine changes presumed to underlie the immunological effects of stressful life experiences have not been delineated. Any number of hormones or the patterning of hormonal responses could influence immunity. Elevated levels of adrenocortical steroids, the most common manifestation of the stress response, are generally immunosuppressive, and there are many stressor-induced changes in immune function that are mediated by adrenal hormones. However, many stress-induced changes in immunity are independent of adrenal activity.

The response to stressful life experiences involves complex interactions among behavior, the nervous system, the endocrine system, and immune response (Rabin, 1999). As a result, the literature on the immunological effects of stress has yielded some equivocal or seemingly inconsistent findings. It should not be surprising, though, that different stressors—commonly thought to elicit a common stress response—can have different effects on the same immune response. Also, one particular stressor can have different effects on different immune responses. Another source of variability may relate to the direct translation of procedures used in immunological research to behavioral studies. For example, a concentration of antigen that is optimal for the study of cellular processes or immunizations against disease may not be optimal for studies designed to investigate the psychobiological interactions that appear to influence immunoregulatory processes. Thus, for the latter purpose, we need studies in which antigen concentrations are at the lower levels to which individuals may be exposed in natural settings. Varying antigen dose would reduce the risk of masking the contribution of those biopsychosocial factors that influence health and illness in the real world.

If we are not always able to predict the direction, magnitude, or duration of the effects of stressful life experiences, it is clear nevertheless that stressful life experiences can influence immune functions; they can increase or decrease susceptibility to immunologically mediated diseases, permit an otherwise inconsequential exposure to some viruses to develop into clinical disease, or contribute to the reactivation of viral infections to which the individual was exposed in the past. Unfortunately, there are relatively few studies that have measured the relationship between susceptibility to a particular disease and those immune responses that are relevant to that disease.

BIOLOGICAL IMPACT OF BEHAVIORALLY INDUCED ALTERATIONS OF IMMUNE FUNCTION

The effects of conditioning and of stressful experiences on immune function have been referred to as "small." The changes in immune function have remained within normal limits, and it is argued, therefore, that the effects of behavior on immune function have no clinical significance. Although there may be reason to question the selective application of the criterion of effect size, a concern for the biological impact of behaviorally induced changes in immune function is quite legitimate. The association between stressful life experiences and susceptibility to disease and the association between stressful life events and changes in immune function do not establish a causal chain linking stress, immune function, and disease. Thus, a central question that remains to be addressed concerns the biological (clinical) significance of behaviorally induced changes in immunity.

There is little, if any, human research in which an altered resistance to disease has been shown to be a direct result of changes in immune function induced by stressful life experiences. Animal studies of experimentally induced or spontaneously occurring diseases, however, are being developed to address this issue. Stressful stimulation delays the production of virus-specific antibodies in mice infected with influenza and suppresses NK cell activity and the development of some T lymphocytes in animals inoculated with herpes simplex virus (HSV). Although physical restraint is ineffective in reactivating HSV infections, disruption of the social hierarchy within a colony of mice increases aggressive behavior, activates the HPA axis,[2] and results in reactivation of HSV in a significant proportion of infected animals. When the spread of a lung tumor is related to NK cell function, several different stressors can decrease NK cell activity and increase lung disease.

Inflammatory processes, an essential component in the healing of wounds, can be modulated by the sympathetic nervous system and HPA axis. It is not surprising, then, that experimentally produced wounds heal more slowly in caretakers of Alzheimer's patients than in control subjects and in students tested before an examination rather than during summer vacation. Mice restrained for several days before and after they are wounded show a diminished inflammatory response, an elevated level of adrenocortical steroids, and a dramatic delay in healing.

Additional work with animals will enable studies of the mechanisms through which stressful life experiences affect health and determine whether disease susceptibility can, as hypothesized, be influenced by behaviorally induced alterations in immune function.

The biological impact of conditioning was examined using mice that spontaneously develop a disease similar to systemic lupus erythematosus in which there is an overreactivity of the immune system. In this case, a suppression of immunological reactivity would be in the biological interests of these animals. CS presentations without active drug were provided on 50% of the pharmacotherapy trials on which animals were scheduled to receive immunosuppressive drug. By capitalizing on conditioned immunosuppressive responses, it was possible to delay the onset of lupus using a cumulative amount of drug that was not, by itself, sufficient to alter progression of the autoimmune disease. Similarly, resistance to experimentally induced arthritis was achieved by exposing animals to a CS previously paired with immunosuppressive treatments. Among mice previously conditioned by pairing a CS with an immunosuppressive drug, reexposure to the CS following transplantation of foreign tissues delayed the immunologically induced rejection of the tissues. There is one clinical case study of a child with lupus who was successfully treated using a conditioning protocol to reduce the total amount of immunosuppressive drug usually prescribed. Although the effects of conditioning have been described as small, conditioned immunological effects can have a profound biological impact on the development of disorders resulting from an overreactive immune system, some cancers, and the survival of tissue transplants.

The issue of clinical significance has occasioned a lot of misplaced breast-beating and apologias in the name of scientific conservatism. Except, perhaps, for extreme and rare circumstances, the notion that a conditioned stimulus or psychosocial conditions could, by themselves, perturb the immune system to an extent that exceeds normal boundaries and leads to overt disease is somewhat simplistic from either an immunological or a behavioral perspective. Given the complexity of the cellular interactions within the immune system and the interactions between the immune and nervous systems, a behaviorally induced deviation from baseline that did not exceed the normal boundaries would seem to be the only response that could reasonably be expected. As far as susceptibility to a particular disease is concerned, however, it would not be unreasonable to theorize that changes capable of altering immune responses relevant to disease could have clinical consequences when interacting with environmental pathogens or when superimposed upon existing pathology or an immune system compromised by host factors such as age or external influences such as immunosuppressive drugs of abuse. The potential importance of psychoneuroimmunological interactions, then, requires that we adopt research strategies that capitalize on individual differences; high-risk populations (e.g., the very young or old, people whose immune systems are compromised, those with genetic predispositions to particular diseases, those with existing disease); systematic variation of the magnitude of the antigen; and the measurement of responses that are demonstrably relevant to particular diseases.

CONCLUSIONS

Psychoneuroimmunology is an interdisciplinary field that has developed and now prospers by ignoring the arbitrary and illusory boundaries of the biomedical sciences. As a result of the integrative research conducted in recent years, a paradigm shift is occurring; researchers can no longer study immunoregulatory processes as the independent activity of an autonomous immune system. These processes take place within a neuroendocrine environment that is sensitive to the individual's perception of and adaptive responses to events occurring in the external world.

Research predicated on the hypothesis that there is a single, integrated defense system could change the way we define and study certain diseases. Theoretically, it is likely that behavioral, neural, and endocrine interventions are relevant in the treatment of some immune system-related diseases (e.g., arthritis) and that immune system activity may contribute to the understanding and treatment of behavioral, neural, and endocrine disorders (e.g., depression or even schizophrenia).

We cannot yet detail the mechanisms mediating the effects of conditioning or stressful life experiences on immune responses, and further studies are needed. However, we do know that neural and endocrine changes are associated with changes in behavior and that there is a network of connections between the brain and the immune system. The existence of these bidirectional pathways reinforces the hypothesis that changes in the immune system constitute an important mechanism through which psychosocial factors could influence health and disease.

Recommended Reading

Ader, R. (1995). Historical perspectives on psychoneuroimmunology. In H. Friedman, T.W. Klein, & A.L. Friedman (Eds.), *Psychoneuroimmunology, stress and infection* (pp. 1–21). Boca Raton, FL: CRC Press.

Ader, R., Madden, K., Felten, D., Bellinger, D.L., & Schiffer, R.B. (1996). Psychoneuroimmunology: Interactions between the brain and the immune system. In B.S. Fogel, R.B. Schiffer, & S.M. Rao (Eds.), *Neuropsychiatry* (pp. 193– 221). Philadelphia: Williams & Wilkins.

Glaser, R., & Kiecolt-Glaser, J.K. (Eds.). (1994). *Handbook of human stress and immunity.* New York: Academic Press.

Schedlowski, M., & Tewes, U. (Eds.). (1999). *Psychoneuroimmunology: An interdisciplinary introduction.* New York. Kluwer Academic/ Plenum.

Acknowledgments—Preparation of this article was supported by a Research Scientist Award (K05 MH06318) from the National Institute of Mental Health.

Notes

1. Address correspondence to Robert Ader, Department of Psychiatry, University of Rochester Medical Center, Rochester, NY 14642.

2. This term comes from the structures involved in the secretion of so-called stress hormones. During a stress response, the brain's hypothalamus (H) releases a chemical that affects the pituitary gland (P). The pituitary then secretes a hormone that causes the adrenal glands (A) to release corticosteroids (cortisol in humans, corticosterone in rodents) into the bloodstream.

References

Ader, R. (1981a). A historical account of conditioned immunobiologic responses. In R. Ader (Ed.), *Psychoneuroimmunology* (pp. 321–354). New York: Academic Press.

Ader, R. (Ed.). (1981b). *Psychoneuroimmunology.* New York: Academic Press.

Ader, R., & Cohen, N. (1975). Behaviorally conditioned immunosuppression. *Psychosomatic Medicine, 37,* 333–340.

Ader, R., & Cohen, N. (2001). Conditioning and immunity. In R. Ader, D.L. Felten, & N. Cohen (Eds.), *Psychoneuroimmunology* (3rd ed., Vol. 2, pp. 3–34). New York: Academic Press.

Herbert, T.B., & Cohen, S. (1993). Depression and immunity: A meta-analytic review. *Psychological Bulletin, 113,* 472–486.

Rabin, B.S. (1999). *Stress, immune function, and health.* New York: Wiley-Liss.

Environmental and Behavioral Influences on Gene Activity

Gilbert Gottlieb[1]

Center for Developmental Science, University of North Carolina at Chapel Hill, Chapel Hill, North Carolina

Abstract

The central dogma of molecular biology holds that "information" flows from the genes to the structure of the proteins that the genes bring about through the formula DNA $\rightarrow$ RNA $\rightarrow$ protein. In this view, a set of master genes activates the DNA necessary to produce the appropriate proteins that the organism needs during development. In contrast to this view, probabilistic epigenesis holds that necessarily there are signals from the internal and external environment that activate DNA to produce the appropriate proteins. To support this view, I review a substantial body of evidence showing that external environmental influences on gene activation are normally occurring events in a large variety of organisms, including humans. This demonstrates how genes and environments work together to produce functional organisms, thus extending the model of probabilistic epigenesis.

Keywords

central dogma; probabilistic epigenesis; predetermined epigenesis

A virtual revolution that has taken place in our knowledge of environmental and behavioral influences on gene expression has not yet seeped into the social sciences in general and the behavioral sciences in particular. Earlier, it was not recognized that environmental and behavioral influences play an important role in triggering gene activity. Paradoxically, in biology there is an explicit dogma, formulated as such, that does not permit environmental influences on gene activity: the central dogma of molecular biology, first enunciated by Crick in 1958.

Although the central dogma may seem quite remote from psychology, I think it lies behind some psychological and behavioral theories that emphasize the sheerly endogenous (internal) development of the nervous system and early behavior (e.g., Elman et al., 1996) and the "innate foundation of the psyche" (e.g., Tooby & Cosmides, 1990), independent of experience or functional considerations. Such theories follow from the essentially dichotomous view that genes and other endogenous factors construct part of the organism and environment determines other features of the organism. The present essay is an attempt to show how genes and environment necessarily cooperate in the construction of organisms, and specifically, to show how genes require environmental and behavioral inputs to function appropriately during the normal course of individual development.

THE CENTRAL DOGMA

The central dogma asserts that "information" flows in only one direction from the genes to the structure of the proteins that the genes bring about. The formula for this information flow is DNA → RNA → protein. (Messenger RNA, or mRNA, is the intermediary in the process of protein synthesis. In the lingo of molecular biology, the process by which RNA is formed from the DNA template is called transcription, and the process by which proteins are formed from the RNA template is called translation.) After retroviruses were discovered in the 1960s (in retroviruses, RNA reversely transcribes DNA instead of the other way around), Crick wrote a postscript to his 1958 article in which he congratulated himself for not claiming that reverse transcription was impossible: "In looking back I am struck not only by the brashness which allowed us to venture powerful statements of a very general nature, but also by the rather delicate discrimination used in selecting what statements to make" (Crick, 1970, p. 562). Any ambiguity about the controlling factors in gene expression in the central dogma was removed in a later article by Crick, in which he specifically said that the genes of higher organisms are turned on and off by other genes (Crick, 1982, p. 515). Figure 1 shows the central dogma of molecular biology in the form of a diagram.

THE GENOME ACCORDING TO CENTRAL DOGMA

The picture of the genome that emerges from the central dogma is one of (a) encapsulation, setting the genome off from influences above the genetic level (supragenetic influences), and (b) a largely feedforward (unidirectional) informational process in which the genes contain a blueprint or master plan for the construction and determination of the organism. In this view, the genome is not seen as part of the holistic, bidirectional developmental-physiological system of the organism, responsive to signals from internal cellular sources such as the cytoplasm of the cell or to extracellular influences such as hormones, and the genome is seen as certainly not responsive to influences from outside the organism, such as stimuli or signals from the external environment.

In this essay, my goal is to show that the normally occurring influences on genetic activity include influences from the external environment, that is, to demonstrate that the genome is not encapsulated and is in fact a part of the organism's general developmental-physiological adaptation to environmental stresses and signals: Genes express themselves appropriately only in responding to internally and externally generated stimulation. Further, in this holistic view, although genes participate in the making of protein, protein is also subject to other influences, and protein must be further stimulated and elaborated to become part of the nervous system (or other systems) of the organism. Thus,

Genetic Activitity According to Central Dogma

$$\text{DNA} \longrightarrow \text{DNA} \overset{?}{\underset{\longrightarrow}{\longleftarrow}} \text{RNA} \longrightarrow \text{Protein}$$

Fig. 1. The central dogma of molecular biology. The right-going arrows represent the central dogma. Retroviruses (represented by the left-going arrow from RNA to DNA) were not part of the dogma, but after their discovery, Crick (1970) said they were not prohibited in the original formulation of the dogma (Crick, 1958).

genes operate at the lowest level of organismic organization, and they do not, in and of themselves, produce finished traits or features of the organism. The organism is a product of epigenetic development, that is, a process that involves not only the genes but also many other supragenetic influences. Because this latter point has been the subject of numerous publications (reviewed in Gottlieb, 1992), I do not deal with it further here, but, rather, restrict this essay to documenting that the activity of genes is regulated in just the same way as the rest of the organism, being called forth by signals from the normally occurring external environment, as well as the internal environment. Although this fact is not well known in the social and behavioral sciences, it is surprising to find that it is also not widely appreciated in biology proper (Strohman, 1997). In biology, the external environment is seen as the agent of natural selection in promoting evolution, not as a crucial feature of individual development. Many biologists subscribe to the notion that "the genes are safely sequestered inside the nucleus of the cell and out of reach of ordinary environmental effects" (Wills, 1989, p. 19).

FROM CENTRAL DOGMA OF MOLECULAR BIOLOGY TO PROBABILISTIC EPIGENESIS

As can be seen in Table 1, a number of different naturally occurring environmental signals can stimulate gene expression in a large variety of organisms from nematodes to humans. To understand the findings summarized in Table 1, the nongeneticist needs to know that there are three levels of evidence of genetic activity in the right-hand column of Table 1: protein expression or synthesis, mRNA activity, and genetic activity itself. As the middle column of the table shows, there are important environmental and behavioral signals affecting genetic activity, even though the activity of the genes is quite remote from these stimuli. After proteins are made, many factors must intervene before neurons or behaviors are realized; the route from protein to neuron or behavior is not direct. The fact that normally occurring environmental events stimulate gene activity during the usual course of development in a variety of organisms means that genes and genetic activity are part of the developmental-physiological system and do not stand outside of that system.

The main purpose of this essay is to place genes and genetic activity firmly within a holistic developmental-physiological framework, one in which genes not only affect each other and mRNA but are affected by activities at other levels of the system, up to and including the external environment. This holistic developmental system of bidirectional, coacting influences is captured schematically in Figure 2. In contrast to the unidirectional and encapsulated genetic predeterminism of the central dogma, a probabilistic view of epigenesis holds that the sequence and outcomes of development are probabilistically determined by the critical operation of various stimulative events that occur both within and outside the organism.

The probabilistic-epigenetic framework presented in Figure 2 not only is based on what we now know about mechanisms of individual development at all levels of analysis, but also derives from our understanding of evolution and natural selection. Natural selection serves as a filter and preserves reproduc-

Table 1. *Normally occurring environmental and behavioral influences on gene activity*

Species	Environmental signal or stimulus	Resulting alteration
Nematodes	Absence or presence of food	Diminished or enhanced neuronal *daf-7* gene mRNA expression, inhibiting or provoking larval development
Fruit flies	Transient elevated heat stress during larval development	Presence of proteins produced by heat shock and thermotolerance (enhanced thermal regulation)
Fruit flies	Light-dark cycle	Presence of PER and TIM protein expression and circadian rhythms
Various reptiles	Incubation temperature	Sex determination
Songbirds (canaries, zebra finches)	Conspecific song	Increased forebrain mRNA
Hamsters	Light-dark cycle	Increased pituitary hormone mRNA and reproductive behavior
Mice	Acoustic stimulation	Enhanced c-*fos* expression, neuronal activity, and organization of the auditory system
Mice	Light-dark cycle	c-*fos*-induced mRNA expression in hypothalamus, circadian locomotor activity
Rats	Tactile stimulation	Enhanced c-*fos* expression and increased number of somatosensory (sense of touch) cortical neurons[a]
Rats	Learning task involving vestibular (balance) system	Change in nuclear RNA base ratios in vestibular nerve cells
Rats	Visual stimulation	Increased RNA and protein synthesis in visual cortex[a]
Rats	Environmental complexity	Increased brain RNA diversity
Rats	Prenatal nutrition	Increase in cerebral DNA (increased number of brain cells)
Rats	Infantile handling, separation from mother	Increased hypothalamic mRNAs for corticotrophin-releasing hormone throughout life
Cats	Visual stimulation	Increased visual cortex[a] RNA complexity (diversity)
Humans	Academic examinations taken by medical students (psychological stress)	Reduced mRNA activity in interleukin 2 receptor (immune system response)

Note. mRNA = messenger RNA; PER and TIM are proteins arising from activity of *per* (*period*) and *tim* (*timeless*) genes; activity of c-*fos* genes leads to production of c-FOS protein. References documenting the findings listed can be found in Gottlieb (1998, Table 2).

[a]Cortex is the outer covering of the brain, or gray matter.

BIDIRECTIONAL INFLUENCES

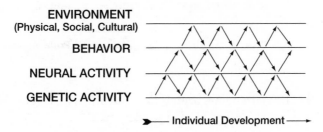

ENVIRONMENT
(Physical, Social, Cultural)

BEHAVIOR

NEURAL ACTIVITY

GENETIC ACTIVITY

➤── Individual Development ──➤

Fig. 2. The probabilistic-epigenetic framework. The diagram depicts the completely bidirectional and coactive nature of genetic, neural, behavioral, and environmental influences over the course of individual development. From *Individual Development and Evolution: The Genesis of Novel Behavior* (p. 152), by G. Gottlieb, 1992, New York: Oxford University Press. Copyright 1992 by Oxford University Press, Inc. Reprinted with permission.

tively successful phenotypes (outcomes of development). These successful phenotypes are a product of individual development, and thus are a consequence of the adaptability of the organism to its developmental conditions. Therefore, natural selection has preserved (favored) organisms that are adaptably responsive to their developmental conditions, both behaviorally and physiologically. Organisms with the same genes can develop very different phenotypes under different developmental conditions, as witness the identical twins shown in Figure 3. These men were raised in different homes and developed striking physical, behavioral, and psychological differences, despite their identical genomes.

Because the probabilistic-epigenetic view presented in Figure 2 does not portray enough detail at the level of genetic activity, it is useful to flesh that out, to show how it differs from the previously described central dogma of molecular biology. As shown in Figure 4, the original central dogma explicitly posited one-way traffic—DNA → RNA → protein—and was silent about any other

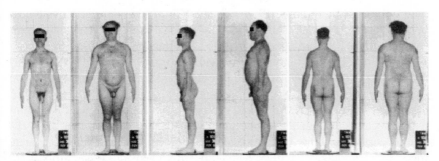

Fig. 3. Remarkable illustration of the enormous phenotypic variation that can result when monozygotic (single-egg) identical twins are reared apart in very different family environments from birth. From *Fetus Into Man* (p. 120), by J.M. Tanner, 1978, Cambridge, MA: Harvard University Press. Copyright 1978 by Harvard University Press, renewed 1989 by J.M. Tanner. Adapted with permission.

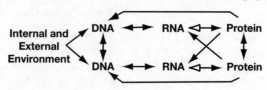

Genetic Activity According to Central Dogma

DNA ⟶ DNA ⟵---⟶ RNA ⟶ Protein
            ?

DNA ⟶ DNA ⟵---⟶ RNA ⟶ Protein
            ?

Genetic Activity According to Probabilistic Epigenesis

Internal and External Environment

DNA ⟷ RNA ⟷ Protein

DNA ⟷ RNA ⟷ Protein

Fig. 4. Influences on genetic activity according to the central dogma (top) and probabilistic epigenesis (bottom). The filled arrows indicate documented sources of influence, and the open arrow from protein back to RNA indicates what remains a theoretical possibility in probabilistic epigenesis but is prohibited in the central dogma (as are protein ⟷ protein influences). Protein → protein influences occur (a) when prions (abnormally conformed proteins) transfer their abnormal conformation to other proteins and (b) when, during normal development, proteins activate or inactivate other proteins (as in the case of phosphorylation, described in the text). The filled arrows from protein to RNA represent the activation of mRNA by protein (e.g., as a consequence of phosphorylation). DNA ⟷ DNA influences are termed epistatic, referring to the modification of the expression of genes depending on the genetic background in which they are located. In the central dogma, genetic activity is dictated solely by genes (DNA → DNA), whereas in probabilistic epigenesis, internal and external environmental events activate genetic expression through proteins (protein → DNA), hormones, and other influences. To keep the diagram manageable, the fact that behavior and the external environment exert their effects on DNA through internal mediators (proteins, hormones, etc.) is not shown; nor is it shown that the protein products of some genes regulate the expression of other genes. (See the text for further discussion of this figure.)

flows of information (Crick, 1958). The bottom of Figure 4 illustrates probabilistic epigenesis, which is inherently bidirectional in the horizontal and vertical levels (Fig. 2). Thus, this diagram has information flowing not only from RNA to DNA, but from protein to protein and from DNA to DNA. The only relationship that is not yet supported is protein → RNA, in the sense of protein altering the structure of RNA, but there are other influences of protein on RNA activity (not its structure) that would support such a directional flow. For example, a process known as *phosphorylation* can modify proteins so that they activate (or inactivate) other proteins (protein → protein), which, when activated, trigger rapid production of mRNA (protein → RNA activity). When mRNAs are transcribed by DNA, they do not necessarily become immediately active but require a further signal to do so. The consequences of phosphorylation could provide that signal (protein → protein → mRNA activity → protein). A process like this appears to be involved in the expression of "fragile X mental retardation protein." This protein is produced as described under normal conditions but is missing in the brain of fragile X mental retardates; thus, fragile X mental retardation represents a failure of gene (or mRNA) expression rather than a positive genetic contribution.[2]

CONCLUSIONS

The central dogma lies behind the persistent trend in biology and psychology to view genes and environment as making identifiably separate contributions to the phenotypic outcomes of development. Quantitative behavior genetics (the study of the heritability of behavior when one does not know how many or which genes are correlated with a given trait) is based on this erroneous assumption. Although genes no doubt play a constraining role in development, the actual limits of these constraints are quite wide and, most important, cannot be specified in advance of experimental manipulation or accidents of nature. There is no doubt that development is constrained at all levels of the system (Fig. 2), not only by genes and environments.

Finally, I do hope that the emphasis here on normally occurring environmental influences on gene activity does not raise the specter of a new, subtle form of "environmentalism." I do not think I would be labeled an environmentalist if I were to say organisms are often adaptably responsive to their environments. So, by calling attention to genes being adaptably responsive to their internal and external environments, I am not being an environmentalist but merely including genetic activity within the probabilistic-epigenetic framework that characterizes the organism and all of its constituent parts.

In view of the findings reviewed here, in the future it would be most important to eschew both genetic determinism and environmental determinism, as we now should understand that it is truly correct (not merely a verbalism) to say that environments and genes necessarily cooperate in bringing about any outcome of individual development.

Recommended Reading

Gottlieb, G. (1997). *Synthesizing nature-nurture: Prenatal roots of instinctive behavior.* Mahwah, NJ: Erlbaum.
Nijhout, H.F. (1990). Metaphors and the role of genes in development. *BioEssays, 12,* 441–446.
Stent, G. (1981). Strength and weakness of the genetic approach to the nervous system. *Annual Review of Neuroscience, 4,* 163–194.
Wahlsten, D., & Gottlieb, G. (1997). The invalid separation of nature and nurture: Lessons from animal experimentation. In R.J. Sternberg & E. Grigorenko (Eds.), *Intelligence, heredity, and environment* (pp. 163–192). New York: Cambridge University Press.

Acknowledgments—The author's research and scholarly activities are supported in part by National Institute of Mental Health Grant P50-MH-52429. This article is an abstract of an article that appeared in the *Psychological Review,* 1998, Vol. 105, pp. 792–802, and is reproduced here with the permission of the American Psychological Association.

Notes

1. Address correspondence to Gilbert Gottlieb, Center for Developmental Science, Campus Box 8115, University of North Carolina, Chapel Hill, NC 27599-8115.

2. "Genetic" disorders, both mental and physical, often represent biochemical deficiencies of one sort or another due to the lack of expression of the genes and mRNAs needed to produce the appropriate proteins necessary for normal development. Thus, the search for "candidate genes" in psychiatric or other disorders is most often a search for genes that are not being expressed, not for genes that are being expressed and causing the disorders. So-called cystic fibrosis genes and manic-depression genes, among others, are in this category. The instances that I know of in which the presence of genes causes a problem are Edward's syndrome and trisomy 21 (Down syndrome), wherein the presence of an extra, otherwise normal, chromosome (18 and 21, respectively) causes problems. In some cases, it is of course possible that the expression of mutated genes can be involved in a disorder, but, in my opinion, it is often the lack of expression of normal genes that is the culprit.

References

Crick, F. (1970). Central dogma of molecular biology. *Nature, 227,* 561–563.

Crick, F. (1982). DNA today. *Perspectives in Biology and Medicine, 25,* 512–517.

Crick, F.H.C. (1958). On protein synthesis. In *The biological replication of macromolecules* (Symposia of the Society for Experimental Biology No. 12., pp. 138–163). Cambridge, England: Cambridge University Press.

Elman, J.L., Bates, E.A., Johnson, M.H., Karmiloff-Smith, A., Parisi, D., & Plunkett, K. (1996). *Rethinking innateness: A connectionist perspective on development.* Cambridge, MA: MIT Press.

Gottlieb, G. (1992). *Individual development and evolution: The genesis of novel behavior.* New York: Oxford University Press.

Gottlieb, G. (1998). Normally occurring environmental and behavioral influences on gene activity: From central dogma to probabilistic epigenesis. *Psychological Review, 105,* 792–802.

Strohman, R.C. (1997). The coming Kuhnian revolution in biology. *Nature Biotechnology, 15,* 194–200.

Tanner, J.M. (1978). *Fetus into man.* Cambridge, MA: Harvard University Press.

Tooby, J., & Cosmides, L. (1990). The past explains the present: Emotional adaptations and the structure of ancestral environments. *Ethology and Sociobiology, 11,* 375–424.

Wills, C. (1989). *The wisdom of the genes: New pathways in evolution.* New York: Basic Books.

Critical Thinking Questions

1. Describe the pathways through which psychosocial and environmental characteristics "get inside the body" to influence disease. Using the model that you developed for Question 1, Section 1 as a starting point, add in the plausible behavioral and biological pathways.

2. Imagine that you're trying to develop a psychological intervention that protects people from developing illnesses when they are exposed to adverse psychosocial or environmental circumstances. What activities would the intervention consist of? What kinds of processes—psychological, behavioral, biological—would you target?

3. In what ways could you use animal models to devise experiments that provide greater insights into the processes through which psychosocial characteristics influence disease susceptibility?

4. After reading this series of articles, to what extent do you think the behavioral and biological response to stressful experience is adaptive? On balance, is it a good or a bad thing that humans respond to stress the way that they do?

5. Genetics has been relatively neglected in health psychology research. How could this exciting area of inquiry be used to better understand the interface of psychology and medicine? For example, how might genetic characteristics help to explain the environments that different people inhabit, or how they respond psychologically and biologically to these settings?

Psychosocial Adaptation
to Medical Illness

The two previous sections have focused on a major research question in health psychology: To what extent do psychosocial and environmental characteristics influence a person's vulnerability to medical illness? Although this is a fascinating question with important implications, health psychologists also feel it is important to take the opposite perspective. Thus, another major research in the field is: How does having a medical illness affect a person's well-being? The readings in this section provide an overview of how people adapt psychologically to health problems.

The first two articles describe individuals' reactions to getting sick. Wrosch et al. focus on the natural changes in health that occur as one ages, and strategies that elderly adults use to deal with these changes. While it is inevitable that people get sicker as they age, their responses to health problems can vary widely. For example, how do health problems affect people's pursuit of life goals? Wrosch et al. argue that certain health problems are controllable, and that in these situations, individuals will adjust better if they try to actively control these problems and continue pursuing their life goals. On the other hand, some health problems are uncontrollable, and in these situations, individuals will adjust better if they disengage from life goals that are now unattainable. This research demonstrates that no psychological state is always good for health and well-being; rather, what is important is to match one's goals realistically to the situation, and to be able to adjust those goals when the situation changes. Compas and Luecken focuses on a life-threatening chronic illness—breast cancer—and discuss the relationship of this devastating condition to psychological distress. They argue that diseases do not have uniform psychological effects on all individuals, but rather that certain factors, such as characteristics of the disease, characteristics of the patients, social relationships, cognitions, and coping, all affect how an individual adapts to the diagnosis and treatment of a life-threatening disease.

Next we move from the level of the individual to the broader social environment, and examine the role of others in affecting individuals' psychological adjustment to illness. Newsom presents an interesting and counterintuitive argument that caregiving is not always positive for the person who is ill. Although most patients are grateful and feel indebted to others who care for them, it is also not uncommon for patients to sometimes have negative reactions to others' attempts to provide help. This could happen if caregivers engage in unsupportive behaviors, or if the patient perceives a caregiver's behavior in a negative way (regardless of what the actual intent was). This article highlights the importance of not assuming that social support will always be beneficial to patients who are ill. Hall et al. discuss the relationship between patients and their physicians. Higher satisfaction with medical care is associated with better health, but it is not clear whether satisfaction with care actually leads to changes in health. Hall et al. present data showing that patients who start out with better health are the ones who are more satisfied with their care. Moreover, Hall et al. demonstrate that when patients are in poorer health, physicians engage them in less social conversation, and this in turn leads to patients being less satisfied with care. Both of these articles reveal that helping someone who is sick can be complicated. As family members, we may think that we are offering help, but we may also be undermining a patient's sense of self-control and self-worth. As physicians, one has to be aware that features of a patient's illness may affect how we feel about and behave toward that patient, which in turn affects patient satisfaction.

The last article in this section presents a biological explanation for people's psychological states when they are sick. Maier and Watkins propose that when the immune system gets activated by bacteria or a virus, chemical messengers of the immune system known as cytokines trigger "sickness behaviors" such as feeling tired, feeling sad, and not engaging in social activity. That is, when the immune system becomes activated, it can send signals to the brain, and in turn, these signals produce changes in behavior, mood, and cognition. These changes may have been evolutionarily adaptive, in that sickness behaviors such as reducing energy and social activity allowed an organism time to recover from infection and reduced the likelihood of attacks from other aggressors. If true, this suggests that negative psychological states such as depression have adaptive value in helping us to recover from acute illnesses.

Health Stresses and Depressive Symptomatology in the Elderly: A Control-Process Approach

Carsten Wrosch,[1] Richard Schulz,[2] and Jutta Heckhausen[3]

[1]*Department of Psychology and Centre for Research in Human Development, Concordia University, Montreal, Quebec, Canada;* [2]*Department of Psychiatry and University Center for Social and Urban Research, University of Pittsburgh; and* [3]*Department of Psychology and Social Behavior, School of Social Ecology, University of California at Irvine*

Abstract

The social and life sciences need to examine pathways of successful aging to master the consequences of increased longevity and physical vulnerability of the elderly population. One of older adults' well-known problems relates to the fact that their quality of life can be threatened by physical health stresses and associated depressive symptomatology. Common health problems among older adults often contribute to depressive symptomatology, and, in turn, depressive symptoms may further compromise older adults' health. It is thus an important task to discover factors that can protect older adults from experiencing the negative emotional consequences of health stresses. Using ideas from the life-span theory of control, we show how to adaptively manage the negative consequences of health problems in the elderly. Active investments in overcoming health problems that are controllable should result in positive outcomes. In contrast, it may be beneficial for older adults to disengage from health goals that are unattainable. By adjusting their control-related behaviors to the controllability of specific health stresses, older adults can maintain their psychological and physical health.

Keywords

aging; control; depression; disengagement; health

More human beings live to old age today than ever before. However, the increased longevity comes at a price. Many older adults experience physical illness and disability, such as arthritis, heart disease, or diabetes. In addition, it is widely recognized that physical disease and depressive symptomatology are positively associated in the elderly, and may reciprocally influence each other. From a psychological point of view, it is thus important to understand how older individuals manage the challenges associated with physical disease and to identify processes that enhance and maintain their psychological and physical health.

In this article, we examine the link between physical disease and depressive symptomatology, and identify adaptive processes for managing physical

Address correspondence to Carsten Wrosch, Concordia University, Department of Psychology, 7141 Sherbrooke St. West, Montreal, Quebec H4B 1R6, Canada; e-mail: wrosch@vax2.concordia.ca.

disease (i.e., control strategies) in the elderly. These processes may prevent older adults from experiencing the negative emotional consequences of health stresses. At the most general level, we argue that adaptive management of health stresses requires older adults to adjust their control strategies to the type of health stressor encountered. Whereas some health stresses are potentially controllable in old age (e.g., pain) and can be overcome when active control processes are used, the controllability of other health stresses is often sharply reduced (e.g., functional disabilities, such as difficulty using the toilet, dressing, or preparing meals) and may require older adults to adjust their health-related goals. The use of control processes that are functionally adjusted to the controllability of specific health stresses may alleviate the negative emotional consequences of health problems and thereby contribute to maintaining physical and psychological health.

HEALTH STRESSES AND DEPRESSIVE SYMPTOMATOLOGY IN THE ELDERLY

One of the most robust findings in the literature is the relation between physical declines and depressive symptomatology in the elderly (Lenze et al., 2001). Indeed, the fact that many older individuals suffer from physical illness and disability places them at risk for clinical depression. For example, depressive symptomatology has been shown to be particularly high among elderly individuals with specific medical conditions, such as rheumatoid arthritis or osteoarthritis, Parkinson's disease, advanced cardiovascular disease, or stroke. Studies that focus on the functional consequences of chronic health problems (e.g., limitations in activities of daily living) also report high levels of depressive symptoms.

The relationship between health and depression is complex. First, poor health can directly influence depressive symptomatology. Those older adults who confront physical health problems are often more likely than their healthier peers to develop subsequent depressive symptoms. Second, depression may contribute to further health problems, either directly or indirectly (Schulz, Martire, Beach, & Scheier, 2000). For example, depression has been shown to contribute to mortality in older adults. In addition, depressive symptomatology can be associated with changes in motivational, behavioral, and biological factors, thereby affecting further health declines. The reciprocal relations between depression and disease suggest that a substantial proportion of older adults is at risk of developing both physical and psychological problems.

HOW TO MANAGE HEALTH STRESSES IN THE ELDERLY

Given the link between health stresses and depressive symptoms in older adults, it is important to explore potential moderators of this relationship. Identifying protective factors may contribute to a better understanding of the relation between health and depression and can be a tool for improving older adults' quality of life. The life-span theory of control (Heckhausen & Schulz, 1995; Schulz & Heckhausen, 1996) provides a conceptual framework for examining psychological and behavioral mechanisms that may help older adults to manage their experience of health threats. This theory distinguishes between primary and secondary control strategies that can be activated to realize important objectives and to manage failure and unattainable goals. Primary control targets the external world and involves attempts to achieve effects in the immediate environment external to the individual. In contrast, secondary control targets the self and is aimed at optimizing the individual's motivation and emotion, which are, in turn, essential resources for further primary control.

One of the important functions that primary and secondary control strategies fulfill is facilitating goal attainment. In particular, three types of control strategies support the attainment of personal goals: actively investing effort and time (i.e., selective primary control), seeking advice and help from other people (i.e., compensatory primary control), and strengthening motivational commitment for goal attainment (i.e., selective secondary control). Control strategies aimed at realizing personal goals should be particularly adaptive if they are used when the circumstances seem to favor goal attainment. Another important function of individuals' control strategies relates to the management of failure and unattainable goals. If it is not possible to realize important life goals, disengagement from them and self-protective secondary control strategies (e.g., attributing failures to external causes or comparing oneself with others who are worse off) may save control resources for attainable goals and help a person to maintain a positive view of the self.

Research examining the adaptive role of control strategies across a wide range of different life domains (e.g., intimate relationships, childbearing, financial issues) has confirmed that the use of control strategies that are adjusted to the controllability of personal goals facilitates a good quality of life. In addition, evidence from a large U.S. study (Midlife Development in the United States, or MIDUS) has demonstrated that self-protective secondary control is particularly strongly associated with subjective well-being among older adults who confront a high number of health problems (Wrosch, Heckhausen, & Lachman, 2000). These findings strongly support a basic tenet of the life-span theory of control: Given that with advancing age people confront decreasing opportunities for overcoming health problems (and achieving other goals), the adaptive value of control strategies that are aimed at goal disengagement and self-protection increases in the elderly.

Figure 1 illustrates a highly simplified model of the relation between physical illness and depression and can be used to conceptualize the adaptive role of control processes in managing health stresses. One pathway in the figure addresses the direct association between physical disease and depression in the elderly. Recent work has suggested that physical illness can directly contribute to depression by causing neuroanatomical and biochemical changes (e.g., disregulated neurotransmission). The other pathway from physical illness to depressive symptomatology emphasizes symptom-related consequences of physical illness. Physical illness, such as arthritis, hypertension, or heart disease, may affect older individuals' lives in at least two ways. First, these conditions often result in functional disabilities that limit people's abilities to carry out normal daily activities. Second, many illnesses generate acute symptoms, such as pain and difficulty breathing, which may further compromise quality of life. In turn, both types of health stresses may increase an older person's risk of experiencing

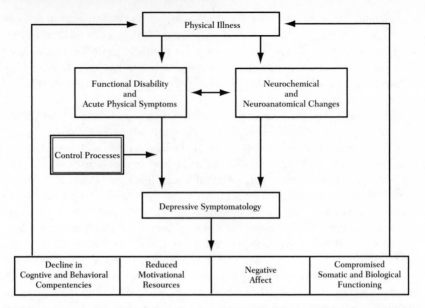

Fig. 1. Conceptual model of the role played by control processes in the association between physical illness and depressive symptomatology in the elderly.

depressive symptoms (e.g., Williamson, Shaffer, & Parmelee, 2000). According to the model in Figure 1, however, this is not necessarily always the case. In particular, we suggest that depressive symptomatology emerges in the elderly when control strategies are unable to adequately address health threats and losses. Thus, the influence of health stresses on depression can be attenuated or even rendered minimal if appropriate control strategies are used.

To identify specific control strategies involved in the adaptive management of health stresses among the elderly, it is necessary to consider that some health stresses are more controllable than others, and that adaptive management of health threats may require older adults to adjust their control processes to the specific opportunities for overcoming each problem. In this regard, an important implication can be drawn from the distinction between functional disabilities and acute physical problems. Functional disabilities are often relatively intractable, and a person's active efforts to overcome them may not be successful. In contrast, in many cases, the acute physical symptoms associated with disease and disability (e.g., pain) are potentially controllable. Thus, active efforts to counteract acute physical symptoms are likely to alleviate disease symptoms and reduce their negative emotional consequences.

A corollary of this proposition is that the use of control strategies that are adjusted to the controllability of specific health stresses may enhance elderly individuals' feelings of well-being in the face of age-related loss. In particular, we suggest that investment in control strategies aimed at overcoming acute physical symptoms should moderate the relation between acute physical symptoms and depressive symptomatology. Such control strategies should facilitate the achievement of those health goals that are still attainable. Older adults who have more intractable functional disabilities, by contrast, may need to activate control strategies that facilitate disengagement from unattainable health goals and protect the self. In situations in which a health problem cannot be overcome, disengagement and self-protection may alleviate distress deriving from trying to attain the unattainable, and free personal resources that can be invested in the pursuit of other meaningful and more attainable goals. In short, elderly individuals should be able to reduce their depressive symptomatology by using control strategies that are appropriate to whether the health stresses they confront are tractable or not.

Finally, it is important to note that the model presented in Figure 1 also includes several feedback loops and thus addresses the reciprocal pathways between depressive symptomatology and disease. Depression can result in declines of cognitive and behavioral competencies, reduced motivation, increased negative affect, and compromised biological functioning, thereby contributing to further health declines. A relevant implication of the proposed feedback loops is that older adults who do not succeed in adaptively controlling their acute physical symptoms and functional disabilities are at risk not only of developing high levels of depression, but also of experiencing further health declines as a consequence of their depression.

Recent research designed to test some of the predictions we have discussed has lent support to this model of health stresses, depression, and control in the elderly. In a recent study, we demonstrated that control strategies aimed at attaining health goals were associated with low levels of depressive symptoms only among older adults who reported high levels of acute physical symptoms (Wrosch, Schulz, & Heckhausen, 2002). In particular, older adults who experienced acute physical symptoms and did not activate strategies targeted at controlling those symptoms experienced elevated levels of depression. Moreover, a follow-up study showed that high levels of health-related control strategies were associated with reduced depression over time, and that high levels of depressive symptoms resulted in reduced active attempts to attain important health goals. These results support our theoretical model by demonstrating that control strategies aimed at attaining health goals are a significant moderator of the association between acute physical symptoms and depressive symptomatology. In addition, the findings point to the conclusion that depressive symptomatology can reduce a person's motivation to actively try to attain potentially controllable health goals, and thereby may compromise older adults' physical and psychological health.

CONCLUSION

The theoretical model and empirical research we have discussed were designed to explore the adaptive functions of control strategies among older adults who experience different types of physical health stresses. In support of the theoretical model, the research suggests that activation of appropriate control strategies may protect older adults from experiencing the negative emotional consequences of health threats. However, other parts of the model need to be tested, and more research is needed to illuminate the complex relations between physical declines, control behaviors, and depressive symptomatology in the elderly.

First, researchers need to examine in more detail how older adults can adaptively manage their functional disabilities and unattainable health goals. The proposed model suggests that self-protective control strategies and goal disengagement could reduce depression among older adults who confront functional disabilities. However, disengagement may have negative consequences under some circumstances. If older adults disengage from unattainable goals and have no alternative goals to pursue, they may feel aimless and empty. A recent study supports this argument: Levels of emotional well-being were compromised among older adults who were able to let go of unattainable goals but reported difficulties with finding new, meaningful activities to pursue (Wrosch, Scheier, Miller, Schulz, & Carver, 2003). Thus, disengagement from unattainable health goals may be adaptive only if it leads to taking up new goals and keeps a person engaged in the pursuit of meaningful and important activities.

Second, as noted earlier, the life-span theory of control proposes three different types of control strategies that are functionally related to attaining important life goals. The research we have discussed did not differentiate among these types. However, future research on the management of health stresses in the elderly should take a more fine-grained approach to assessing the adaptive value of different control strategies across different phases of the disease and treatment process. For example, in the early stages of a potentially curable health problem, strategies related to seeking help or advice from a health expert may be particularly important. Increased motivational commitment for overcoming a health problem, by contrast, may be particularly important when individuals are confronted with a long-lasting or painful treatment process.

Third, research is needed to clarify the mechanisms linking older adults' control behaviors, depressive symptoms, and physical health. In this regard, the activation of control strategies may influence not only depression, but also other variables that play an important role in the causal link between depressive symptomatology and disease. As discussed earlier, depressive symptomatology may further compromise a person's health through behavioral, motivational, and biological processes. Our theoretical framework suggests that control-related management of health stresses influences the biological and psychological consequences of depressive symptomatology and thereby may affect older adults' health.

Finally, an important implication for future research concerns the design of interventions for elderly populations. The control strategies identified by our model could be taught to individuals confronting various health challenges. Indeed, it can be argued that some therapies (e.g., problem-solving therapy) operate on this principle, because they are designed to help the individual identify problems, think through solutions, and then act on them. In addition, it may be beneficial for older adults to learn to recognize that specific health conditions are not controllable, so that they invest their efforts in maintaining a certain level of functioning despite their uncontrollable health conditions. Moreover, disengagement and self-protection may enable them to avoid the negative emotional consequences of illnesses by refocusing their resources on the pursuit of other meaningful and more attainable goals. In sum, by enabling elderly individuals to avoid a downward spiral characterized by high levels of health stresses, maladaptive control behaviors, and depressive symptomatology, intervention programs may contribute to increasing older adults' psychological and physical health and significantly reducing the costs for public health services.

Recommended Reading

Williamson, G.M., Shaffer, D.R., & Parmelee, P.A. (Eds.). (2000). (See References)
Wrosch, C., Schulz, R., & Heckhausen, J. (2002). (See References)

REFERENCES

Heckhausen, J., & Schulz, R. (1995). A life-span theory of control. *Psychological Review, 102*, 284–304.
Lenze, E.J., Rogers, J.C., Martire, L.M., Mulsant, B.H., Rollman, B.L., Dew, M.A., Schulz, R., & Reynolds, C.F., III. (2001). The association of late-life depression and anxiety with physical disability: A review of the literature and prospectus for future research. *American Journal of Geriatric Psychiatry, 9*, 113–135.
Schulz, R., & Heckhausen, J. (1996). A life span model of successful aging. *American Psychologist, 51*, 702–714.
Schulz, R., Martire, L.M., Beach, S.R., & Scheier, M.F. (2000). Depression and mortality in the elderly. *Current Directions in Psychological Science, 9*, 204–208.
Williamson, G.M., Shaffer, D.R., & Parmelee, P.A. (Eds.). (2000). *Physical illness and depression in older adults: A handbook of theory, research, and practice.* New York: Kluwer Academic/Plenum Publishers.
Wrosch, C., Heckhausen, J., & Lachman, M.E. (2000). Primary and secondary control strategies for managing health and financial stress across adulthood. *Psychology and Aging, 15*, 387–399.
Wrosch, C., Scheier, M.F., Miller, G.E., Schulz, R., & Carver, C.S. (2003). Adaptive self-regulation of unattainable goals: Goal disengagement, goal reengagement, and subjective well-being. *Personality and Social Psychology Bulletin, 29*, 1494–1508.
Wrosch, C., Schulz, R., & Heckhausen, J. (2002). Health stresses and depressive symptomatology in the elderly: The importance of health engagement control strategies. *Health Psychology, 21*, 340–348.

Psychological Adjustment to Breast Cancer

Bruce E. Compas[1] and Linda Luecken
Department of Psychology, University of Vermont, Burlington, Vermont (B.E.C.), and Department of Psychology, Arizona State University, Tempe, Arizona (L.L.)

Abstract

Breast cancer remains a highly prevalent and extraordinarily stressful experience for hundreds of thousands of women each year in the United States and around the world. Psychological research has provided a picture of the emotional and social impact of breast cancer on patients' lives, and of factors associated with better versus worse adjustment. Psychosocial interventions have been beneficial in decreasing patients' distress and enhancing their quality of life. Recent research also suggests that psychological factors may be related to potentially important biological disease-related processes. In addition to providing an understanding of the psychological factors in breast cancer, research in this area has provided a framework for research on adaptation to health-related stress in general.

Keywords

breast cancer; psychological adjustment; coping

Breast cancer is a major public-health problem for women in the United States and internationally. Annually, more than 180,000 women in the United States are diagnosed with breast cancer, and more than 40,000 die from the disease; currently, a woman in the United States has a one in eight chance of developing the disease in her lifetime (American Cancer Society, 2001). The extraordinarily stressful aspects of the disease and its treatment have made research on its psychological effects a high priority.

Early research on the psychological effects of breast cancer dealt with a disease that typically had a relatively poor prognosis and was treated with aggressive forms of surgery (e.g., total mastectomy) and adjuvant therapies (e.g., chemotherapy) that were accompanied by debilitating negative side effects. The picture of psychological adjustment to breast cancer offered by early studies was, not surprisingly, one characterized by significant distress and trauma. Notable advances in early detection, diagnostic methods, and surgical and medical treatments have improved the prognosis of the disease, and new forms of treatment (e.g., anti-emetic medications) have dramatically reduced adverse side effects that formerly plagued many patients. Approximately 50% of women with breast cancer can now expect to survive at least 15 years, and over 95% of women with localized disease will survive 5 years or more (American Cancer Society, 2001).

Despite these advances, however, the diagnosis of, treatment of, and recovery from breast cancer remain highly stressful. Psychological research has played an essential role in helping investigators understand the impact of breast cancer on the lives of patients and their families, develop interventions to decrease distress and enhance quality of life, and understand possible relationships between psychological factors and biological disease processes. In addition, research on the psychological aspects of breast cancer provides a valuable paradigm for studying coping with health-related stress in general.

PSYCHOLOGICAL IMPACT OF BREAST CANCER

The psychological effects of breast cancer have been documented by using patients' self-reported mood and psychological symptoms to assess their psychological distress, sexual functioning, and overall quality of life; more rarely, investigators have used structured diagnostic interviews to assess psychiatric diagnoses. Findings indicate that the diagnosis of breast cancer is associated with heightened levels of negative emotions and psychological distress, especially symptoms of anxiety and depression. Elevated symptoms of anxiety and depression near the time of diagnosis are typically reported in 30% to 40% of patients, a rate that is approximately three to four times that found in the general population (e.g., Epping-Jordan et al., 1999). Rates of psychiatric diagnoses among breast cancer patients are less clear, as studies have varied widely in the methods used. Recent evidence suggests, however, that the rates of psychiatric diagnoses may not differ from those found in community studies. For example, Andrykowski, Cordova, Studts, and Miller (1998) found that rates of posttraumatic stress disorder (6% current and 4% lifetime) among newly diagnosed patients were comparable to rates in the general population.

There is considerable evidence that breast cancer and its treatment are associated with problems with body image, sexuality, and sexual functioning. For example, a recent study of patients 1 to 2 months after surgery reported avoidance of and decrease in sexual activity and disruption in arousal, orgasm, and satisfaction with sexual activity following all types of breast surgery (Yurek, Farrar, & Andersen, 2000). Women who received modified radical mastectomies with reconstructive surgery had greater disruptions in sexual functioning than women who received modified radical mastectomies without reconstruction and women who received lumpectomy surgery (Yurek et al., 2000). These findings are consistent with results of a meta-analysis[2] that found that lumpectomy (which conserves the breast) was associated with small but significant advantages in body image and sexual adjustment compared with mastectomy (Moyer, 1997).

Prospective studies in which symptoms of psychological distress are measured at multiple points during treatment have provided a relatively consistent picture of the course of adjustment to breast cancer: Psychological distress is highest near the time of diagnosis and declines over the ensuing months (e.g., Carver et al., 1993; Epping-Jordan et al., 1999). The steepest drop in distress occurs during the first 3 months after diagnosis and surgery, or before the completion of adjuvant therapy for most patients. However, although the mean level of distress generally declines over the course of treatment and recovery, some patients continue to experience high levels of anxiety and depression many months or even years after diagnosis.

PREDICTORS OF ADJUSTMENT

The process and course of adjustment to breast cancer have been studied in relation to five broad factors: characteristics of the disease, characteristics of the patient, social relationships and interpersonal resources, cognitive appraisals and attributions (e.g., perceptions of the disease and its causes, sense of control over the course of the disease), and coping methods. These factors have been examined in prospective studies to determine their contribution to increases or decreases in psychological symptoms and quality of life over the course of diagnosis, treatment, and recovery.

There is little evidence of a direct association of psychological distress with disease prognosis and type of treatment (e.g., surgical procedures, chemotherapy). The association between disease characteristics and psychological distress is far from simple, however, as it may change over the course of treatment and recovery. For example, one study (Compas et al., 1999) found that cancer stage (as an indicator of severity of the disease) was not associated with distress near the time of diagnosis, but was related to distress 6 months later. These findings suggest that patients' prognoses may become more salient once treatment is completed, as patients with a positive prognosis may recover psychologically more rapidly than patients with a poor prognosis and greater risk of recurrence.

Patients' characteristics that have been examined as predictors of distress include demographic factors (e.g., age, education) and personality characteristics (e.g., optimism). There is consistent evidence that age is inversely related to distress, such that younger women report more symptoms of anxiety and depression than older women (Stanton et al., 2000). Less formal education is associated with poorer psychological adjustment, including attempts to cope with the stress of breast cancer by avoiding emotions, thoughts, or information related to the disease (Epping-Jordan et al., 1999). Among the various personality characteristics that have been studied, dispositional optimism, or the tendency to expect positive outcomes, has been most consistently associated with lower symptoms of anxiety and depression and higher quality of life (e.g., Carver et al., 1993; Epping-Jordan et al., 1999).

In addition to patients' personal characteristics, social relationships and interpersonal resources available to patients are associated with the course of adjustment to breast cancer. Foremost among these resources is the quality of social support available to women during their treatment and recovery. Emotional support (other individuals' verbal and nonverbal communication of caring and concern for the patient) shows the most consistent relationship to lower distress and higher quality of life. Evidence for beneficial effects of emotional support has been stronger in descriptive studies of naturally occurring support in patients' lives than in studies of the effects of peer-led support groups (Helgeson & Cohen, 1996).

Cognitive processes, including the patient's thoughts concerning her control over the disease or role in causing it, are also central in adaptation to breast cancer. As we have already noted, holding relatively optimistic beliefs about future outcomes is associated with better psychological adjustment (Carver et al., 1993). The tendency to attribute one's cancer to one's own stable characteristics (characterological self-blame) or to one's behavior is related to higher current psychological distress, and characterological self-blame is uniquely related to increases in distress over time.

The ways that patients attempt to cope with their disease and the effects of treatment are central in determining the course of psychological distress and adjustment. Coping methods that involve disengagement from (avoidance of) the source of stress or one's negative emotions are predictive of poorer psychological adjustment and poorer health outcomes (e.g., Carver et al., 1993; Epping-Jordan et al., 1999). In contrast, coping methods that reflect engagement with the stressor and one's emotions are generally related to more positive psychological outcomes (e.g., Carver et al., 1993; Stanton et al., 2000). Furthermore, coping responses function as both mediators and moderators[3] of the effects of other factors on adjustment. At least two prospective studies have found that coping mediates the relationship between optimism and distress—optimism is associated with greater acceptance and humor, and pessimism is associated with greater avoidance and wishful thinking (Carver et al., 1993; Epping-Jordan et al., 1999), and these differences in coping style are in turn associated with different levels of distress. Coping also moderates the association between perceptions of personal control and distress in adjustment to breast cancer (Osowiecki & Compas, 1999). Distress is lowest when patients who have a sense of personal control over their cancer cope by using active, problem-oriented methods of coping. Research on predictors of adjustment to breast cancer has identified a set of processes that warrant attention in research on adaptation to other health-related stressors.

PSYCHOLOGICAL INTERVENTIONS FOR BREAST CANCER

Individual and group interventions have been developed to enhance quality of life and decrease distress in breast cancer patients. Treatment techniques have included training patients in relaxation and guided-imagery techniques, providing them with educational information, providing them the opportunity to express emotions, encouraging the exchange of social support with other patients, and training patients in cognitive and behavioral coping skills for dealing with a range of outcomes (e.g., nausea, pain, emotional distress, changes in quality of life, progression of the illness). Early work focused on behavioral methods for managing the nausea and vomiting associated with chemotherapy. Since the advent of antiemetic medications, psychological treatments have focused increasingly on using group methods to decrease patients' psychological distress and enhance their quality of life. The two treatment models that have been developed and examined most extensively in research are cognitive-behavioral (e.g., stress management, cognitive coping skills; e.g., Antoni et al., 2001) and supportive-expressive (focusing on the expression and processing of emotion; e.g., Classen et al., 2001).

Reviews of psychosocial interventions for cancer patients have shown that such interventions are effective for patients with various kinds of cancer, including breast cancer. Psychosocial interventions consistently show beneficial effects on emotional adjustment, functional adjustment, and treatment- and disease-related symptoms (e.g., nausea, pain). However, no specific type of intervention with breast cancer patients has met the criteria to be considered an "empirically supported" treatment (i.e., beneficial effects in at least two randomized trials conducted by independent investigators).

PSYCHOLOGICAL PROCESSES AND BIOLOGICAL OUTCOMES

Perhaps the most provocative and intriguing area of research involves the possible association between psychological processes and biological disease processes and outcomes. Numerous studies have shown that stress and emotional distress are associated with increased output of the stress-related hormone cortisol, and with suppression of immune function. Stress and the psychological states of depression and anxiety have been associated with compromised immune function in breast cancer patients. In contrast, higher quality social support is associated with lower cortisol output in women with metastatic breast cancer (e.g., Turner-Cobb, Sephton, Koopman, Blake-Mortimer, & Spiegel, 2000). Although results from these and other studies suggest that psychological factors can influence immune functioning, the impact on cancer outcomes has yet to be determined.

Preliminary evidence suggests that psychosocial interventions for breast cancer patients may have beneficial physiological effects, including lowered cortisol, improved immune function, and enhanced survival. One well-known study reported significant survival advantages for women with metastatic breast cancer following participation in psychosocial support groups (Spiegel, Bloom, Kraemer, & Gottheil, 1989). However, several recent studies have failed to find an effect of psychosocial intervention on disease progression or survival time (e.g., Goodwin et al., 2001). Thus, potential physiological or survival benefits of psychosocial intervention for breast cancer patients remain speculative and deserve further investigation.

FUTURE DIRECTIONS

Further research is needed to build on current understanding of psychological processes in breast cancer in several ways. First, several critical issues pertaining to psychological interventions remain unresolved. The mechanisms that account for the observed benefits of psychological interventions remain unclear. Interventions that facilitate emotional expression and support, as well as those that build coping skills, have yielded beneficial effects. However, the active components in these interventions remain unclear. The most controversial area of research involves the effects of psychological interventions on disease progression and survival. Second, research on breast cancer can benefit from closer integration with research advances in other areas of psychological science. For example, breast cancer is a disease primarily of older women. Understanding adjustment to breast cancer can be informed by basic research and theory on psychological aspects of aging. Also, research on cognitive and affective processes in adjustment to breast cancer will benefit greatly by drawing on emerging methods for measurement that have been developed in cognitive science and the study of emotions. Finally, as breast cancer treatments continue to improve and patients continue to live longer, attention may need to shift from the immediate effects of diagnosis and treatment to the longer-term effects during extended survival.

Recommended Reading

Baum, A., & Andersen, B.L. (Eds.). (2001). *Psychosocial interventions for cancer.* Washington, DC: American Psychological Association.
Compas, B.E., Haaga, D.A., Keefe, F.J., Leitenberg, H., & Williams, D.A. (1998). Sampling of empirically supported psychological treatments from health psychology: Smoking, chronic pain, cancer, and bulimia nervosa. *Journal of Consulting and Clinical Psychology, 66,* 89–112.
Luecken, L., & Compas, B.E. (in press). Stress, coping, and immune function in breast cancer. *Annals of Behavioral Medicine.*
Suinn, R.M., & VandenBos, G.R. (Eds.). (1999). *Cancer patients and their families: Readings on disease course, coping, and psychological interventions.* Washington, DC: American Psychological Association.

Acknowledgments—Preparation of this manuscript was supported in part by Grant RO1CA67936 from the National Cancer Institute.

Notes

1. Address correspondence to Bruce E. Compas, Department of Psychology, University of Vermont, Burlington, VT 05405; e-mail: bruce.compas@uvm.edu.
2. In a meta-analysis, the findings of multiple studies are analyzed quantitatively by comparing them using a common unit of measurement.
3. Mediators are factors that account for the association between two other variables, whereas moderators are factors that alter the relationship between two other variables.

References

American Cancer Society. (2001). *Cancer facts and figures.* Atlanta, GA: Author.
Andrykowski, M.A., Cordova, M.J., Studts, J.L., & Miller, T.W. (1998). Posttraumatic stress disorder after treatment for breast cancer: Prevalence of diagnosis and use of the PTSD Checklist–Civilian Version (PCL–C) as a screening instrument. *Journal of Consulting and Clinical Psychology, 66,* 586–590.
Antoni, M.H., Lehman, J.M., Klibourn, K.M., Boyers, A.E., Culver, J.L., Alferi, S.M., Yount, S.E., McGregor, B.A., Arena, P.L., Harris, S.D., Price, A.A., & Carver, C.S. (2001). Cognitive-behavioral stress management intervention decreases the prevalence of depression and enhances benefit finding among women under treatment for early stage breast cancer. *Health Psychology, 20,* 20–32.
Carver, C.S., Pozo, C., Harris, S.D., Noriega, V., Scheier, M.F., Robinson, D.S., Ketcham, A.S., Moffat, F.L., & Clark, K.C. (1993). How coping mediates the effect of optimism on distress: A study of women with early stage breast cancer. *Journal of Personality and Social Psychology, 65,* 375–390.
Classen, C., Butler, L.D., Koopman, C., Miller, E., DiMiceli, S., Giese-Davis, J., Fobair, D., Carlson, R.W., Kraemer, H.C., & Spiegel, D. (2001). Supportive-expressive group therapy and distress in patients with metastatic breast cancer. *Archives of General Psychiatry, 58,* 494–501.
Compas, B.E., Stoll, M.F., Thomsen, A.H., Oppedisano, G., Epping-Jordan, J.E., & Krag, D.N. (1999). Adjustment to breast cancer: Age-related differences in coping and emotional distress. *Breast Cancer Research and Treatment, 1233,* 195–203.
Epping-Jordan, J.E., Compas, B.E., Osowiecki, D.M., Oppedisano, G., Gerhardt, C., Primo, K., & Krag, D.N. (1999). Psychological adjustment to breast cancer: Processes of emotional distress. *Health Psychology, 18,* 315–326.

Goodwin, P.J., Leszcz, M., Ennis, M., Koopmans, J., Vincent, L., Guther, H., Drysdale, E., Hundleby, M., Chochinov, H.M., Navarro, M., Speca, M., Masterson, J., Dohan, L., Sela, R., Warren, B., Paterson, A., Pritchard, K.I., Arnold, A., Doll, R., O'Reilly, A.E., Quirt, G., Hood, N., & Hunter, J. (2001). The effect of group psychosocial support on survival in metastatic breast cancer. *The New England Journal of Medicine, 345,* 1719–1726.

Helgeson, V.S., & Cohen, S. (1996). Social support and adjustment to cancer: Reconciling descriptive, correlational, and intervention research. *Health Psychology, 15,* 135–148.

Moyer, A. (1997). Psychosocial outcomes of breast conserving surgery versus mastectomy: A meta-analytic review. *Health Psychology, 16,* 284–298.

Osowiecki, D.M., & Compas, B.E. (1999). A prospective study of coping, perceived control and psychological adjustment to breast cancer. *Cognitive Therapy and Research, 23,* 169–180.

Spiegel, D., Bloom, J.R., Kraemer, H.C., & Gottheil, E. (1989). Effect of psychosocial treatment on survival of patients with metastatic breast cancer. *Lancet, 2,* 888–891.

Stanton, A.L., Danoff-Burg, S., Cameron, C.L., Bishop, M., Collins, C.A., Kirk, S.B., Sworowski, L.A., & Twillman, R. (2000). Emotionally expressive coping predicts psychological and physical adjustment to breast cancer. *Journal of Consulting and Clinical Psychology, 68,* 875–882.

Turner-Cobb, J.M., Sephton, S.E., Koopman, C., Blake-Mortimer, J., & Spiegel, D. (2000). Social support and salivary cortisol in women with metastatic breast cancer. *Psychosomatic Medicine, 62,* 337–345.

Yurek, D., Farrar, W., & Andersen, B.L. (2000). Breast cancer surgery: Comparing surgical groups and determining individual differences in postoperative sexuality and body change stress. *Journal of Consulting and Clinical Psychology, 68,* 697–709.

Another Side to Caregiving:
Negative Reactions to Being Helped

Jason T. Newsom[1]

Institute on Aging, Portland State University, Portland, Oregon

Abstract

Until recently, caregiving research focused almost exclusively on caregivers of older adults with health problems, and there was little focus on care recipients perceptions of the care they receive. The present article reviews relevant research on reactions to caregiving assistance. Several recent studies indicate that help in these contexts can be viewed negatively by care recipients. As many as two thirds of physically impaired older adults who receive assistance with daily activities, such as preparing meals, climbing stairs, or dressing, experience negative reactions to some of the help they receive. Negative reactions seem to have important consequences for the care recipient, because they are associated with higher depression concurrently and 1 year later. Because some of the findings are inconsistent with theoretical models of negative responses to help, an alternative framework, based on social-support and social-conflict research, is briefly proposed.

Keywords

care receiving; caregiving; aging; negative interactions; helping; social support

With thousands of scholarly articles written on the topic, research on caregiving has become an important focus in a wide range of disciplines. Caregiving researchers have extensively studied the stressful consequences for caregivers who provide assistance to physically or cognitively impaired older adults. It is surprising, however, to discover that only a handful of studies have focused on caregiving from the perspective of the recipient who receives the care. Most studies, in fact, do not even collect data from care recipients. A series of recent studies indicates that many recipients experience some negative reactions to assistance with daily activities. Although too few studies have been conducted to provide a truly accurate picture of the prevalence of negative reactions, there is enough evidence to raise serious concerns. Negative reactions appear to be neither rare nor inconsequential. Reports indicate that one third to two thirds of recipients report some negative reactions to help, and a number of studies have shown that these reactions are associated with depression or other measures of psychological distress.

CURRENT FINDINGS ON NEGATIVE REACTIONS

Negative reactions to help have been measured and defined in a variety of ways. In studies using general measures, care recipients have reported emotional strain or unpleasant feelings in response to help provided with various daily activities (Newsom, Adams, Rahim, Mowry, & Rogers, 1998; Newsom & Schulz, 1998), negative perceptions of caregiving behaviors (Clark & Stephens, 1996), and dissatisfaction with help received (Thomas, 1993). Some care recipients have also reported lowered self-esteem in response to help, feelings of rejection, feelings of dependency, anger, resentment, concerns about reciprocity, and feelings of incompetence (see Table 1 for examples from one study). Responses involving negative self-attributions (e.g., feeling embarrassed, feeling weak or incapable, a loss of self-esteem) seem to be the specific feelings most related to general ratings of unpleasantness in response to help (Newsom et al., 1998).

One hypothesis is that too little or too much help may tend to increase negative reactions. When asked about unhelpful actions by their spouses, stroke patients in the study by Clark and Stephens (1996) frequently said that their spouses over- or underestimated the amount of help needed. Along with my colleague Richard Schulz, I investigated this hypothesis further by comparing activities with which recipients reported having difficulty with caregivers reports of help provision for those activities (Newsom & Schulz, 1998). Too little, but not too much, help was associated with general negative reactions to help. Although the results were statistically significant, underhelping was only modestly related to negative reactions and was not a significant predictor when other factors, such as level of impairment, were taken into account.

Poor-quality care or other negative behaviors of the caregiver are also considered to be potential causes of negative reactions, although these are unlikely to be the only causes. Quality of care is difficult to define or measure, but open-ended reports by care recipients suggest that helping is sometimes judged to be incorrect (Clark & Stephens, 1996). Recipients also tend to report a variety of negative caregiver behaviors that are apparently related to their health problems. Some of these negative behaviors include criticisms (Clark & Stephens, 1996; Parmelee, 1983), hostility (Parmelee, 1983), demandingness (Clark & Stephens, 1996), and insensitivity (Martire et al., 1998). My colleagues and I found that negative caregiver behaviors, such as reluctance, resentfulness, discourteousness, and criticisms, were relatively infrequently reported (about 10% of participants) but were important predictors of general negative reactions to help (Newsom et al., 1998). Negative caregiver behaviors may also lead to temporary decrements in self-esteem (Clark & Stephens, 1996).

It is possible that accounts of caregivers behaviors are partially a function of

Table 1. *Reports of specific cognitive and emotional reactions to a spouse's help (from Newsom, Adams, Rahim, Mowry, & Rogers, 1998)*

Negative Reaction to help	Percentage agreeing or strongly agreeing
Concerned about spouse being injured providing help	66
Felt dependent on spouse	54
Felt indebted to spouse	30
Wished could give more in return	31
Felt would never be able to return favor	27
Felt like a weak or incapable person	26
Did not feel like a person of worth, at least as much as others	23
Did not feel able to do things as well as most others of same age	23
Wished they could have more respect for self	23

biased perceptions of the recipients rather than a reflection of poor-quality care. Personality characteristics, such as pessimism, or depression may color care recipients reports of their caregivers behaviors. More information about this hypothesis is needed, but evidence suggests that recipients reports are not wholly inaccurate. Caregivers reports of critical attitudes toward their spouses illness are predictive of recipients levels of depression (Stephens et al., 1998). In addition, longitudinal data indicate that negative reactions predict depression when initial levels of depression are controlled for statistically (Newsom & Schulz, 1998).

Certain types of individuals may be especially likely to report negative reactions to help. Those with greater levels of impairment tend to experience more negative reactions. It may be that these individuals are more likely to experience negative reactions because they feel dependent or feel they are less able to reciprocate. Lower perceived control and lower self-esteem are predictive of general negative reactions, but the effects occur primarily for individuals who receive high levels of assistance. Lower marital satisfaction and greater marital conflict are also associated with negative reactions, but current research is unable to distinguish whether marital quality is a causal factor or a consequence of negative reactions.

Several findings suggest that there may be serious consequences of negative reactions to caregiving assistance. General measures of negative reactions to help are associated with greater depression and lower life satisfaction. Longitudinal results over a 1-year period suggest that negative reactions to caregiving may cause depression, with effects that are fairly long-lasting (Newsom & Schulz, 1998). A variety of specific reactions, including feelings of incompetence, lack of control, rejection, and less freedom of choice in response to help, have also been found to be correlated with depression and lower life satisfaction (Martire et al., 1998).

MAKING SENSE OF THE LITERATURE

Helping

The study of reactions to aid from others is not new. Extensive laboratory research on reactions to help has been conducted, and findings indicate that negative reactions to help are not uncommon (Fisher, Nadler, & Whitcher-Alagna, 1982). The factors that have been found to lead to negative responses to aid in laboratory studies include an inability to reciprocate and thus indebtedness to the helper, restriction of freedom, greater perceived control over life events, and higher self-esteem (Nadler & Fisher, 1986). The primary theoretical framework to explain results in this area is the threat-to-self-esteem model (Fisher et al., 1982). This model states that help is perceived as threatening, because help implies that the aid recipient is inferior or is incapable of completing the task alone.

The threat-to-self-esteem model, however, is inconsistent with findings on care recipient's reactions to help in several ways. Those with lower self-esteem tend to experience greater negative reactions to caregivers help, and this contradicts laboratory helping studies indicating that individuals with higher self-esteem are more likely to react negatively to help. The threat-to-self-esteem model also predicts that those with greater perceived control will be more likely to react negatively to help, but in studies of care recipients, those with lower perceived control were more likely to have negative responses.

A recent study by Daubman (1995) suggests that there may be limitations to the threat-to-self-esteem model. Her findings indicate that when help recipients have little or no hope for improvement on a task, those with low self-esteem and low perceived control are more likely to perform poorly on the task when help is provided than when it is not. This situation may be similar to many caregiving situations in which the task involves physical activities. In many instances, care recipients may feel there is little hope for improvement in these activities.

A Social-Support Negative-Interaction Framework

The social-support and social-conflict literature (Rook, 1992) may provide a more useful context for understanding care recipients negative reactions. Assistance with daily activities can be viewed as instrumental social support (i.e., material or physical assistance). Negative reactions to help may result either from positive support that is interpreted negatively or from behaviors that are not intended to be supportive (e.g., criticisms). Thus, just as perceptions of social support do not necessarily correspond to actual support, subjective perceptions of caregiving interactions may not be consistent with the objective interactions. In caregiving studies, the actual amount of help provided is unrelated or, in some cases, positively related to negative reactions (Newsom & Schulz, 1998). Subjective perceptions of social interactions are considered to be more important for mental and physical health outcomes than actual levels of support or conflict, and, similarly, caregivers behaviors may have less impact on mental health than subjective responses to assistance (Martire et al., 1998).

Barrera and Baca (1990), studying the link between actual and subjective support, conceptualized two ways supportive and conflictual social interactions may have their effects. Variables that have a direct effect on perceptions will lead to more positive or more negative perceptions of social interactions independently of other factors. For instance, extraverts rate social interactions more positively than introverts, and individuals with greater interpersonal competence are more satisfied with support than those with less interpersonal competence. Other factors may moderate the relationship between actual social interactions and subjective perceptions. With moderator effects, the relationship between provided support and satisfaction with support, for example, may be stronger for certain individuals than for others.

Many findings from the caregiving literature concerning care recipients can be interpreted using a framework similar to the one provided by Barrera and Baca. For example, fewer negative reactions are associated with high self-esteem and low fatalism (related to low perceived control), and these findings are consistent with several studies in the support literature that demonstrate increased benefit from support for individuals with high self-esteem and perceived control. The amount of assistance may also affect perceptions of caregivers negative behaviors. Social conflict, in general, tends to be viewed more negatively when it involves an individual providing more support (Okun & Keith, 1998), because expectations that the person providing support will be supportive are violated (Rook, 1992).

Figure 1 summarizes five general types of variables that may lead to nega-

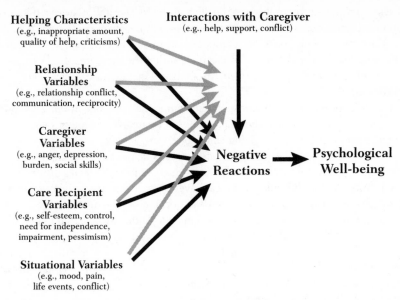

Helping Characteristics
(e.g., inappropriate amount, quality of help, criticisms)

Interactions with Caregiver
(e.g., help, support, conflict)

Relationship Variables
(e.g., relationship conflict, communication, reciprocity)

Caregiver Variables
(e.g., anger, depression, burden, social skills)

Care Recipient Variables
(e.g., self-esteem, control, need for independence, impairment, pessimism)

Situational Variables
(e.g., mood, pain, life events, conflict)

Negative Reactions

Psychological Well-being

Fig. 1. Direct and moderator effects of five factors that may affect negative reactions to caregiving assistance. Black arrows represent direct effects, and gray arrows represent moderation of the relation between help and negative reactions.

tive reactions to assistance: helping characteristics, the caregiver recipient relationship, characteristics of the caregiver, characteristics of the care recipient, and situational variables. Each category of variables may directly influence negative reactions (black arrows) or moderate (gray arrows) the relationship between actual assistance and subjective responses to that assistance.

FUTURE DIRECTIONS

One way to improve our understanding of negative reactions to caregiving will be to expand the range of care recipients studied. Nearly all research in this area has focused on spousal caregiving, and more information is needed about negative reactions when care is delivered by adult children, professionals, or multiple parties. Research on professional care, for example, might contribute to and draw from recent work on doctor patient relationships. To date, all studies have involved recipients with physical impairments, and research on patients with cognitive impairments or communication difficulties is greatly needed. Measuring negative reactions will be a greater challenge in these situations, but there are a variety of observational techniques and new survey methods using visual aids that may be useful. Existing studies also tend to focus on physical assistance, but investigating other types of support provided by caregivers, such as emotional or cognitive support, would provide valuable new avenues of research (e.g., Stephens et al., 1998).

More longitudinal research is needed to elucidate the causes of negative reactions to assistance. Nearly all studies have been cross-sectional, and several sticky issues about causality remain. For instance, marital quality, self-esteem, and perceptions of control appear to be related to negative reactions to care, but it is not known whether these factors are causes, consequences, or merely correlates of negative reactions. It is also critical that the measures used can clearly distinguish between hypothesized causes, the reactions themselves, and their consequences.

The time is also ripe to consider developing interventions in this area. Some fruitful areas may include the improvement of caregiver-recipient communication, marital relations, caregiving skills, or coping strategies of care recipients. It is imperative, however, that such interventions be guided by research. It would be inappropriate, for instance, to focus on the care provider if negative reactions stem from marital difficulties, the caregiver's burden, or the recipient's personality characteristics. Because causal factors may affect negative reactions in unexpected or complex ways, interventions not guided by research may be ineffective or even harmful in some cases. For example, encouraging people to be more self-reliant and encouraging people to be more reliant on others have both been shown to have harmful effects under specific conditions. Thus, interventions designed to invariably reduce dependence, for instance, may not be beneficial for all impaired older adults.

Although research in this area has added a valuable new perspective on caregiving, readers should be cautioned against concluding that caregivers are not good at what they do or that caregiving is not typically valued. Most care recipients who participate in studies of caregiving express a profound sense of gratitude to their family for their assistance, and, on average, approximately half of participants do not report any negative reactions. Moreover, when recipients are asked about caregivers helpful and unhelpful behaviors, approximately two thirds of the behaviors they list are helpful ones (Clark & Stephens, 1996). Although care recipients are likely to underreport negative interactions with caregivers for a variety of reasons (e.g., indebtedness, social desirability), it is reasonable to assume that informal, in-home caregiving is of great benefit to recipients in most instances. Thus, one valuable direction for future research will be to investigate the beneficial aspects of care from the recipient s perspective.

Recommended Reading

Fisher, J.D., Nadler, A., & DePaulo, B.M. (1983). *New directions in helping: Vol. 1. Recipient reactions to aid.* New York: Academic Press.

Kahana, E., Biegel, D.E., & Wykle, M.L. (1994). *Family caregiving across the lifespan.* Thousand Oaks, CA: Sage.

Rook, K.S., & Pietromonaco, P. (1987). Close relationships: Ties that heal or ties that bind. In W.H. Jones & D. Perlman (Eds.), *Advances in personal relationships* (Vol. 1, pp. 1–35). Greenwich, CT: JAI Press.

Spacapan, S., & Oskamp, S. (1992). *Helping and being helped.* Newbury Park, CA: Sage.

Wills, T.A. (1991). Social support and interpersonal relationships. In M.S. Clark (Ed.), *Review of personality and social psychology: Vol. 12. Prosocial behavior* (pp. 265–289). Newbury Park, CA: Sage.

Acknowledgments—Work on this article was supported in part by grants from the National Institute on Aging (AG15159 and AG14130). This article benefited from ideas and discussions with several of my colleagues: David Morgan, Karen Rook, and participants of the University of Oregon Psychology Brown Bag series. Helpful comments on an earlier draft were also provided by Beth Green, John Reich, and Margaret Neal.

Note

1. Address correspondence to Jason T. Newsom, Institute on Aging, Box 751, Portland State University, Portland, OR 97207-0751. A more detailed version of this article is available through the author's World Wide Web page at http://www.ioa.pdx.edu/newsom/home/homepage.htm.

References

Barrera, M., Jr., & Baca, L.M. (1990). Recipient reactions to social support: Contributions of enacted support, conflicted support, and network orientation. *Journal of Social and Personality Relationships, 7*, 541–551.

Clark, S.L., & Stephens, M.A.P. (1996). Stroke patients' well-being as a function of caregiving spouse's helpful and unhelpful actions. *Personal Relationships, 3*, 171–184.

Daubman, K.A. (1995). Help which implies dependence: Effects on self-evaluations, motivation, and performance. *Journal of Social Behavior and Personality, 10*, 677–692.

Fisher, J.D., Nadler, A., & Whitcher-Alagna, S. (1982). Recipient reactions to aid. *Psychological Bulletin, 91*, 27–54.

Martire, L.M., Stephens, M.A.P., Druley, J.A., Berthoff, M.A., Fleisher, C.L., & Wojno, W.C. (1998, August). *Older women coping with osteoarthritis: Negative reactions to spousal support*. Paper presented at the annual meeting of the American Psychological Association, San Francisco.

Nadler, A., & Fisher, J.D. (1986). The role of threat to self-esteem and perceived control in recipient reactions to help: Theory development and empirical validation. In L. Berkowitz (Ed.), *Advances in experimental social psychology* (Vol. 19, pp. 81–122). New York: Academic Press.

Newsom, J.T., Adams, N.L., Rahim, A., Mowry, H., & Rogers, J. (1998, November). *Approaches to measuring care recipient's negative reactions to assistance*. Poster presented at the annual meeting of the Gerontological Society of America, Philadelphia.

Newsom, J.T., & Schulz, R. (1998). Caregiving from the recipient's perspective: Negative reactions to being helped. *Health Psychology, 17*, 172–181.

Okun, M.A., & Keith, V.M. (1998). Effects of positive and negative social exchanges with various sources on depressive symptoms in younger and older adults. *Journal of Gerontology: Psychological Sciences, 53B*, 4–20.

Parmelee, P.A. (1983). Spouse versus other family caregivers: Psychological impact on impaired aged. *American Journal of Community Psychology, 11*, 337–349.

Rook, K.S. (1992). Detrimental aspects of social relationships: Taking stock of an emerging literature. In H.O.F. Veiel & U. Baumann (Eds.), *The meaning and measurement of social support* (pp. 157–169). Washington, DC: Hemisphere.

Stephens, M.A.P., Druley, J.A., Martire, L.M., Fleisher, C.L., Berthoff, M.A., & Wojno, W.C. (1998, November). *Older couples coping with wives osteoarthritis: Problematic support from husbands*. Poster presented at the annual meeting of the Gerontological Society of America, Philadelphia.

Thomas, J.L. (1993). Concerns regarding adult children's assistance: Comparison of young-old and old-old parents. *Journal of Gerontology: Social Sciences, 48*, 315–322.

Illness and Satisfaction With Medical Care

Judith A. Hall,[1] Debra L. Roter, and Michael A. Milburn

Department of Psychology, Northeastern University, Boston, Massachusetts (J.A.H.); Department of Health Policy and Management, Johns Hopkins School of Public Health, Baltimore, Maryland (D.L.R.); and Department of Psychology, University of Massachusetts, Boston, Massachusetts (M.A.M.)

Abstract

Patients who have worse physical or mental health are less satisfied with their medical care than patients in better health. This article describes research that explores the causal underpinnings of this correlation. Does poor health cause dissatisfaction, or does dissatisfaction cause poor health? And is the dissatisfaction of sicker patients attributable to their own state of mind, or rather to how they are treated by their doctors? It appears that, predominantly, dissatisfaction follows from poorer health rather than vice versa, and moreover that sicker patients' negative outlook is a pervasive cause of their lower satisfaction. However, there is also evidence that physicians' reactions to sicker patients, in the form of curtailed social conversation, also play a role in the reduced satisfaction of these patients.

Keywords

patient satisfaction; health status; physician behavior

After several decades of measuring medical patients' satisfaction with medical care, investigators now understand a fair amount about the patient and physician variables that correlate with satisfaction. For example, older patients tend to be more satisfied than younger ones, but women and men are equivalently satisfied (Hall & Dornan, 1990). Patients are more satisfied when their physicians spend more time with them, inform them more, engage in more discussion of social-emotional issues, and are more technically competent (Hall, Roter, & Katz, 1988), and also when their physicians like them more (Like & Zyzanski, 1987). Patients who are more satisfied adhere more faithfully to their treatment regimens and are less likely to change physicians (DiMatteo & DiNicola, 1982).

Patients' health has also been found to be related to satisfaction. People with better health, both mental and physical, are more satisfied. Although the associations are not strong in magnitude, they occur across a range of definitions of health. Greater satisfaction has been found to be related to better functional health (ability to perform activities of daily living), better health ratings made by physicians, fewer hospitalizations, fewer symptoms or diagnoses, better self-perceived overall health, better emotional health, and greater social activity (for reviews, see Hall, Feldstein, Fretwell, Rowe, & Epstein, 1990; Pascoe, 1983).

Although most research on correlates of satisfaction has not addressed the causal paths that might be involved, investigations of health status and satisfaction have attempted to do so. In the remainder of this article, we describe what research has revealed so far about the possible causal relations between health and satisfaction.

WHICH COMES FIRST: THE HEALTH OR THE SATISFACTION?

The first logical question to ask is the direction of causality: Does better health lead to greater satisfaction, or does satisfaction lead to better health? Both paths are plausible. On the one hand, if patients credit their physicians with positive health outcomes, it follows that they might be more satisfied as a result. On the other hand, greater satisfaction could produce better health if satisfaction leads to increased compliance with medical recommendations (among other possibilities). The notion of patients "rewarding" their physicians with compliance in exchange for satisfying care is consistent with a social-exchange perspective on physician-patient interaction (Roter & Hall, 1992).

In a 1-year longitudinal study of more than 500 elderly patients enrolled in a health maintenance organization, we (Hall, Milburn, & Epstein, 1993) asked whether health led to satisfaction or vice versa. Analysis suggested that better initial health led to positive changes in satisfaction, but not vice versa. Thus, it appears that, in general, greater satisfaction does not produce improvements in health, though our findings do not rule out the possibility that satisfaction can influence health in some cases.

WHO IS RESPONSIBLE: THE PATIENT OR THE PHYSICIAN?

Theoretical questions are not laid to rest with the finding that health predicts satisfaction more than vice versa. One still wants to know by what mechanism health influences satisfaction. Several distinct possibilities can be explored.

The Patient

In 1982, Linn and Greenfield suggested that the source of the health-satisfaction correlation is the patient. According to this view, the patient's health has a direct impact on how the patient views his or her medical care. Illness may produce negative affect that becomes attached to the care provider; furthermore, if conscientious medical treatment does not produce noticeable improvements, a sick patient may be inclined to blame the provider. Given this logic, it is not surprising that Linn and Greenfield argued that investigators studying the relation of satisfaction to the process, content, or structure of medical care should control for health status (along with other sociodemographic correlates of satisfaction) when performing such analyses, to avoid the error of looking to the health care system to explain problems that actually reside in the patient.

Indirect evidence supports this "grouchy patient" hypothesis. Satisfaction with medical care is associated with satisfaction with other dimensions of life, including marriage, leisure, money, government, consumer issues, one's community, and public organizations (Carmel, 1985; Roberts, Pascoe, & Attkisson, 1983). If having worse health predicts dissatisfaction with these nonmedical aspects of life, then it seems quite possible that dissatisfaction with medical care has more to do with the individual's global negative outlook than with anything in particular about that medical care.

The Physician

A different causal possibility was raised by Greenley, Young, and Schoenherr (1982). After finding that patients with worse mental health were less satisfied with their medical care, these investigators suggested that physicians' negative responses to mentally distressed patients might actually be the source of the dissatisfaction. In contrast to the previously described direct hypothesis, this explanation is indirect. It posits that poor health has an impact on the physician, who then (through his or her behavior) influences the patient's satisfaction. Patients' poor health might cause negative reactions in physicians if sicker patients behave disagreeably or are unresponsive, or simply have a disagreeable appearance or sensory qualities (e.g., are unwashed or unkempt). Physicians might also have a negative response to patients whose medical problems can be attributed to the patients' own behavior or lifestyle (e.g., drug-abusing patients or those who refuse to stop smoking). If this indirect physician-mediation explanation is true, then statistically removing the effects of health on satisfaction before studying medical care, as Linn and Greenfield (1982) suggested, would be a serious error.

A large amount of evidence supports the plausibility of the physician-mediation explanation. First, patients who are in worse physical or mental health do behave in a more negative way; they engage in less social conversation, they are perceived as more angry and anxious, and their voice quality is more submissive and lacking in optimism (Hall, Roter, Milburn, & Daltroy, 1996). Thus, there is evidence that sicker patients may indeed be a negative stimulus.

Second, research indicates that the more mentally or physically sick patients are, the more physicians respond to them in ways that can be considered negative, or at least ambivalent (Hall et al., 1996). When with these patients, physicians engage in less social conversation, disagree more, and are rated as more negative overall, and as having a more negative voice quality. However, it is important to note that physicians interacting with sicker patients also engage in more positive and concerned behaviors, such as making more positive verbal statements, imparting more information, and talking more about emotional issues, than when interacting with healthier patients. Thus, physicians appear to engage in an interesting mixture of negatively and positively toned behaviors when interacting with sicker patients.

A third line of support for the physician-mediation explanation concerns the link between physicians' behavior and patients' satisfaction. Numerous studies show that the behavior of the physician does predict satisfaction, as alluded to earlier (Hall et al., 1988).

The fourth category of findings that support the physician-mediation explanation rests on physicians' own reports of how they react to their sicker patients. Several studies have produced the rather remarkable finding that physicians have less liking for, and are less satisfied with, their patients the sicker the patients are (Hall, Epstein, DeCiantis, & McNeil, 1993; Hall et al., 1996).

Although these four kinds of evidence, taken together, may seem to constitute strong support for the physician-mediation hypothesis, they are only circumstantial because testing the mediation hypothesis requires linking health status, physicians' behavior, and satisfaction all in one study. It is also desirable to test the direct and physician-mediation explanations simultaneously. That is, the hypothesis that lower satisfaction stems directly from poorer health and the hypothesis that poorer health influences the physician's behavior, which then influences satisfaction, are not mutually exclusive hypotheses. Recent research has addressed these goals (Hall, Milburn, Roter, & Daltroy, 1998).

A Test of the Two Hypotheses

We tested the direct and indirect hypotheses in two studies (Hall et al., 1998). Study 1 involved 114 patients visiting rheumatologists, and Study 2 involved 649 patients seeing their physicians (internal medicine or family practice) for routine continuing care. In both studies, health status (both physical and mental) was assessed via reports from both the physician and the patient, numerous communication behaviors were coded or rated by independent observers from audiotapes of the medical visits, and satisfaction was measured immediately after each medical visit. Having measurements of health, satisfaction, and communication all on the same samples of patients and physicians permitted us to test the two hypotheses simultaneously.

The direct hypothesis was supported: When we controlled for other possible variables, there was significant evidence in both studies that health directly influenced satisfaction. In Study 1, there was no support for the physician-mediation hypothesis. However, in Study 2, there was significant support for that hypothesis with respect to the amount of social conversation (i.e., casual, nonmedical talk) provided by the physician. The results indicated that poorer patient health led to less social conversation by the physician, which in turn led to lower satisfaction.

Why would curtailing social conversation lead to reduced satisfaction in sicker patients? Given the extreme time pressures on physicians, perhaps they must limit social conversation to compensate for the time required to deal with a more complex array of medical or social-emotional problems. Alternatively, physicians may reason that a sicker patient expects an "all business" interaction; or physicians treating sicker patients may experience more negative affect and therefore be less inclined to engage in chitchat, which, almost by definition, is pleasant in tone. In any case, physicians may consider such pleasantries to be expendable given the need for their medical expertise and the high cost of their time.

Unfortunately, because a certain amount of social conversation is an expected part of a social interaction, especially between people who rarely see each other, patients may resent its curtailment. Not only is social conversation an expected phase in social interaction, but, we believe, it also serves specific functions in the context of physician-patient interaction. In the initial phase of a medical visit, when most of the social conversation takes place, important aspects of the physician-patient relationship are established or reinforced. Through conversation about personal opinions, family, or work, the physician acknowledges the patient as a unique person and not just an anonymous "case" or a set of symptoms interchangeable with those of any other patient. Also, social conversation has a more symmetrical and fraternal quality than the rest of a medical visit, when the physician controls the dialogue, usually by means of yes/no questions. Beginning an interaction with comments on the weather or the local sports teams, or with an expression of interest in the other person's family or personal life, implies a level of equality that is otherwise not present in typical physician-patient exchanges.

We are not suggesting that more social conversation is necessarily better; in all likelihood, too little and too much social conversation are both problematic, with too much suggesting that the physician has an inappropriate degree of personal interest or is neglecting his or her job. We are instead suggesting that a certain amount of a behavior that might on first glance seem idle and time-wasting may actually be very important from the social psychological point of view. It is thus ironic that well-meaning physicians, while trying to give the best care they can, may end up producing dissatisfaction in their sicker patients.

CONCLUSION

To summarize, both the direct and the physician-mediation hypotheses received support in our recent research. Sicker patients' grouchiness does seem to account for some of their dissatisfaction, but so does at least one category of physicians' response to sicker patients. It is important to keep in mind that finding only a limited physician-mediation effect does not mean that physicians' behavior does not have a pervasive impact on patients' satisfaction. Our research tested specifically the hypothesis that health status influences satisfaction by way of physicians' behavior. A physician's behavior with a particular patient has many sources other than the patient's state of health, however. These include other characteristics of the patient (such as social class or age), the patient's behavior, the physician's habitual way of interacting with patients, and circumstantial factors such as fatigue or stress. Therefore, our finding that physicians' behavior plays a limited role in the health-satisfaction correlation should not be construed as meaning that physicians' behavior is unimportant. Indeed, there is abundant evidence from this and other research that physicians' behavior is related to satisfaction.

Recommended Reading

Hall, J.A., Milburn, M.A., Roter, D.L., & Daltroy, L.H. (1998). (See References)
Roter, D.L., & Hall, J.A. (1992). (See References)

Acknowledgments—The research on direct and indirect paths of causation reported in this article was supported by a grant from the Agency for Health Care Policy and Research to the first author.

Note

1. Address correspondence to Judith A. Hall, Department of Psychology, Northeastern University, Boston, MA 02115; e-mail: hall1@neu.edu.

References

Carmel, S. (1985). Satisfaction with hospitalization: A comparative analysis of three types of service. *Social Science & Medicine, 21*, 1243–1249.
DiMatteo, M.R., & DiNicola, D.D. (1982). *Achieving patient compliance: The psychology of the medical practitioner's role.* New York: Pergamon Press.

Greenley, J.R., Young, T.B., & Schoenherr, R.A. (1982). Psychological distress and patient satisfaction. *Medical Care, 20,* 373–385.

Hall, J.A., & Dornan, M.C. (1990). Patient sociodemographic characteristics as predictors of satisfaction with medical care: A meta-analysis. *Social Science & Medicine, 30,* 811–818.

Hall, J.A., Epstein, A.M., DeCiantis, M.L., & McNeil, B.J. (1993). Physicians' liking for their patients: Further evidence for the role of affect in medical care. *Health Psychology, 12,* 140–146.

Hall, J.A., Feldstein, M., Fretwell, M.D., Rowe, J.W., & Epstein, A.M. (1990). Older patients' health status and satisfaction with medical care in an HMO population. *Medical Care, 28,* 261–270.

Hall, J.A., Milburn, M.A., & Epstein, A.M. (1993). A causal model of health status and satisfaction with medical care. *Medical Care, 31,* 84–94.

Hall, J.A., Milburn, M.A., Roter, D.L., & Daltroy, L.H. (1998). Why are sicker patients less satisfied with their medical care? Tests of two explanatory models. *Health Psychology, 17,* 70–75.

Hall, J.A., Roter, D.L., & Katz, N.R. (1988). Meta-analysis of correlates of provider behaviors in medical encounters. *Medical Care, 26,* 657–675.

Hall, J.A., Roter, D.L., Milburn, M.A., & Daltroy, L.H. (1996). Patients' health as a predictor of physician and patient behavior in medical visits: A synthesis of four studies. *Medical Care, 34,* 1205–1218.

Like, R., & Zyzanski, S.J. (1987). Patient satisfaction and the clinical encounter: Social psychological determinants. *Social Science & Medicine, 24,* 351–357.

Linn, L.S., & Greenfield, S. (1982). Patient suffering and patient satisfaction among the chronically ill. *Medical Care, 20,* 425–431.

Pascoe, G.C. (1983). Patient satisfaction in primary health care: A literature review and analysis. *Evaluation and Program Planning, 6,* 185–210.

Roberts, R.E., Pascoe, G.C., & Attkisson, C.C. (1983). Relationship of service satisfaction to life satisfaction and perceived well-being. *Evaluation and Program Planning, 6,* 373–383.

Roter, D.L., & Hall, J.A. (1992). *Doctors talking with patients/patients talking with doctors: Improving communication in medical visits.* Westport, CT: Auburn House.

The Immune System as a Sensory System: Implications for Psychology

Steven F. Maier[1] and Linda R. Watkins
Department of Psychology, University of Colorado, Boulder, Colorado

Abstract

The brain and immune system form a bidirectional communication network in which the immune system operates as a sense organ to provide the brain with information about infection and injury, thereby allowing the brain to coordinate a defense. Activated immune cells release proteins called cytokines, which signal the brain by both blood and neural routes. Information that reaches the brain across this sensory channel produces large changes in neural activity, behavior, mood, and cognitive functioning. Appreciation of the functioning of this network may illuminate poorly understood aspects of stress, depression, and intraindividual variability in behavior, mood, and cognition.

Keywords

immune system; cytokines; stress; depression

It is widely recognized that psychological variables alter the functioning of the immune system. However, pathways between the brain and immune system have proven to be bidirectional, so that processes within the immune system also influence and regulate psychological processes. Recent work shows that products of immune cells released in response to infection and tissue injury potently alter neural activity, thereby regulating behavior, mood, and cognition. We believe that recognition of these *immune-to-brain* pathways provides important new insights about a variety of psychological phenomena, including stress, pain, depression, and aspects of cognitive functioning. The core idea is that the immune system, in addition to its other functions, is actually a sense organ (Blalock & Smith, 1985). In this article, we describe some of the implications of this newly appreciated sensory pathway for psychology.

NEURAL, BEHAVIORAL, MOOD, AND COGNITIVE CHANGES FOLLOWING IMMUNE ACTIVATION

Neural activity, behavior, mood, and cognitive processes change dramatically within 1 to 3 hr following activation of immune cells by viruses, bacteria, or agents used to stimulate immune cells experimentally (e.g., lipopolysaccharide [LPS], a constituent of the cell wall of certain bacteria). Interestingly, the pattern of neural changes is similar to that produced by exposure to many different environmental stressors. For example, the neurotransmitters norepinephrine and serotonin are released in the brain in the hypothalamus and hippocampus, respectively, in response to both activation of immune cells and environmental stressors.

Behavioral changes following administration of LPS or viruses are large and dramatic (Dantzer, Bluthe, Kent, & Goodall, 1993). In animals, they include reduced activity and exploration, reduced social behavior, anorexia, increases in anxiety-related behaviors, anhedonia (a loss of normal pleasures), sleep disturbances, hyperalgesia (increased pain sensitivity), and interference with memory for learning tasks that depend on the hippocampus, but no interference with tasks that do not depend on the hippocampus.[2] Finally, immune activation leads to a physiological "stress response"—activation of the hypothalamopituitary-adrenal (HPA) axis and the sympathetic nervous system.[3] Humans show the same behavioral and physiological changes, and in addition have difficulty with tasks that require flexible thinking and report feelings of fatigue and depressed mood.

It is important to understand that these changes are adaptive responses that promote recovery from infection (Hart, 1988) and not reflections of weakness produced by illness. For example, defense against infection requires large amounts of energy. The HPA response releases cortisol, and the sympathetic response releases catecholamines (the transmitters that are released from the terminals of sympathetic nerve fibers and carry the message to the heart, respiratory organs, etc.). Both cortisol and catecholamines function to produce energy (e.g., by converting glycogen to glucose, the form of energy that can be used by the organs of the body, including the brain), while many of the behavioral changes reduce the energy used by behavior.

HOW DOES IMMUNE ACTIVATION PRODUCE THESE CHANGES?

The fact that the administration of viruses and bacteria induces the alterations just described does not mean that the immune system is the mediating link. Indeed, many aspects of immune responding are too delayed to be able to account for these rapid responses to infection. However, phagocytic white blood cells (cells that "eat" microbes) called macrophages are rapidly activated by broad classes of pathogens. When activated, macrophages release a variety of products, including the cytokines interleukin-1 (IL-1), interleukin-6 (IL-6), and tumor necrosis factor-alpha (TNF-α), which are proteins that can circulate through the body. IL-1 and IL-6 were given their names because they were thought to function for communication between white blood cells, or leukocytes (*inter leukin* stands for "between leukocytes"). These cytokines are responsible for initiating the sequelae of infection described in the previous section. This is known because injecting them into an animal produces the full pattern of sickness responses, and blocking their action with receptor antagonists (i.e., substances that block their receptors and so oppose the action of the cytokines) blocks or blunts the sickness responses after infection. Indeed, in humans, the administration of cytokines produces even the reports of fatigue, depressed mood, and confused thinking that are characteristic of infection. IL-1 is the most potent of the cytokines, and we therefore limit our discussion to it.

How do cytokines such as IL-1 get the "I am infected" message to the brain? This is an issue because the cells that line the blood vessels that course through the brain are specialized and have tight gaps between them, preventing anything but the smallest molecules from crossing into the brain. This is called the blood-brain barrier, and IL-1 is too large to cross this barrier in significant quantities.

There are a number of mechanisms involved in IL-1 getting its message to the brain. One is that blood-borne IL-1 is able to bind to receptors for IL-1 that are on the surface of the insides of the blood vessels that go through the brain. The binding of IL-1 to these receptors leads cells associated with the blood vessels to produce and release small molecules that are then able to diffuse into the brain and bind to receptors in the brain. Interestingly for psychologists, IL-1 is also able to activate peripheral nerves in structures in which IL-1 is released (e.g., lymph nodes). These peripheral nerves (i.e., nerves that are outside the brain and send signals to it) then send a neural "I am sick" message to the brain. After all, this is the way sense organs in general communicate to the brain.

There is much to be learned about what happens when the message gets to the brain, but one interesting thing that does happen is that brain cells make their own IL-1. It is then released and binds to IL-1 receptors on neurons and nonneuronal cells in the brain called glia. Thus, peripheral immune activation produces IL-1 in the periphery, which then sends a message to the brain, which causes IL-1 to be made and released in the brain—peripheral IL-1 begets central IL-1. This central IL-1 is involved in the production of sickness responses, because administration of IL-1 into the brain produces sickness responses and blockade of IL-1 receptors in the brain blocks many aspects of the sickness response to infection. Moreover, the production of IL-1 in the brain leads the brain to activate pathways, going from the brain to the body, that further activate peripheral immune processes that are involved in fighting infections and further activate macrophages. Thus, there is a bidirectional pathway between the brain and the immune system, with immune activation signaling the brain and brain processes in turn regulating peripheral immune function.

STRESS AND DEPRESSION

We have already noted that the patterns of neural activity and neurotransmitter (e.g., norepinephrine) changes produced by stressors and immune activation are quite similar. By definition, stressors produce HPA and sympathetic nervous system activation, just as does infection. In addition, the behavioral impact of infection summarized earlier is very similar to the behavioral impact of exposure to a stressor. Indeed, each and every behavioral change associated with infection has also been demonstrated to follow exposure to a stressor such as restraint or presence of a predator's odor. But, is the resemblance more than superficial? After all, infection produces many consequences that would appear to be restricted to sickness. For example, fever, increased white blood cell count, and the liver's production of proteins that help fight infection are part of the early response to infection. It might not seem likely that stressors produce these symptoms of infection. However, we (Maier & Watkins, 1998) have found all of these to be produced by a variety of different stressors. Perhaps most surprisingly, stressors are even able to activate macrophages!

How could this happen? One obvious possibility is that stressors activate the same brain circuitry that is involved in mediating sickness. If the communication pathway is bidirectional, then stressors would both produce the same brain-mediated responses as does infection and also activate the outflow pathways back to the immune system. One particularly intriguing possibility is that stressors induce IL-1 in the brain, and, indeed, blocking brain IL-1 receptors has been shown to block or reduce some behavioral and physiological consequences of stressor exposure. Infection taps into the circuit by the infectious agent acting on macrophages and other immune cells, whereas stressors must enter the circuit at a different locus, namely, one within the brain. However, if the circuit is bidirectional, as we argue, the ultimate impact will be the same.

What of depression? Numerous investigators have noted the similarity between the symptoms of depression and the sequelae of exposure to potent stressors, and a role for stress in precipitating depressive episodes has long been known. We have already noted the similarity in outcomes between infection and stressors, and so this naturally raises the possibility that immune activation is involved in precipitating depression. Indeed, the behavioral changes that occur during infection are strikingly similar to the symptoms of depression. Furthermore, there is a growing literature (Maes, 1995) documenting that depressed patients show signs that are normally characteristic of infection, including the presence of activated immune cells and high levels of cytokines circulating in the blood. It is interesting to note in this context that depression is a very frequent concomitant of autoimmune diseases such as arthritis, which involve immune activation at their core. The American Psychiatric Association's *Diagnostic and Statistical Manual of Mental Disorders* even has a diagnostic category called "depression from a general medical condition," which of course involves immune activation. Finally, it can be noted that chronic antidepressant treatment has been reported to reduce the IL-1 response to LPS, as well as the fever and anhedonic responses to LPS.

We are not suggesting that immune activation and the induction of cytokines are necessary causes of depression. Rather, we are suggesting that they may be sufficient, and recall that administration of cytokines to humans does produce reports of severely depressed mood. Furthermore, we are suggesting that whatever the root causes of depression might be (e.g., a pessimistic explanatory style combined with the experience of negative life events), they tap into the bidirectional immune-to-brain circuitry described in this article, and that many of the symptoms of depression may be a reflection of the immune activation that results. After all, why should depression be associated with the particular physical symptoms that occur rather than a different set? Why should depression be linked, as has recently been reported, with reduced mineral density in bone? In this connection, it can be noted that IL-1 promotes development and activation of the cells (called osteoclasts) that cause bone resorption and reduced mineral density in bone.

WHY SHOULD THERE BE THESE RELATIONSHIPS WITH IMMUNITY AND WHAT DO THEY IMPLY?

The early immune response to an infectious agent and the sickness response evolved much earlier than did the stress response. Even the most primitive organisms must defend against infection, and macrophage-like cells and cytokine molecules are present even in the most primitive species. Defense against infection requires the production of large amounts of energy and the coordination of diverse bodily functions, including behavior. From early in evolution, cytokines such as IL-1 have been involved in initiating the production of energy in response to infection and have also participated in the coordination of the body's defense by communicating with neural tissue, even in organisms that do not have discrete brains. The stress response as scientists conceive it in mammals is really a fight-or-flight response to external threat and evolved much later. However, the fight-or-flight response also requires the production of energy, and a mechanism already existed to produce energy. Evolution often works by coopting an existing mechanism to perform a new function, and in this case all that was needed was to initiate the sickness machinery through a new source—external threat instead of infection. Coopting the sickness machinery would also have had the secondary benefit of priming nonspecific immune defense in case injury and consequent tissue damage and infection occurred. Of course, the other outputs of the sickness circuitry would then also follow stressor exposure. It has been argued that infection is a stressor, but we are suggesting that stressors can be viewed as infection. This approach may provide some insight into why the sequelae of exposure to stressors are what they are, and how the stress response is adaptive.

This line of reasoning may also suggest how depressed mood is adaptive and how it evolved. Recall that sickness responses promote recovery from infection. Many of the discrete behavioral changes associated with sickness decrease the energy consumed by behavior and also reduce the chances that a sick organism will expose itself to predation or aggressive encounters, and depressed mood may further promote these outcomes. Thus, depressed mood may have begun as an aid to recovery from infection and injury, then later become responsive to stress as stressors came to tap into the same bidirectional immune-to-brain circuitry.

IMPLICATIONS

There is considerable day-to-day variation in an individual's behavior, mood, and cognitive functioning. However, psychology has not given much attention to the explanation of intraindividual differences, even though these differences may be large. We argue that events in the immune system might drive much of this variability. It is important to keep in mind that immune-activating events that induce behavioral and other changes do not have to be events that produce overt infection. In an experiment with potentially profound implications, Besedovsky and his colleagues (Besedovsky, Sorkin, Keller, & Muller, 1975) injected rats with sheep red blood cells. These cells are harmless, but they are a foreign protein and so lead to an immune response. At the peak of the immune response to this harmless protein, there was a dramatic rise in blood levels of corticosteroids and catecholamines—a pronounced stress response, with brain activity and behavior changing as well. Individuals frequently encounter foreign proteins and mount immune responses, and remain unaware of these events. Thus, much of the variability in behavior, mood, and cognitive efficiency that all people experience may have its roots in the immune system. It is now commonplace to consider hormones as important regulators of brain and behavior, and we believe that in a few short years it will be equally common to view products of immune cells, such as cytokines, in this fashion.

Many questions, however, remain unanswered and will be the topics of future research. Only a few can be highlighted here. One concerns the role of IL-1 in stress, mood, and depression. Does IL-1 in the brain really play a causal role? An answer to this question will require blocking IL-1 production or the functioning of IL-1 receptors and ascertaining the effects of such blockade on stress responses, mood, and depression. A particularly attractive idea for future research is that immune activation sensitizes the brain's IL-1 response to stressors for a period of time, so that stressors have a more severe and prolonged effect in individuals who have recently mounted an immune response. Infection and IL-1 administration also alter cognitive functions, but the precise nature of these alterations and their relationship to current cognitive theory is unknown. Finally, we have pretended as if all infections and immune challenges produce the same immune response and mix of immune products. Actually, different immune activators (e.g., gram-positive bacteria, gram-negative bacteria, viruses of different classes) produce activation of different populations and subpopulations of cells, along with different products from those cells in different temporal sequences. Is the brain simply informed in each case that "I am sick," or is the communication more specific, with correspondingly more fine-grained modulation of brain and behavior? The tools exist to answer such questions, and the next few years should produce exciting advances in this new field of immune products and behavior.

Recommended Reading

Connor, T.J., & Leonard, B.E. (1998). Depression, stress, and immunological activation: The role of cytokines in depressive disorders. *Life Sciences, 62*, 583–606.
Kent, S., Bluthe, R.M., Kelley, K.W., & Dantzer, R. (1992). Sickness behavior as a new target for drug development. *Trends in Pharmacological Sciences, 13*, 24–28.
Maier, S.F., & Watkins, L.R. (1998). (See References)
Ottaviani, E., & Franceschi, C. (1996). The neuroimmunology of stress from invertebrates to man. *Progress in Neurobiology, 48*, 421–440.
Watkins, L.R., & Maier, S.F. (in press). The pain of being sick: Implications of immune-to-brain communication for understanding pain. *Annual Review of Psychology.*
Yirmiya, R. (1997). Behavioral and psychological effects of immune activation: Implications for "depression due to a general medical condition." *Current Opinion in Psychiatry, 10*, 470–476.

Notes

1. Address correspondence to Steven F. Maier, Department of Psychology, Campus Box 345, University of Colorado, Boulder, CO 80309; e-mail: smaier@psych.colorado.edu.

2. The hippocampus is a structure that has diverse functions in mediating learning and memory. One of these is that the hippocampus is involved in developing memory representations of environmental or stimulus contexts, and the activation of immune cells by viruses or LPS interferes selectively with the formation of memory for contexts.

3. During a stress response, neurons within the hypothalamus (H) secrete corticotropin-releasing factor into blood vessels at the base of the brain that connect to the pituitary gland. This substance causes the pituitary (P) to secrete into the bloodstream

a hormone that acts on the adrenal glands (A), causing them to secrete the stress hormone cortisol into the bloodstream—hence the term HPA axis. Cortisol is the classic stress hormone and mediates many of the effects of stress. Stress also activates neurons in the brain that control peripheral nerves that regulate the heart, respiration, and so forth—the sympathetic nervous system. Indeed, many researchers define stress by the activation of these two systems.

References

Besedovsky, H.O., Sorkin, E., Keller, M., & Muller, J. (1975). Changes in blood hormone levels during immune response. *Proceedings of the Society for Experimental Biology and Medicine, 150*, 466–470.

Blalock, J.E., & Smith, E.M. (1985). A complete regulatory loop between the immune and neuroendocrine systems. *Federation Proceedings, 44*, 108–111.

Dantzer, R., Bluthe, R.M., Kent, S., & Goodall, G. (1993). Behavioral effects of cytokines: Insight into the mechanisms of sickness behavior. In E.G. DeSouza (Ed.), *Neurobiology of cytokines* (pp. 130–151). San Diego: Academic Press.

Hart, B.L. (1988). Biological basis of the behavior of sick animals. *Neuroscience and Biobehavioral Reviews, 12*, 123–137.

Maes, M. (1995). Evidence for an immune response in major depression: A review and hypothesis. *Progress in Neuro-Psychopharmacology and Biological Psychiatry, 19*, 11–38.

Maier, S.F., & Watkins, L.R. (1998). Cytokines for psychologists: Implications of bidirectional immune-to-brain communication for understanding behavior, mood, and cognition. *Psychological Review, 105*, 83–107.

Critical Thinking Questions

1. Newsom discusses how a process that is normally thought of as positive—social support—may have detrimental effects. Similarly, Maier and Watkins discuss how a process that is normally thought of as negative—depression—may have adaptive value. Discuss other psychological states or traits and some ways in which they might operate in a counterintuitive manner.

2. Imagine you have a family member or close friend who is going to start providing care for a relative with a chronic illness. Drawing on the articles by Wrosch et al. and Newsom, what kind of advice would you give them about how to proceed? What can a caregiver do to help a patient adapt most successfully to unfortunate circumstances?

3. Feelings of control are vital to well-being. What can caregivers and physicians do to foster these feelings in patients who are struggling with chronic and sometimes debilitating illnesses?

4. Maier and Watkins argue that sickness behavior is an adaptive response, one that maximizes a person's chances of surviving from an infectious disease. Nevertheless, when many of us develop the cold or the flu, the first thing we do is take medicine to lower our fever and diminish symptoms of the illness. Is this a wise or unwise strategy when it comes to our recovery?

5. Think back to the readings from Sections 1 and 2. How can you integrate what you've learned in this section with those readings? Can a person's psychological responses to getting sick influence the course of his/her disease? Sketch a model that integrates psychological responses to illness, intervening behavioral and biological pathways, and the course of disease.

Psychosocial Approaches to Improve Health and Manage Disease

The articles in the preceding sections address two broad questions: "How does a person's psychology affect health?" and "How does health affect a person's psychology?" In this section, we consider whether modifying psychological characteristics can lead to changes in health. That is, can psychosocial interventions make a difference in terms of a person's vulnerability to disease or chances of surviving once he /she has an illness?

Lewis-Claar and Blumenthal provide a nice overview of research on psychosocial interventions in the context of cancer and heart disease. Researchers have tried to modify a number of processes discussed in earlier sections of this book, including stress, coping skills, and social support. Overall, studies have shown convincingly that psychosocial interventions improve the quality of life in patients with chronic illnesses. However, there is little support for the notion that psychosocial interventions decrease vulnerability to disease or prolong survival.

In light of this, some researchers have focused on whether we can change health practices such as cigarette smoking or medication adherence, with the rationale that improving behavior will likely reduce rates of illness and mortality. Christensen and Johnson review findings related to patient adherence to medical treatments. Adherence is a critical factor in health, in that advances in medicine will always be limited by the extent to which patients adhere to prescribed medication regimens. Christensen and Johnson argue that the role of patient characteristics (such as personality) must be considered within the context of the treatment itself. The best outcomes will be achieved when we can match a treatment to a patient's preferences for care. Schwarzer discusses the psychological factors that give rise to risky behaviors such as cigarette smoking and alcohol abuse. Here we learn that there are two components to changing health behaviors: we need to understand the factors that underlie a person's motivation to change, and we need to understand the factors that underlie how goals get translated into actions (self regulation).

Toward the goal of better understanding and more effectively changing health behaviors, Nell takes an evolutionary approach and argues that there may be good reasons why individuals, particularly young men, engage in risky behaviors. If there are adaptive social and evolutionary reasons why risky behaviors emerge in young men in our society, then it is important to acknowledge these in interventions aimed at reducing risk taking.

Keefe and France use the example of pain to highlight the importance of integrating biological, psychological, and social factors in medical care. All of these factors are important to understand when designing interventions to reduce pain. For example, both treatments that have targeted psychological correlates of pain (e.g., poor coping skills), as well as treatments that have targeted social factors in pain (e.g., spouse-assisted interventions) have been found to be beneficial for reducing suffering and disability. One of the most interesting findings is that early intervention is key to preventing future pain problems. This finding suggests that we should not wait until something is "broken" to "fix" it; rather, by anticipating health problems and stopping them early, we may be able to save patients from additional suffering and save our society from additional health care costs.

Lastly, Allen proposes an intriguing approach to intervention, based on research showing that social support is beneficial for health. Rather than to assume that social support has to come from other people, Allen raises the idea that pets can be a source of social support and act as a buffer against the negative consequences of stress. We may not think of pets as traditional forms of social support because they cannot provide advice or verbal emotional support, nor can they provide tangible support (e.g., giving you a ride to the doctor). However, pets are a source of unconditional and nonjudgmental social support (they don't criticize you), and there may be times when this is beneficial for physiological systems, and in the long term, for physical health.

The Value of Stress-Management Interventions in Life-Threatening Medical Conditions

Robyn Lewis Claar[1] and James A. Blumenthal

Duke University Medical Center, Durham, North Carolina

Abstract

Emotional stress has been associated with the development and progression of several chronic medical conditions. Recently, researchers have assessed the impact of stress-management interventions on patients' psychological functioning, quality of life, and various disease outcomes, including survival. This review summarizes the value of stress-management techniques in the treatment of two important, life-threatening conditions: coronary heart disease and cancer. Results from randomized clinical trials indicate that psychological interventions can improve patients' psychological functioning and quality of life. However, there is limited evidence to suggest that these interventions significantly reduce morbidity and mortality.

Keywords

coronary heart disease; cancer; psychological interventions; stress management

Many studies have demonstrated that higher levels of emotional stress are associated with poorer health outcomes in a variety of medical conditions, including coronary heart disease, cancer, gastrointestinal disorders, and chronic pain. As a result, research has focused on the benefits of stress management for patients' physical health. Stress-management techniques are designed to alter patients' cognitive and emotional responses to stressful events and reduce the physiological arousal that often accompanies these responses. These techniques may include cognitive restructuring, guided imagery, and relaxation.[2]

There has been much debate recently about the effects of stress management on quality of life and adverse clinical events. In this review, we briefly summarize research on the value of stress-management techniques in treating two important health conditions: coronary heart disease and cancer.

CORONARY HEART DISEASE

Research has demonstrated that stress and negative emotions can affect the development and course of cardiovascular disease by altering underlying pathophysiological processes (see Fig. 1). For example, stress can lead to excessive nervous system activation that may trigger myocardial ischemia (a temporary, inadequate supply of blood to the heart) and cardiac arrhythmias. In addition, stress may promote unhealthy lifestyle behaviors, such as poor diet, smoking, physical inactivity, and nonadherence to medical therapies; these behaviors, in turn, may alter physiological processes, resulting in the development and progression of disease. Stress-management interventions, which may alter physiological and behavioral processes relevant to disease, may ultimately reduce disease morbidity and mortality.

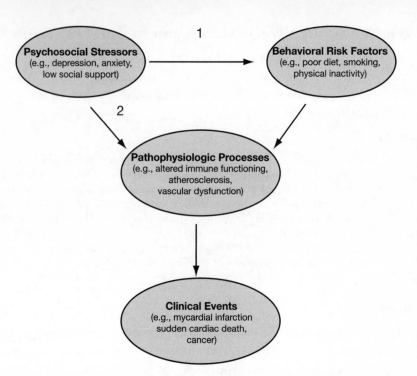

Fig. 1. Two pathways through which psychosocial stressors may contribute to the development and promotion of disease. First, stressors may contribute to behavioral risk factors, such as poor diet. These behavioral risk factors, in turn, lead to pathophysiological processes, such as atherosclerosis (blockages in the arteries of the heart) and vascular dysfunction. Second, stressors may directly promote pathophysiological processes. In either case, pathophysiological processes can lead to clinical events such as myocardial infarction (heart attack) and death.

A meta-analysis[3] of 23 studies assessing the effectiveness of stress-management interventions in coronary artery disease suggests that psychosocial interventions combined with standard care may reduce morbidity and mortality, as well as psychological distress (Linden, Stossel, & Maurice, 1996). Results indicated small, but significant, group differences that favored the inclusion of psychological interventions to reduce patient mortality and improve quality of life. However, this meta-analysis was based on studies with small sample sizes and nonrestrictive selection criteria that had a variety of methodological weaknesses. Moreover, the psychological interventions were delivered in addition to other interventions, such as medication and exercise. Although the results indicate the effectiveness of psychological interventions over and above usual care, it is not possible to discern the unique contribution of the psychological interventions in reducing morbidity and mortality.

Friedman et al. (1986) conducted one of the first clinical trials of stress-management interventions in Type A cardiac patients. (Type A behavior, a constellation of behavior and personality traits such as hostility, aggressiveness, and ambitiousness, is often associated with coronary heart disease patients.) Participants were randomly assigned to a cardiac counseling intervention (consisting of recommendations regarding diet, exercise, and medication, and information about cardiovascular pathophysiology) or a behavioral counseling intervention that included relaxation training, cognitive restructuring, and other cognitive-behavioral techniques aimed at reducing Type A behavior. After 4.5 years, the Type A modification intervention, which was successful in decreasing Type A behavior, reduced nonfatal myocardial infarctions (MIs) by 44% relative to the cardiac counseling intervention. Overall mortality and mortality due to cardiovascular causes were not different between the cardiac and behavioral counseling groups.

Frasure-Smith and Prince (1985) conducted a randomized trial of monthly telephone monitoring of psychological symptoms in 553 male patients following their MIs. In the intervention condition, patients who reported high levels of distress received a follow-up telephone call or home visit to provide additional counseling. After 1 year, patients in the intervention group reported reduced distress and exhibited significantly lower levels of cardiac morbidity and mortality compared with men in the usual-care control condition. A 7-year follow-up revealed that there were fewer MI recurrences, but not lower mortality rates, among patients in the intervention group.

Given these promising results, Frasure-Smith et al. (1997) conducted a larger randomized controlled trial with a similar nursing-based telephone intervention. The participants were 1,376 male and female post-MI patients. In contrast to the original study, however, this study showed no significant difference in survival after 1 year between patients in the intervention and control groups. In fact, mortality rates were higher for women in the intervention group than for women in the control group. However, the intervention did not significantly reduce patients' symptoms of depression or anxiety. It is not surprising, therefore, that the intervention did not reduce mortality.

In one of the largest randomized trials of stress management for cardiac patients, Jones and West (1996) assessed the effectiveness of a group psychological intervention in more than 2,000 post-MI patients. The intervention consisted of relaxation, stress-management, and coping-skills training over a 7-week period. At 6-month follow-up, there were no clinically significant differences in depression or anxiety between patients in the intervention group and those in the control group. In addition, at 12-month follow-up, there were no differences between the groups in the incidence of nonfatal MI or mortality. However, the stress-management intervention was brief, and as in the Frasure-Smith et al. (1997) study, failed to alter levels of self-reported stress, including anxiety and depression.

Recently, the National Institutes of Health sponsored a multicenter clinical trial, called ENRICHD (Enhancing Recovery in Coronary Heart Disease), that examined the impact of cognitive behavior therapy (CBT) on psychological functioning, morbidity, and mortality in 2,481 post-MI patients with clinical depression, low patient-perceived social support, or both. CBT is a type of psychotherapy that focuses on the link between thoughts and behavior and helps patients to modify their unrealistic or irrational thoughts to produce more adaptive behavior. This randomized controlled trial examined whether treating patients' depression and improving their social support reduced the risk of recurrent MI and death. Patients were randomly assigned to usual care or a CBT intervention for up to 6 months. Patients with moderate to severe depression who did not show a significant reduction in depressive symptoms after 5 weeks in the CBT intervention also received an antidepressant for up to 1 year. Patients in the CBT intervention experienced greater reductions in depression and larger improvement in social support compared with patients in the usual-care condition. However, the CBT intervention was not associated with decreased morbidity and mortality after a 2-year follow-up.

In summary, results of these studies suggest that stress-management techniques may improve quality of life in cardiac patients and reduce psychosocial risk factors such as Type A behavior, depression, and low social support. However, there is a paucity of data from well-controlled studies showing that stress-management interventions reduce morbidity and mortality. Because large numbers of patients need to be studied over long time periods to assess the impact of stress management on hard clinical end points (i.e., discrete, objective disease states that are well defined, including heart attack and death), some studies have examined surrogate markers of coronary heart disease. For example, a stress-management intervention was associated with decreased myocardial ischemia induced by mental stress in 107 patients with stable coronary disease (Blumenthal et al., 1997). In addition, 5 years following the intervention, patients in the stress-management intervention experienced a significant reduction in adverse cardiac events, such as recurrent MI and surgical procedures to restore blood flow.

CANCER

Much like the research with cardiovascular disease, research on cancer has used a biobehavioral model of stress and disease processes as a framework for understanding how stress affects physiological processes in cancer progression (see Fig. 1). According to this model, psychological stress is associated with alteration of the immune system, as well as negative lifestyle behaviors such as poor diet, nicotine use, and nonadherence to medical regimens. These factors may ultimately affect the course of the disease. Research suggests that psychological interventions can reduce stress, improve health behaviors, and possibly improve immune functioning. However, research on the impact of stress management on hard clinical end points, such as death, is more limited.

Spiegel, Bloom, Kraemer, and Gottheil (1989) conducted one of the first intervention studies examining the impact of a psychological intervention on patients' survival. Participants were 85 women with breast cancer who were randomly assigned to a control group or a weekly, 1-year intervention that provided group supportive-expressive therapy, a treatment that encourages patients with life-threatening illnesses to express their feelings and illness-related concerns. Participants in the intervention group lived 18 months longer than patients in the control group; however, there were no significant differences in survival at the 10-year follow-up.

In a subsequent analysis of the Spiegel et al. (1989) study, Fox (1998) proposed that unmeasured confounding variables affected the survival of patients in the control group, and that without such differences, the survival of the two groups would not have been significantly different at 18 months. Fox compared the survival curves of the control patients in the Spiegel et al. study with survival curves from a large national sample of cancer patients and found that the patients in the control group had a lower rate of survival than the national sample. Thus, the significant difference between the survival rates for the control and intervention groups in the Spiegel et al. study may be explained by the lower survival of patients in the control group rather than the effectiveness of the intervention in decreasing mortality in the treatment group.

Fawzy et al. (1990) examined the impact of a psychological intervention on immune functioning and disease end points. Patients with malignant melanoma were randomly assigned to a control group or a 10-session psychological intervention that included coping-skills training, progressive relaxation, and group support. Participants in the intervention group not only improved their coping behaviors relative to participants in the control group, but also had increases in their natural killer cell activity,[4] which has been shown to be associated with increased immune functioning and decreased cancer progression. Six-year follow-up data indicated that only 9% of the participants in the intervention group died, compared with 29% of the participants in the control group (Fawzy et al., 1993).

In contrast, more recent randomized trials of psychological interventions for women with breast cancer have not shown significant health benefits. Cunningham et al. (1998) randomly assigned women with breast cancer to a control condition or a psychological intervention consisting of 35 weekly sessions of support and CBT. Five years after the intervention, there were no significant differences in survival between the two groups. The researchers noted that limited statistical power may account for the lack of significant effects: Their small sample made it difficult to detect a difference even if one existed. In addition, the inclusion of other psychological interventions for patients in the control group may have mitigated significant group differences: Patients in the control group used relaxation audiotapes, and one quarter of participants in the control group attended support groups. Because patients in the control group also had the benefit of psychological interventions, group differences may have been reduced.

In a study of 124 women, Edelman and her colleagues (Edelman, Bell, & Kidman, 1999; Edelman, Lemon, Bell, & Kidman, 1999) also examined the impact of CBT on the survival of women with breast cancer. Patients in the intervention group attended eight weekly sessions, which included coping-skills training, cognitive restructuring, and relaxation exercises; these participants also attended three monthly follow-up sessions to reinforce their use of coping strategies. Results showed a short-term reduction in depression for participants in the intervention group; however, these improvements were no longer evident at assessments 3 and 6 months later. In addition, there were no significant differences in survival between the two groups.

Recently, Goodwin and her colleagues (2001) replicated the Speigel et al. (1989) study in a sample of 235 women with breast cancer. Women were randomly assigned to a control group or the supportive-expressive group therapy intervention, which consisted of 90-min weekly meetings for at least 1 year. Although women in the intervention group reported lower levels of depression, anxiety, and pain than women in the control group, there were no significant differences in overall survival. Thus, although the beneficial effects of the intervention on psychological functioning indicate that the intervention was effectively delivered, it did not improve patients' survival.

In summary, the cancer research has yielded results similar to those of the cardiovascular research: There is considerable evidence that psychological and stress-management interventions reduce distress and improve quality of life in patients with cancer. However, there appears to be little evidence for the effectiveness of these interventions in reducing morbidity and mortality. However, studies have been limited by methodological problems, such as small sample sizes and unmeasured confounding variables. Cunningham and his colleagues (1998) proposed that in order for psychological functioning to affect cancer progression, it must be accompanied by physiological changes that significantly affect tumor growth at the tissue level. In fact, there are data to suggest that psychological interventions may induce significant changes in immune functioning. For example, Cruess et al. (2000) found that women with breast cancer who attended a 10-week cognitive-behavioral stress-management group intervention had significantly lower levels of cortisol (a "stress" hormone that also helps regulate the immune system and infection) than control patients.

CONCLUSION

With respect to cancer and coronary heart disease, research suggests that psychosocial interventions can improve patients' quality of life and reduce symptoms of depression and anxiety when these interventions are delivered by trained clinicians over an adequate time period. However, examination of the randomized clinical trials that have assessed hard clinical end points, such as nonfatal MI or disease-specific mortality, reveals little evidence that psychological interventions reduce morbidity and mortality. Although some studies have demonstrated positive findings (e.g., Friedman et al., 1986; Spiegel et al., 1989), they have been limited by methodological problems, such as small sample sizes, use of multiple therapies in the same group of participants, inadequate randomization, and reliance on outcome ratings provided by people who knew which patients received therapy. Randomized controlled trials are needed to determine the value of stress-management interventions in treating patients with life-threatening health conditions. However, these trials will require large numbers of patients, who can be recruited only from a large network of hospitals, and lengthy follow-up intervals. The expense and logistical difficulty of recruiting patients and developing interventions should not be underestimated. The study of surrogate markers of disease, such as myocardial ischemia, subclinical coronary atherosclerosis, vascular functioning, and immune functioning, may be a viable alternative to large-scale randomized clinical trials and may provide valuable insight into the impact of stress management on important pathophysiological processes relevant to health and disease.

Recommended Reading

Andersen, B.L. (2002). Biobehavioral outcomes following psychological interventions for cancer patients. *Journal of Consulting and Clinical Psychology, 70,* 590–610.

Relman, A.S., & Angell, M. (2002). Resolved: Psychosocial interventions can improve clinical outcomes in organic disease (con). *Psychosomatic Medicine, 64*, 558–563.

Rozanski, A., Blumenthal, J.A., & Kaplan, J. (1999). Impact of psychological factors on the pathogenesis of cardiovascular disease and implications for therapy. *Circulation, 99*, 2192–2217.

Smith, T.W., & Ruiz, J.M. (2002). Psychosocial influences on the development and course of coronary heart disease: Current status and implications for research and practice. *Journal of Consulting and Clinical Psychology, 70*, 548–568.

Acknowledgments—This review was supported by National Institutes of Health Grants MH49679, HL65503, HC55142, and HL59672.

Notes

1. Address correspondence to Robyn Lewis Claar, Duke University Medical Center, Department of Psychiatry and Behavioral Science, Box 3119, Durham, NC 27710; e-mail: claar002@mc.duke.edu.

2. Cognitive restructuring is a technique to alter maladaptive thought patterns and replace them with more adaptive cognitions. Guided imagery is a technique in which patients are coached to create calming, peaceful images to induce relaxation. Relaxation techniques include deep breathing and progressive muscle relaxation in which various muscle groups are tensed and relaxed.

3. Meta-analysis is a statistical technique for comparing and combining effects found in several studies using a common unit of analysis.

4. Natural killer cells are a specialized type of cell that can recognize and destroy cancer cells and virus-infected cells.

References

Blumenthal, J.A., Jiang, W., Babyak, M., Krantz, D.S., Frid, D.J., Coleman, R.E., Waugh, R., Hanson, M., Applebaum, M., O'Connor, C., & Morris, J.J. (1997). Stress management and exercise training in cardiac patients with myocardial ischemia: Effects on prognosis and evaluation of mechanisms. *Archives of Internal Medicine, 157*, 2213–2223.

Cruess, D.G., Antoni, M.H., McGregor, B.A., Kilbourn, K.M., Boyers, A.E., Alferi, S.M., Carver, C.S., & Kumar, M. (2000). Cognitive-behavioral stress management reduces serum cortisol by enhancing benefit among women being treated for early stage breast cancer. *Psychosomatic Medicine, 62*, 304–308.

Cunningham, A.J., Edmonds, C.V.I., Jenkins, G.P., Pollack, H., Lockwood, G.A., & Warr, D. (1998). A randomized controlled trial of the effects of group psychological therapy on survival in women with metastatic breast cancer. *Psycho-Oncology, 7*, 508–517.

Edelman, S., Bell, D.R., & Kidman, A.D. (1999). A group cognitive behaviour therapy programme with metastatic breast cancer patients. *Psycho-Oncology, 8*, 295–305.

Edelman, S., Lemon, J., Bell, D.R., & Kidman, A.D. (1999). Effects of group CBT on the survival time of patient with metastatic breast cancer. *Psycho-Oncology, 8*, 474–481.

Fawzy, F.I., Cousins, N., Fawzy, N.W., Kemeny, M.E., Elashoff, R., & Morton, D. (1990). A structured psychiatric intervention for cancer patients: I. Changes over time in methods of coping and affective disturbance. *Archives of General Psychiatry, 47*, 720–725.

Fawzy, F.I., Fawzy, N.W., Hyun, C.S., Elashoff, R., Guthrie, D., Fahey, J.L., & Morton, D.L. (1993). Malignant melanoma: Effects of a structured psychiatric intervention, coping, and affective state on recurrence and survival six years later. *Archives of General Psychiatry, 50*, 681–689.

Fox, B.H. (1998). A hypothesis about Spiegel et al.'s (1989) paper on psychosocial intervention and breast cancer survival. *Psycho-Oncology, 7*, 361–370.

Frasure-Smith, N., Lesperance, F., Prince, R.H., Verrier, P., Garber, R.A., Juneau, M., Wolfson, C., & Bourassa, M.G. (1997). Randomised trial of home-based psychosocial nursing intervention for patients recovering from myocardial infarction. *Lancet, 350*, 473–479.

Frasure-Smith, N., & Prince, R. (1985). The ischemic heart disease life stress monitoring program: Impact on mortality. *Psychosomatic Medicine, 47*, 431–445.

Friedman, M., Thoresen, C.E., Gill, J.J., Ulmer, D., Powell, L.H., Price, V.A., Brown, B., Thompson, L., Rabin, D.D., Breall, W.S., Bourg, E., Levy, R., & Dixon, T. (1986). Alteration of type A behavior and its effect on cardiac recurrences in post myocardial infarction patients: Summary results of the recurrent coronary prevention project. *American Heart Journal, 112*, 653–665.

Goodwin, P.J., Leszcz, M., Ennis, M., Koopmans, J., Vincent, L., Guther, H., Drysdale, E., Hundleby, M., Chochinov, H.M., Navarro, M., Speca, M., & Hunter, J. (2001). The effect of group psychosocial support on survival in metastatic breast cancer. *New England Journal of Medicine, 345*, 1719–1726.

Jones, D.A., & West, R.R. (1996). Psychological rehabilitation after myocardial infarction: Multicentre randomised controlled trial. *British Medical Journal, 313*, 1517–1521.

Linden, W., Stossel, C., & Maurice, J. (1996). Psychosocial interventions for patients with coronary artery disease: A meta-analysis. *Archives of Internal Medicine, 156*, 745–752.

Spiegel, D., Bloom, J.R., Kraemer, H.C., & Gottheil, E. (1989). Effect of psychosocial treatment on survival of patients with metastatic breast cancer. *Lancet, 2*, 888–891.

Patient Adherence With Medical Treatment Regimens: An Interactive Approach

Alan J. Christensen[1] and Jamie A. Johnson

Department of Psychology, The University of Iowa, Iowa City, Iowa

Abstract

Inadequate patient adherence to treatment regimens is a ubiquitous problem in health care and carries a profound personal, societal, and economic cost. This article illustrates a general theoretical framework we believe to be useful for the interpretation, conception, and design of adherence research. The core tenet of this framework is that factors that influence adherence can be better understood by considering the interactive effects of patients' characteristics, type of adherence intervention, and characteristics of the illness and medical treatment context. This framework represents an extension and application of previous theory and research from personality, social, and clinical psychology concerning the value of an interactionalist perspective. We illustrate the framework using some of our past work involving treatment adherence among patients with chronic renal failure.

Keywords

patient adherence; interactive framework; personality; aptitude-treatment interaction

Over the past several decades, the potential ability of medical professionals to diagnose and treat physical disorders has been propelled by an exponential increase in biomedical knowledge and new technologies. Ironically, the potential effectiveness of these advances continues to be challenged by a most fundamental requirement, behavior change on the part of the patient. Whether medical intervention requires a patient to follow a prescribed medication regimen, involves making a necessary dietary or other lifestyle change, or simply requires an individual to attend a scheduled appointment or procedure, the patient's adherence is, in virtually all cases, a necessary condition for safe, effective, and efficient treatment.

Inadequate patient adherence is a pervasive problem and one that carries a profound personal, societal, and economic cost. Although estimates of patient nonadherence vary across regimens, settings, and populations, the available data suggest that between 20 and 80% of patients do not adhere to the basic requirements of their medical treatment regimen (Dunbar-Jacob & Schlenk, 2001). For example, in a study involving patients with longstanding, serious hypertension, electronic monitoring suggested that 61% of these patients failed to take their antihypertensive medications as prescribed (Lee et al., 1996). The rate of nonadherence appears to be highest for preventive regimens in asymptomatic patients, slightly lower for chronic regimens in symptomatic populations, and lowest for time-limited regimens in acutely ill patients.

Estimates of the economic costs of nonadherence range from $25 billion annually in additional treatment costs and hospital admissions to more than $100 billion a year when lost productivity and total economic impact are considered

(Berg, Dischler, Wagner, Raia, & Palmer-Shevlin, 1993). Patient nonadherence has been linked to increased sickness, treatment failures, and hospitalization, and to higher mortality across many clinical populations. Among patients being medically treated for hypertension, for example, the risk of being hospitalized or dying from coronary heart disease is 4 times greater for individuals who fail to continue to take antihypertensive medications as prescribed than for individuals who comply with their medication regimen (Psaty, Koepsell, Wagner, LoGerfo, & Inui, 1990). It is believed that as many as 75% of renal transplant failures in the second year following transplant may be due to nonadherence with the immunosuppressive medication regimen (Kiley, Lam, & Pollak, 1993). An increasing concern in the treatment of HIV and AIDS is the recognition that patients' lack of adherence with antiretroviral regimens is resulting in virus mutations that are increasingly resistant to drug therapy (Catz & Kelly, 2001). Similar concerns have arisen with regard to bacterial infections, as many antibiotics are becoming less effective at fighting common bacteria such as streptococcus and tuberculin.

DETERMINANTS OF ADHERENCE: AN INTERACTIVE VIEW

Given the prevalence and consequences of patient nonadherence, it is not surprising that considerable attention has been devoted to identifying patients' characteristics that are associated with nonadherence, as well as to designing and implementing intervention strategies that might facilitate adherence. Despite considerable resources being devoted to these two issues, the collective empirical progress of this work has been modest at best. For example, comprehensive reviews of the adherence literature have generally concluded that there is little or no predictable or consistent association between patients' characteristics (i.e., personality traits, expectancies or beliefs, sociodemographic factors) and adherence to treatment (e.g., Dunbar-Jacob & Schlenk, 2001).

Over the past several years, we have worked with our colleagues to formulate an alternative interpretation to explain the lack of progress and marked inconsistency in this area of adherence research (Christensen, 2000). Specifically, we have proposed that the associations between patients' characteristics and adherence may vary predictably with features of the disease context or treatment regimen (i.e., that the person-context interaction needs to be considered). From this perspective, a lack of consistency across heterogeneous treatment settings and populations may simply reflect expected behavioral patterns arising from the interaction between individuals' characteristics and the medical treatment or illness context. To explore this possibility, an interactive approach is necessary (see Fig. 1). The basic assumption in this perspective is that relevant contextual or treatment-related features should be assessed explicitly, and that the interaction of these factors with patient variables should be tested directly.

At a general level, this person-by-context interactive framework has a long history in the science of psychology. According to the interactionalist perspective in personality and social psychology, attempts to identify personality traits that predict behavior are of limited usefulness unless one also considers the context an individual is facing (Higgins, 1990). From this perspective, it is the interactive effect of person factors and contextual factors that most strongly influences

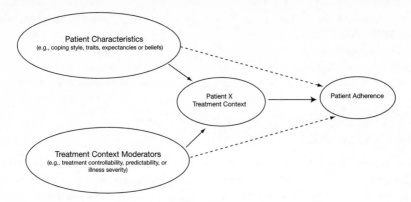

Fig. 1. Conceptual representation of the patient-by-treatment-context interactive framework. The dashed lines reflect the fact that research generally does not find that patient characteristics or contextual features have a significant effect on adherence. Adapted from Christensen (2000).

behavior. Within clinical psychology, the interactionalist perspective has been apparent in the research on the outcome of psychotherapy (Dance & Neufeld, 1988). In this literature, studies that have adopted an interactive perspective (often referred to as "aptitude-treatment interaction" studies) consider the possibility that a given intervention strategy may be more effective for certain subgroups of patients than for others. This approach serves as an alternative to the common practice of treating all patients with a given disorder or target problem as a homogeneous group, ignoring potential differences among them. One of the more consistent patterns that has emerged from studies adopting an interactive framework is that individuals with more active and internally focused coping styles show a better response to treatments that emphasize self-control than to treatments that emphasize therapist control (Dance & Neufeld, 1988).

Our research group's studies involving patients with end-stage renal disease (ESRD) illustrate the potential value of the interactive framework in understanding influences on adherence behavior (e.g., Christensen, 2000; Christensen, Smith, Turner, & Cundick, 1994; Christensen, Smith, Turner, Holman, & Gregory, 1990). The large majority of patients with ESRD face the prospect of lifelong medical treatment with a form of renal dialysis. In addition to undergoing frequent and time-consuming dialysis sessions, these patients are required to adhere to a multifaceted behavioral regimen that includes making substantial dietary changes, following strict fluid-intake restrictions, and taking one or more medications on a regular basis. Our past work has suggested that adherence is best when the patient's characteristic or preferred style of coping is consistent with the contextual features or behavioral demands of the particular type of dialysis treatment the patient is undergoing. For example, patients with highly active or vigilant styles or coping preferences exhibit better adherence when undergoing a form of dialysis that is primarily patient controlled and carried out at home, whereas patients with a less active style or a tendency to disengage from stressful situations show better adherence when undergoing staff-administered dialysis in a hospital or clinic.

Thus, it is the degree of congruence between the patient's coping style and the behavioral requirements or constraints of the medical treatment context that appears important. Because the vast majority of past adherence studies have examined only the main effects of a given patient characteristic, they have been unable to detect potential effects of the person-context interaction.

ENHANCING PATIENT ADHERENCE: APPLYING THE INTERACTIVE FRAMEWORK

In the most comprehensive review to date, Roter et al. (1998) examined the results reported in 153 studies that investigated a variety of behavioral (e.g., reinforcement of adherent behavior), psychoeducational (e.g., instruction in the reasons the treatment regimen is necessary), and affective-based (e.g., help managing emotional distress that may undermine adherence intervention strategies) intervention strategies designed to promote patients' adherence to their treatment regimens. These studies involved more than 20 different medical conditions and treatment regimens. The central conclusion of this quantitative review was that various interventions had a weak to modest, but significant effect on indicators of patient adherence, but that no single intervention strategy appeared consistently stronger than any other. There was some indication that interventions combining cognitive, behavioral, and affective components may be more effective than single-focus interventions.

Perhaps not surprisingly, the conclusion that different approaches to facilitating adherence have essentially equivalent effectiveness mirrors the typical conclusion of research on the outcomes of psychotherapy—different treatments have equivalent efficacy. However, it is important to note that virtually none of the adherence-related studies to date have considered the possibility that the efficacy of a given intervention approach varies across subgroups of patients. We believe that the patient-context interactive framework is useful for identifying potential moderators of intervention success. For example, findings from the broader psychotherapy-outcome literature, as well as from our own adherence research, suggest that self-control-based strategies (e.g., self-monitoring, self-evaluation, and self-reinforcement of adherence behavior) may be particularly effective in enhancing adherence among patients who characteristically have active styles of coping with illness or treatment-related issues. In contrast, a more structured intervention or one that features more control by the treatment provider (e.g., behavioral contracting, external inducements, instruction by the provider) may benefit patients with more passive styles.

Other characterizations of individual differences are also conceptually relevant and may be important to consider. One possibly useful framework is the Five Factor Model of personality. From the perspective of this model, variability in personality traits can be distilled to five underlying dimensions: neuroticism (reflecting generalized emotional distress or chronic negative affect), extraversion (reflecting sociability, assertiveness, and cheerfulness), openness to experience (reflecting imaginativeness, intellectual curiosity, and unconventionality), agreeableness (reflecting altruism, trust of other people's intentions, and cooperativeness), and conscientiousness (reflecting self-discipline or self-control, dependability, and will to achieve). The potential importance of the Five Factor

Model of personality as an organizing framework for patient assessment has been highlighted in both the adherence (Wiebe & Christensen, 1996) and the psychotherapy (Anderson, 1998) literatures. For example, patients high on the agreeableness trait may respond better to group-based interventions or interpersonally oriented strategies for promoting adherence, whereas those low on this trait may benefit from an individualized, less confrontive approach. Each of these general intervention approaches has been previously investigated by adherence researchers but has not yet been considered within an interactive framework.

MOVING FORWARD: CHALLENGES AND RECOMMENDATIONS FOR FUTURE RESEARCH

Rather than attempting to review and critique the large literature on patient adherence, we have illustrated a general theoretical framework we believe will be useful for the conception and design of future adherence studies. Adoption of an interactive approach encourages adherence researchers to do two things. First, it encourages them to systematically consider aspects of the illness and medical treatment context that are potentially relevant to behavioral or psychological processes. Although much of our work has focused on the contextual issue of how much patient control a treatment offers, many other aspects of the illness or treatment context may be important to consider. In our own work, we have found that existing data and theory from the broader literature on the effects of stress (e.g., work on urban or environmental stress; Glass & Singer, 1972) can provide very useful direction in this regard. That is, relevant characteristics of the illness and medical treatment context generally parallel factors that have been identified in the broader literature as being moderators of the effects of stress (e.g., controllability of treatment delivery, predictability of treatment response).

Second, the interactive framework encourages researchers to consider the possibility that the utility of a given intervention may vary across different diseases or treatment settings. Thus, we believe this framework will prove useful in the design, implementation, and testing of intervention strategies. For example, patients facing diseases or treatments that allow them a substantial degree of control over their own treatment delivery (e.g., diabetes management) seem more likely to benefit from interventions promoting self-management, whereas patients whose illness and treatments allow them less control (e.g., most forms of cancer) may benefit from less instrumental, more emotion-focused intervention strategies.

Perhaps more than any other issue in our increasingly interdisciplinary science, the problem of patient adherence clearly falls at the intersection of physical health and behavior. We hope that the framework and ideas presented here prove useful to researchers and providers addressing this most vexing problem. As medical technologies continue to expand, so too will the opportunities for psychological science and practice to play a pivotal role in determining the effectiveness of these technologies. Ultimately, human behavior is likely to remain the *sine qua non* of health care delivery for many years to come.

Recommended Reading

Christensen, A.J. (2000). (See References)

Dance, K.A., & Neufeld, R.W.J. (1988). (See References)
Roter, D.L., Hall, J.A., Merisca, R., Nordstrom, B., Cretin, D., & Svarstad, B. (1998). (See References)
Wiebe, J.S., & Christensen, A.J. (1996). (See References)

Acknowledgments—Preparation of this manuscript was supported in part by National Institute of Diabetes and Digestive and Kidney Diseases Grant DK49129 awarded to Alan Christensen.

Note

1. Address correspondence to A.J. Christensen, Department of Psychology, E11 Seashore Hall, The University of Iowa, Iowa City, IA 52242; e-mail: alan-christensen@uiowa.edu.

References

Anderson, K.W. (1998). Utility of the five-factor model of personality in psychotherapy aptitude-treatment interaction research. *Psychotherapy Research, 8*, 54–70.

Berg, J.S., Dischler, J., Wagner, D.J., Raia, J.J., & Palmer-Shevlin, N. (1993). Medication compliance: A healthcare problem. *Annals of Pharmacotherapy, 27*, S3–S22.

Catz, S.L., & Kelly, J.A. (2001). Living with HIV disease. In A. Baum, T. Revenson, & J. Singer (Eds.), *Handbook of health psychology* (pp. 841–849). Mahwah, NJ: Erlbaum.

Christensen, A.J. (2000). Patient-by-treatment context interaction in chronic disease: A conceptual framework for the study of patient adherence. *Psychosomatic Medicine, 62*, 435–443.

Christensen, A.J., Smith, T.W., Turner, C.W., & Cundick, K.E. (1994). Patient adherence and adjustment in renal dialysis: A person by treatment interactional approach. *Journal of Behavioral Medicine, 17*, 549–566.

Christensen, A.J., Smith, T.W., Turner, C.W., Holman, J.M., & Gregory, M.C. (1990). Type of hemodialysis and preference for behavioral involvement: Interactive effects on adherence in end-stage renal disease. *Health Psychology, 9*, 225–236.

Dance, K.A., & Neufeld, R.W.J. (1988). Aptitude-treatment interaction research in the clinical setting: A review of attempts to dispel the "patient uniformity myth." *Psychological Bulletin, 104*, 192–213.

Dunbar-Jacob, J., & Schlenk, E. (2001). Patient adherence to treatment regimens. In A. Baum, T. Revenson, & J. Singer (Eds.), *Handbook of health psychology* (pp. 571–580). Mahwah, NJ: Erlbaum.

Glass, D.C., & Singer, J.E. (1972). *Urban stress.* New York: Academic Press.

Higgins, E.T. (1990). Personality, social psychology, and person-situation relations: Standards and knowledge activation as a common language. In L.A. Pervin (Ed.), *Handbook of personality: Theory and research* (pp. 301–338). New York: Guilford.

Kiley, D.J., Lam, C.S., & Pollak, R. (1993). A study of treatment compliance following kidney transplantation. *Transplantation, 55*, 51–56.

Lee, J.Y., Kusek, J.W., Greene, P.G., Bernhard, S., Norris, K., Smith, D., Wilkening, B., & Wright, J.T. (1996). Assessing medication adherence by pill count and electronic monitoring in the African American Study of Kidney Disease and Hypertension (AASK) pilot study. *American Journal of Hypertension, 9*, 719–725.

Psaty, B.M., Koepsell, T.D., Wagner, E.H., LoGerfo, J.P., & Inui, T.S. (1990). The relative risk of incident coronary heart disease associated with recently stopping the use of betablockers. *Journal of the American Medical Association, 263*, 1653–1657.

Roter, D.L., Hall, J.A., Merisca, R., Nordstrom, B., Cretin, D., & Svarstad, B. (1998). Effectiveness of interventions to promote patient compliance. *Medical Care, 36*, 1138–1161.

Wiebe, J.S., & Christensen, A.J. (1996). Patient adherence in chronic illness: Personality and coping in context. *Journal of Personality, 64*, 815–835.

Social-Cognitive Factors in Changing Health-Related Behaviors

Ralf Schwarzer[1]

Department of Psychology, Freie Universität Berlin, Berlin, Germany

Abstract

Changing health-related behaviors requires two separate processes that involve motivation and volition, respectively. First, an intention to change is developed, in part on the basis of self-beliefs. Second, the change must be planned, initiated, and maintained, and relapses must be managed; self-regulation plays a critical role in these processes. Social-cognition models of health behavior change address these two processes. One such model, the health action process approach, is explicitly based on the assumption that two distinct phases need to be studied longitudinally, one phase that leads to a behavioral intention and another that leads to the actual behavior. Particular social-cognitive variables may play different roles in the two stages; perceived self-efficacy is the only predictor that seems to be equally important in the two phases.

Keywords

health behavior; self-regulation; self-efficacy; risk perception; social-cognition model

Many health conditions are caused by such risky behaviors as problem drinking, substance use, smoking, reckless driving, overeating, and unprotected sexual contact. Fortunately, human beings have, in principle, control over their conduct. Health-compromising behaviors can be eliminated by self-regulatory efforts, and health-enhancing behaviors, for instance, physical exercise, weight control, preventive nutrition, dental hygiene, or condom use, can be adopted instead. The adoption of health-promoting behaviors is often viewed rather simplistically as a response to a threat to health. According to this view, individuals who become aware that their lifestyle puts them at risk for a threatening disease may make a deliberate decision to refrain from risky behaviors. This commonsense view of behavioral change is based on the questionable belief that humans are rational beings who respond to a perceived risk in the most reasonable manner. However, many studies show that perception of a risk, by itself, is a poor predictor of behavioral change. This state of affairs has encouraged health psychologists to identify other alterable variables that may play a role in changing health-related behaviors and to design more complex models of the processes of change (for reviews, see Conner & Norman, 1996; Schwarzer, 1992; Wallston, 1994; Weinstein, 1993).

In this article, I review the processes involved in changing health-related behaviors. The first section addresses the motivation process, and the second addresses the self-regulatory processes of planning, initiation, maintenance, and relapse management. Finally, I discuss modeling health-related behavior change.

MOTIVATION TO CHANGE

Before people change their habits, they need to become motivated to do so. This is a process leading toward an explicit intention (e.g., "I intend to quit smoking this weekend"). Three variables are considered to play a major role in this process, (a) risk perception, (b) outcome expectancies, and (c) perceived self-efficacy.

Perceiving a health threat seems to be the most obvious prerequisite for the motivation to end a risky behavior. People who are not aware at all of the risky nature of their actions will not develop the motivation to change them. Scaring people into healthy behaviors, however, has not been shown to be effective. In general, the initial perception of risk seems to put people on track for developing a motivation to change, but later on other factors are more influential.

People not only need to be aware of the existence of a health threat, they also need to understand the contingencies between their actions and subsequent outcomes. These *outcome expectancies* are among the most influential beliefs in the motivation to change. A smoker may find more good reasons to quit smoking (e.g., "If I quit smoking, then I will save money") than to continue smoking. This imbalance does not directly lead to action, but it can help lead to an intention to quit. Although the pros and cons, which represent a number of positive and negative outcome expectancies, typically play a role in rational decision making, they need not be explicitly worded and evaluated—they can also be rather diffuse mental representations, loaded with emotions. Depending on the theoretical perspective, outcome expectancies may be viewed as methods or means-ends relationships; regardless of the term used, the idea is that people know proper strategies to produce desired effects.

The efficacy of a method has to be distinguished from individuals' belief in their personal efficacy in applying the method. *Perceived self-efficacy* refers to individuals' beliefs in their capabilities to exercise control over challenging demands and over their own functioning (Bandura, 1997). These beliefs are critical when people approach novel or difficult situations or try to adopt strenuous self-regimens. People attribute capabilities to themselves when they forecast that they will change their behavior (e.g., "I am certain that I can quit smoking even if my friend continues to smoke"). Such optimistic self-beliefs influence the goals people set for themselves, what courses of action they choose to pursue, how much effort they invest in given endeavors, and how long they persevere in the face of barriers and setbacks. Some people harbor self-doubts and cannot motivate themselves. They see little point in even setting a goal if they believe they do not have what it takes to succeed. Thus, the intention to change a habit that affects health depends to some degree on a firm belief in one's capability to exercise control over that habit.

Health interventions that focus on arousing fear of disease, informing about health-compromising habits, or increasing perceived personal vulnerability are less effective than health interventions that raise belief in personal efficacy (Meyerowitz & Chaiken, 1987). Perceived self-efficacy operates in concert with risk perception, outcome expectancies, and other factors in influencing the motivation to change. There is a large body of evidence documenting the influence of these three predictors on the development of an intention to change behavior. Because most studies are based on cross-sectional research designs, little is known about the causal sequence and interplay of these factors. It is assumed that initial risk perception sets the stage for the development of an intention to change behavior,

whereas outcome expectancies and perceived self-efficacy may play a more important role later. At the point in the process when studies typically measure behavioral intentions, the latter two factors emerge as the major predictors, whereas
risk perception often seems only weakly related to behavioral intentions.

SELF-REGULATORY PROCESSES

Unfortunately, research on behavioral intentions is more prevalent than research
that addresses whether behaviors actually change (for reviews, see Bandura,
1997; Schwarzer & Fuchs, 1995, 1996). After people have adopted a goal of
behavioral change, they need to take action and, later, maintain the changes in
the face of obstacles and failures. Thus, goal setting and goal pursuit can be
understood as two distinct processes, the latter of which requires a great deal
of self-regulatory effort.

Entrenched habits seldom yield to a single attempt at change. Renewed
efforts are needed in order to achieve success. Strong self-beliefs can keep
people on track and help them to persevere when temptations arise.

The pursuit of a goal of behavioral change can be subdivided into a
sequence of activities, such as planning, initiation, maintenance, relapse management, and disengagement, although these are not clearly distinct categories.
The importance of *planning* was recently emphasized by Gollwitzer (1999), who
reviewed research on what he called "implementation intentions." These plans
specify the when, where, and how of a desired action and have the structure
"When situation S arises, I will perform response R." They form cognitive links
between situational circumstances or opportunities and the goal behavior. Gollwitzer argued that goals do not induce actions directly, but that they may lead
to highly specific plans, which in turn induce actions. For example, the pursuit
of goals for promoting health, such as strenuous physical exercise, and preventing disease, such as cancer screening, is facilitated by mental simulation
(e.g., by imagining success scenarios).

If the appropriate opportunity for a desired action is clearly defined in terms
of how, when, and where, the probability for procrastination is reduced. People
take *initiative* when the critical situation arises, and they give the action a try.
This requires that they firmly believe they are capable of performing the action.
People who do not hold such beliefs see little point in even trying.

A health-related behavior is adopted and then *maintained* not through an act
of will, but rather through the development of self-regulatory skills and strategies.
In other words, individuals embrace a variety of means to influence their own
motivation and behaviors. For example, they set attainable subgoals, create incen-
tives for themselves, draw from an array of options for coping with difficulties,
and mobilize support from other people. Processes they can use to control their
actions include focusing attention on the task while ignoring distractors, resisting temptations, and managing unpleasant emotions. Perceived self-efficacy is
required in order to overcome barriers and stimulate self-motivation repeatedly.

Individuals who can get themselves started on the path toward change are
quickly confronted with the problem of whether they can be resolute. Adherence to a self-imposed healthy behavior is difficult because performance fluc-

tuates, and improvements may be followed by plateaus, setbacks, and failures. Competent *relapse management* is needed to recover from setbacks. Some people rapidly abandon their newly adopted behavior when they fail to get quick results. When entering high-risk situations (e.g., a bar where people smoke), they cannot resist temptation because they lack a strong belief in their self-efficacy. The competence to recover from a relapse is different from the competence enlisted for commencing an action. Damage control and renewal of motivation are constantly needed within the context of health self-regulation.

Disengagement from the goal can be evidence for lack of persistence and, thus, can indicate self-regulatory failure. But in case of repeated failure, disengagement or scaling back the goal might become adaptive, depending on the circumstances. For example, if the goal was set too high, or if the situation has changed and become more difficult than before, it is seldom worthwhile to continue the struggle. In the case of health-compromising behaviors, however, giving up is not a tenable option. Instead, the individual needs to develop improved self-regulatory skills and take new approaches to the problem. Failure can be a useful learning experience and lead to increased competence, if the individual interprets the episode optimistically and practices constructive self-talk to renew the motivation (Baumeister & Heatherton, 1996).

SOCIAL-COGNITION MODELS OF CHANGING HEALTH-RELATED BEHAVIOR

In summary, changing health-related behaviors involves an initial motivation process that results in setting goals and subsequent self-regulation processes that address the pursuit of these goals. Health psychologists are attempting to model these processes in order to understand how people become motivated to change their risky behaviors, and how they become encouraged to adopt and maintain healthy actions. In the past, the focus of such models was on identifying a parsimonious set of variables that predict people's success in changing their behavior. These variables included constructs such as attitudes, social norms, threat, personal vulnerability, and behavioral intentions. The most prominent approaches were the health belief model, the theory of planned behavior, and protection motivation theory (for an overview and critique of these and other models, see Conner & Norman, 1996; Schwarzer, 1992; Wallston, 1994; Weinstein, 1993).

The *health action process approach* (Schwarzer, 1992, 1999; Schwarzer & Fuchs, 1995, 1996; Schwarzer & Renner, 2000) pays particular attention to what happens after people formulate intentions to change their behavior and conveys an explicit self-regulation perspective. It suggests a distinction between motivation processes that come into play before goals are set and volition processes that come into play afterward. Particular social-cognitive variables may play different roles in predicting the outcomes of these two phases (see Fig. 1 for a schematic of this model).

In the initial *motivation phase*, a person develops an intention to act. Risk perception, which may include not only the perceived severity of possible health threats, but also one's personal vulnerability to fall prey to them, is merely a distant antecedent in this phase. Risk perception in itself is insufficient to enable a person to form an intention. Rather, it sets the stage for further elaboration of thoughts about consequences and competencies. Thus, outcome expectancies and perceived self-efficacy, operating in concert, contribute substantially to the development of an intention to change (Fig. 1).

This pattern of influence changes after goal setting, when people enter the *self-regulation phase*, in which they pursue their goal by planning the details, trying to act, investing effort and persistence, possibly failing, and finally recovering or disengaging. According to the health action process approach, progressing through this phase consists of moving from one substage to the next, and this movement is facilitated by perceived self-efficacy. Thus, at each point there are two predictors of success, namely, the successful completion of the previous substage and an optimistic sense of control over the next one. Risk perception and outcome expectancies no longer exert much influence once goals have been set, although there may be other influential variables in the self-regulation phase that have not yet been identified.

CONCLUSIONS

The major models of health-related behavior identify variables that predict the dependent variables of behavioral intentions and actual behaviors. These models share several common predictors, among them risk perception, outcome expectancies, and perceived self-efficacy. The names for these factors are different in different theories, however. For example, behavioral beliefs can be equated to outcome expectancies, and perceived behavioral control is more or less the same as perceived self-efficacy. Communication among theorists and among researchers has been undermined by lack of conceptual clarity, on the

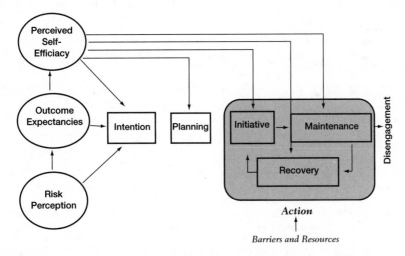

Fig. 1. The health action process approach. The schematic shows the three predictors of behavioral change (in ovals) and the stages of change (in rectangles); the shaded rectangle highlights the action phase of behavioral change.

one hand, and use of different names for similar constructs, on the other. A consensus in identifying and labeling constructs is required.

Although these models assume underlying processes, most studies have used cross-sectional designs in which intentions and self-reported behaviors are predicted by other variables. However, such static prediction does not reflect changes over time, for example, transition from one stage to the next or recycling through phases. Most important, only a few of these models account for the self-regulation phase, in which goals are translated into action. Change in health-related behavior, then, is reduced to the motivation phase, while the action phase is omitted. Research on volitional constructs is needed.

The model described here outlines the complex mechanisms that operate when individuals become motivated to change their habits, when they adopt and maintain a new habit, and when they attempt to resist temptations and recover from setbacks. The model applies to all health-compromising and health enhancing behaviors and could even be adjusted to apply to behavior change more generally. Longitudinal research is needed so that changes can be assessed more precisely. Moreover, there is a need for applied research on matching intervention strategies to stages of change.

Recommended Reading

Bandura, A. (1997). (See References)
Carver, C.S., & Scheier, M.F. (1998). On the self-regulation of behavior. New York: Cambridge University Press.
Conner, M., & Norman, P. (Eds.). (1996). (See References)

Note

1. Address correspondence to Ralf Schwarzer, Freie Universität Berlin, Psychologie, Habelschwerdter Allee 45, 14195 Berlin, Germany; e-mail: health@zedat.fu-berlin.de.

References

Bandura, A. (1997). *Self-efficacy: The exercise of control.* New York: Freeman.
Baumeister, R.F., & Heatherton, T.F. (1996). Self-regulation failure: An overview. *Psychology Inquiry,* 7(1), 1–15.
Conner, M., & Norman, P. (Eds.). (1996). *Predicting health behaviour: Research and practice with social cognition models.* Buckingham, England: Open University Press.
Gollwitzer, P.M. (1999). Implementation intentions: Strong effects of simple plans. *American Psychologist, 54,* 493–503.
Meyerowitz, B.E., & Chaiken, S. (1987). The effect of message framing on breast self-examination attitudes, intentions, and behavior. *Journal of Personality and Social Psychology, 52,* 500–510.
Schwarzer, R. (1992). Self-efficacy in the adoption and maintenance of health behaviors: Theoretical approaches and a new model. In R. Schwarzer (Ed.), *Self-efficacy: Thought control of action* (pp. 217–242). Washington, DC: Hemisphere.
Schwarzer, R. (1999). Self-regulatory processes in the adoption and maintenance of health behaviors: The role of optimism, goals, and threats. *Journal of Health Psychology, 4,* 115–127.
Schwarzer, R., & Fuchs, R. (1995). Changing risk behaviors and adopting health behaviors: The role of self-efficacy beliefs. In A. Bandura (Ed.), *Self-efficacy in changing societies* (pp. 259–288). New York: Cambridge University Press.
Schwarzer, R., & Fuchs, R. (1996). Self-efficacy and health behaviours. In M. Conner & P. Norman (Eds.), *Predicting health behaviour: Research and practice with social cognition models* (pp. 163–196). Buckingham, England: Open University Press.

Schwarzer, R., & Renner, B. (2000). Social-cognitive predictors of health behavior: Action self-efficacy and coping self-efficacy. *Health Psychology, 19*, 487–495.

Wallston, K.A. (1994). Theoretically based strategies for health behavior change. In M.P. O'Donnell & J.S. Harris (Eds.), *Health promotion in the workplace* (2nd ed., pp. 185–203). Albany, NY: Delmar.

Weinstein, N.D. (1993). Testing four competing theories of health-protective behavior. *Health Psychology, 12*, 324–333.

Why Young Men Drive Dangerously: Implications for Injury Prevention

Victor Nell[1]

Institute for Social and Health Sciences, University of South Africa, Johannesburg, South Africa

Abstract

Why is risk consistently underestimated, and why do young men in particular take exceptionally high risks and think of themselves as invulnerable? Two explanatory paths are proposed. The first is that risk taking in young males has been shaped by evolutionary forces to provide a fitness value. The second pathway is through myth and the other narrative forms that affirm the ego's immortality and invulnerability. Because of its evolutionary base, risk taking is emotionally driven: Emotions are pre-verbal and irrational, which means that persuasive prevention cannot be more than weakly successful. Three prevention challenges emerge from this analysis: to determine what it is that young drivers fear, to attach affectively experienced fears to defined driving behaviors, and to devise injury-prevention programs that acknowledge that young males' risk taking is not "stupid," but driven by adaptive needs that are as significant to today's young adults as they were to our distant ancestors.

Keywords

risk taking; immortality; evolution; fear; sensation seeking; driving

Injury prevention is a young, epidemiologically sophisticated, but largely atheoretical discipline. In this survey, I seek to augment injury-prevention theory by sketching the evolved motivational structures and cultural reinforcers that escalate risk taking in young men, and the implications of this approach for the development of strategies for attenuating risk.

These are socially significant issues. For example, 1987 data for the United States show that although there are 26.9 deaths per 100,000 individuals per year among early adolescents (ages 10-14), the death rate for late adolescence (ages 15–19) is 84.6 deaths per 100,000 individuals per year—more than three times higher. As teenagers move from early to late adolescence, males die at twice the rate of females, with a 525% increase in deaths by homicide and legal intervention. In 1994, irrespective of age, 2.86 times as many males as females died in automobile crashes, and twice as many males as females involved in car accidents had a blood alcohol content in excess of 0.10 g/L blood (U.S. Department of Transportation, 1996, Table 16). Among 16- to 20-year-olds, 44.31 males per 100,000 population were in fatal automobile crashes, compared with 20.43 per 100,000 females; in the 21- to 24-year-old age group, the incidences were 42.52 and 14.02 among males and females, respectively (U.S. Department of Transportation, 1996, Table 56). Although the total number of traffic fatalities has a U-shaped relation to age, peaking in youth and old age, fatalities related to both age and a risk-taking behavior, for example, automobile fatalities that occur while the driver is speeding, decline linearly from youth to old age (Fig. 1).

164

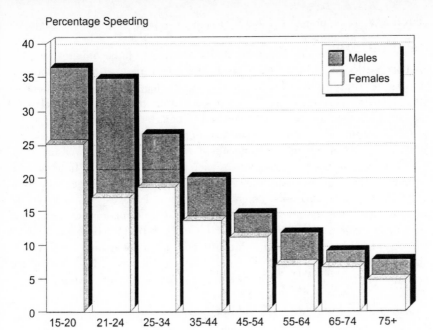

Fig. 1. Percentage of drivers who were speeding in fatal crashes in 1996, by age and sex. From U.S. Department of Transportation (1996, Fig. 4).

RISK TAKING AS AN ADAPTATION

What is the motivational basis for risk taking among young males? To answer this question, it is useful to consider human evolution, the personality trait of sensation seeking, and myth.

Intraspecific Competition

Intraspecific competition is as old as life itself. In the "prebiotic soup" of the Hadean era some 4 million years ago, self-replicating systems of RNA molecules competed for the available precursor materials to construct copies of themselves; in the next evolutionary step, one of these RNA molecule families developed protein synthesis (Alberts et al., 1989, p. 8). The first primordial cell, from which all life on earth is descended, was a benthic procaryote born 3 billion years ago: "This cell, outreproducing its competitors, took the lead in the process of cell division and evolution" that made the world we know (Alberts et al., 1989, p. 10).

Beginning in the Mesozoic some 200 million years ago, competition has continued to drive mammalian evolution. Moving from intraspecific competitiveness to intraspecific aggression is a small step, and aggression emerges as a fitness value at the earliest evolutionary levels. It is especially prominent in *Phylum chordata*, and universal in the carnivore and primate orders. Human beings are innately aggressive (Wilson, 1978/1995, p. 99), and when young males reach the mating and fighting age, the biological platform that supports aggres-

165

sion is at its peak, preparing them for the survival tasks of a ruthlessly competitive social environment.

If risk were correctly appraised, and if death were to become real and terrifying, aggression—which always carries the risk of injury or death—would be impossible. Fear would triumph, and the fearful creature's genes would perish. Evolution has, on the contrary, so arranged matters that young males of virtually all species are biochemically prepared to fight for territorial advantage and physical dominance in order to win for themselves the most desirable mate. Insects, reptiles, ungulates, and primates show the same pattern (Wilson, 1975, pp. 323, 442-443, 493). Primates are notoriously aggressive: "If hamadryas baboons had nuclear weapons, they would destroy the world in a week" (Wilson, 1978/1995, p. 104; also see Wrangham & Peterson, 1996, especially pp. 5–18). For humans, there is a weight of historical and contemporary evidence that human aggression, risk taking, and blood lust, from the Assyrian lion hunts in the seventh century B.C. to the Roman arena (from the second century B.C. through to the fifth century A.D.) and today's genocides in Rwanda and the Balkans, has not changed over the centuries or become "more civilized."

Sensation Seeking and Risk Taking

The heightened sense of invulnerability of late adolescence correlates with heightened sensation seeking, "a trait defined by the seeking of varied, novel, and intense sensations and experiences and the willingness to take physical, social, legal, and financial risks for the sake of such experiences" (Zuckerman, 1994, p. 27). There are strong relations between sensation seeking and risky driving, with a direct linear relationship between reported driving speed and scores on measures of sensation seeking; Zuckerman (1994, p. 139) found the highest sensation-seeking scores among subjects who said they would drive over 75 mph on a clear road with a 55-mph limit. As noted in the introduction, crash statistics confirm these laboratory data.

The Biochemistry of Sensation Seeking

Given that risk taking and sensation seeking are universally higher in young males than in young females and attenuate with age (Zuckerman, 1994, pp. 104–105), they must have a biochemical basis. There is indeed a strong inverse relation between platelet monoamine oxidase (MAO, an enzyme regulating arousal and activity levels) and high scores on the Sensation Seeking Scale (Zuckerman, 1994, Table 11.3, p. 298). Low MAO levels also predict many real-life behaviors related to high sensation seeking (such as tobacco, drug, and alcohol use). Levels of the MAO enzyme gradually increase with age in the human brain, as well as in platelets and plasma, and are lower in men than in women. The situation is similar with the gonadal hormones. Male sensation seekers have unusually high levels of testosterone (Zuckerman, 1994).

Handicap as an Advantage in Sexual Selection

It seems preposterous to claim that risk taking, which is so often fatal or injurious, has a fitness value. This problem is as old as evolutionary theory. In his letters, Darwin wrote, "The sight of a feather in a peacock's tail, whenever I gaze at it, makes me sick" (cited in Cronin, 1991, p. 113). Such ornaments, unlike male strength and quickness, are in fact handicaps to their bearers, as are the enormous jaws of the *Chiasognathus grantii* beetle of South Chile, which have a feeble bite, and stags' antlers. But these and other handicapping male traits might attract a female because they are handicaps, signaling a mating advantage to females of the species. That is, young men who do crazy things are saying in one voice with the peacock and the buck that prances when the lion approaches, "Look at me! I have so much strength and skill that I am fearless, I will survive no matter how much I drink or how fast I drive"; the handicaps (which include substance use) convey the message that the male can support high costs (Cronin, 1991).

Myth, Narrative, and the News

These evolutionary predisposers to risk taking are culturally reinforced by myth and its narrative derivatives. The hero's quest and redemption in grand myth are echoed by the fearless protagonists of the Norse sagas, and the invincible James Bonds of formulaic fiction and boys' adventure stories: In these everyday narratives—of which newspaper and television news are a subcategory—immortality is domesticated as hope, endlessly reaffirming the immortality of His Majesty the Ego (Nell, 2001). Narrative forms thus nurture the immortality delusion, giving further support to risk-taking behavior.

FEAR AS A RISK ATTENUATOR

What stands between risk taking and death is fear. At moderate intensity, fear is adaptive, preparing the organism to avoid or confront threat; at its highest intensity, fear is a paralyzing dread. Because intense fear is rarely felt in modern societies, its potency is underestimated. As a result, it is easy to confuse thinking about fear and feeling fear: This distinction between cognitive and emotional states is tellingly captured by contrasting hypnotic trance, daydreaming, and entertainment-industry inputs—in which the reader or listener may believe (a cognitive state)—with dreaming, which has an imperative reality—"I do not have the dream, it is the dream that has me" (Nell, 1988). The imperative reality of dreams arises from the emotional rather than the cognitive mechanisms that drive dreams—in other words, from subcortical rather than cortical circuits.[2]

The Neuroanatomy of Fear

There is convergent evidence from studies of the routes followed by neurotransmitters in the brain that fear responses are triggered by the central nucleus of the amygdala, which is part of the evolutionarily old limbic system[3] (LeDoux, 1998, p. 205). For both humans and animals, the advantage of these unconscious emotional reactions is that they provide a subcortical and therefore extremely rapid route from stimulus to fear response. LeDoux hypothesized that for both posttraumatic stress disorder and the phobias—as with other forms of panic—there are direct connections from subcortical processing areas to the amygdala. Learned fear is indelible. The fear response may with time extinguish, but will recur at its original intensity if triggered by the conditioned stimulus.

The memory of dread is elusive because it is implicit and nonverbal. Because the amygdala matures before the hippocampus, memories of childhood trauma are purely emotional and have no verbal declarative content (LeDoux, 1998); this rather than the Freudian mechanism of repression accounts for the elusiveness of early childhood experiences, and their power to invade and color the present.

"Fear Appeals Don't Work"

Despite the unequivocal evidence that fear is the most potent negative reinforcer, there is a widespread perception in traffic-safety circles that "fear appeals" do not work. An influential early study (Janis & Feshbach, 1953, as cited in Boster & Mongeau, 1984) found a negative relationship between the strength of the fear appeal and subsequent conformity with the recommendations. Boster and Mongeau (1984) found very small correlations between fear and attitudes toward risky driving ($r = .21$), and between fear and driving behavior (.10).

Given fear's potency, these findings make no sense. First, though shock and aversion are physiologically arousing, they are not fear, and it is specious to claim that exposing drivers to videos of crash victims and autopsies, as was done in these studies, is a fear appeal. Second, fear is an affective rather than a cognitive state. Safety videos—for example, the now-famous television advertisements on safe driving developed a decade ago by the Victoria Transport Accident Commission in Australia—operate in the rational and not the emotional modality. Such programs do not arouse fears of mortality, and the viewer's feelings of immortality are comfortably preserved. If fear appeals have not worked, it is because fear itself has not been tried.

DIRECTIONS FOR FUTURE RESEARCH

Can Fear Be Applied to the Reduction of Dangerous Driving?

Though fear is a potent negative reinforcer, there are three challenges that must be met if fear is to be used effectively in safe-driving programs. The first prevention challenge is to determine what it is that young drivers fear so as to develop feeling, rather than thinking, strategies—strategies that address the immortality delusion by triggering mortality fears in the experiential rather than the rational system (Epstein, 1994). Theoretical social psychology must determine what it is that young drivers do fear. Death is too remote to be feared: "One's own death is beyond imagining," wrote Freud (1915/1985), "and whenever we try to imagine it, we can see that we really survive as spectators . . . . At bottom, nobody believes in his own death" (p. 77; Nell, 2001). Why, then, is mortal danger flooded with fear and horror, and so desperately resisted? An evolutionary hypothesis is that in the environment of evolutionary adaptation, the most feared event was death by predation. Fear would thus have been attached not to death, but to the mutilation and pain that preceded death. Because "the brain systems that generate emotional behaviour are highly conserved through many levels of evolutionary history" (LeDoux, 1998, p. 17), this fear remains. Thus, fear of pain rather than fear of death would be an effective risk attenuator.

The second prevention challenge is to build on the huge existing literature on fear conditioning so as to apply mortality fears in socially and ethically acceptable ways to closely targeted risk behaviors and to demonstrate that fear thus applied will remain specific to these behaviors. This gives rise to a twofold ethical problem. First, fear conditioning evokes images of Stanley Kubrick's 1971 movie, *Clockwork Orange*, with Malcolm McDowell as the young hooligan strapped to a chair, eyes held forcibly open, while prison psychologists make him vomit while he watches scenes of violence. Risk attenuation cannot infringe on social norms regarding individual liberty and limits on state power. Second, mobility is a basic human right and a principle mechanism of economic development: Fear conditioning cannot be allowed to generalize in ways that might contaminate driving's utility and pleasure.

The Personal and Social Value of Risk Taking

Prevention that regards youthful risk taking as "stupid" will not prosper. At the individual level, risk is part of life. A life without risk is a life not worth living, empty of mastery, achievement, and social status. Injury-prevention initiatives are unlikely to succeed if they fail to acknowledge the youthful imperative to increase social status by courting danger to demonstrate courage. Driving represents "the most common form of sensation seeking in young men" (Zuckerman, 1994, p. 138) because it bypasses the genetic endowments of strength and speed and makes the demonstration of courage available to all young men, including the slow and the weak.

Risk taking is also a highly prized social virtue. Violent inter-band rivalry in the earliest phases of evolution made it essential for a group to have a contingent of "dawn warriors . . . . healthy, adventurous, and potentially violent young men" (Bailey, 1995, p. 542). Warrior traits are highly adaptive in combat: "The most brutal warrior hawks have the advantage over their less 'sociopathic' adversaries" (p. 542). Paramedics, fire-fighters, and police are drawn from these dawn warriors, and military establishments build on these traits, teaching young men to kill with their bare hands; sports coaches and corporate teambuilders teach that nice guys come last, and extol the killer instinct; bloodshed and death are the entertainment industry's principal commodity. Young people perceive the hypocrisy of asking them to give up their guns and disband their gangs while the social establishment entrenches risk taking and exploits it in the service of established authority.

Recognition of the fitness value and social utility of risk taking has the potential to bring about a re-conceptualization of violence-prevention interventions, beginning with an acknowledgment of the hypocrisy of dismissing risk taking as adolescent immaturity. A third prevention challenge is thus to recognize that boys in early adolescence need to create their own hero's journey from childhood to adulthood that echoes the journeys of Odysseus and Luke Skywalker. Their need in making this journey is not for a protective mother, but for Iron John (Bly, 1990)—who knew both courage and fear.

Recommended Reading

Bly, R. (1990). (See References)

Marks, I., & Nesse, R. (1997). Fear and fitness: An evolutionary analysis of anxiety disorders. In S. Baron-Cohen (Ed.), *The maladapted mind: Classic readings in evolutionary psychopathology* (pp. 57–72). Hove, England: Psychology Press.

Mohan, D., & Tiwari, G. (Eds.). (2000). *Injury prevention and control*. London: Taylor and Francis.

Nell, V. (2001). (See References)

Wilson, E.O. (1995). (See References)

Notes

1. Address correspondence to Victor Nell, University of South Africa Institute for Social and Health Sciences, P.O. Box 72477, Parkview 2122, Johannesburg, South Africa; e-mail: victor. nell@iafrica.com.

2. The ancient subcortical regions of the brain are preverbal, and similarly organized in all mammals. The cortex is part of the more recently evolved neomammalian brain. It is the seat of language and reasoning, and reaches its most elaborate development in humans.

3. The limbic system, within which the amygdala and hippocampus are located, is an ancient brain structure in the old mammalian brain. It is located deep within the temporal lobe, and among its many functions is the mediation of emotional experience. Implicit emotional memories are thought to be mediated by the amygdala, and explicit, conscious memories by the hippocampus.

References

Alberts, B., Bray, D., Lewis, J., Raff, M., Roberts, K., & Watson, J.D. (1989). *Molecular biology of the cell* (2nd ed.). New York: Garland.

Bailey, K.G. (1995). The sociopath: Cheater or warrior hawk. *Behavioural and Brain Sciences, 18*, 542–543.

Bly, R. (1990). *Iron John: A book about men*. Reading, MA: Addison-Wesley.

Boster, F.J., & Mongeau, P. (1984). Fear-arousing persuasive messages. In R.N. Bostrom & B.H. Westley (Eds.), *Communication yearbook* 8 (pp. 330–375). Newbury Park, CA: Sage.

Cronin, H. (1991). *The ant and the peacock: Altruism and sexual selection from Darwin to today.* Cambridge, England: Cambridge University Press.

Epstein, S. (1994). Integration of the cognitive and psychodynamic unconscious. *American Psychologist, 49*, 709–724.

Freud, S. (1985). Thoughts for the times on war and death. In J. Strachey (Ed.), *Civilisation, society and religion* (pp. 57–90). Harmondsworth, England: Pelican. (Original work published 1915)

LeDoux, J. (1998). *The emotional brain*. London: Weidenfeld and Nicholson.

Nell, V. (1988). *Lost in a book: The psychology of reading for pleasure*. New Haven, CT: Yale University Press.

Nell, V. (2001). Mythic structures in narrative: Life, death, and immortality. In T. Brock, M. Green, & J. Strange (Eds.), *Narrative impact: Social and cognitive foundations* (pp. 17–37). Mahwah, NJ: Erlbaum.

U.S. Department of Transportation. (1996). *Traffic Safety CD-ROM, 1975–1994* (BTS-CD-10). Washington, DC: Bureau of Transportation Statistics.

Wilson, E.O. (1975). *Sociobiology: The new synthesis*. Cambridge, MA: Harvard.

Wilson, E.O. (1995). *On human nature*. Harmondsworth, England: Penguin. (Original work published 1978)

Wrangham, R., & Peterson, D. (1996). *Demonic males: Apes and the origins of human violence.* Boston: Houghton Mifflin.

Zuckerman, M. (1994). *Behavioural expressions and biosocial bases of sensation seeking*. Cambridge, England: Cambridge University Press.

Pain: Biopsychosocial Mechanisms and Management

Francis J. Keefe[1] and Christopher R. France

Department of Psychology, Ohio University, Athens, Ohio

Abstract

Traditionally, pain has been viewed as a sensory event warning of tissue damage or illness. This explanation fails to account for many of the experiences of people suffering from clinically painful conditions. Over the past two decades, a new biopsychosocial perspective on pain has emerged. This perspective emphasizes that pain is a dynamic process that not only is influenced by biological, psychological, and social mechanisms of pain, but also produces biological, psychological, and social changes that can affect future responses to pain. This review presents findings from recent studies of the biological, psychological, and social mechanisms of pain and discusses the implications of these findings for pain research, assessment, prevention, and treatment, as well as for health care policy.

Keywords

pain; pain assessment; pain treatment; biopsychosocial factors and pain

For centuries, pain has been viewed as a warning sign of tissue damage (Melzack & Wall, 1996). This view holds that pain is the sensory end product of a specialized pain pathway in which pain messages are carried by nerves from the site of injury or tissue damage through the spinal cord to the brain. According to this view, pain should be proportional to tissue damage, with individuals having extensive disease (e.g., severe joint damage due to arthritis) having the most pain. This traditional perspective is how most people think about pain and, until recently, has dominated biomedical treatments whose goal is to correct underlying tissue damage. The traditional model of pain, however, has a number of important limitations (Melzack & Wall, 1996). First, the level of pain is rarely directly proportional to underlying tissue damage. Studies have shown that soldiers in the battlefield may report little or no pain from wounds that should be very painful. Second, treatments designed to correct underlying tissue damage often fail to abolish persistent pain. Even after specialized neurosurgical procedures that sever the pain pathway, pain can persist. Finally, the traditional model ignores the profound influence of psychological and social factors on the pain experience.

PAIN MECHANISMS AND MANAGEMENT: A BIOPSYCHOSOCIAL PERSPECTIVE

The biopsychosocial model maintains that pain is a complex phenomenon that is affected by biological mechanisms (e.g., underlying disease processes), psychological mechanisms (e.g., thoughts, beliefs, and feelings), and social mechanisms (e.g., family or work environment, sociocultural milieu). This model views pain as a dynamic process that not only is influenced by biological, psychological, and social mechanisms, but also produces biological, psychological, and social changes that, in turn, affect future responses to pain.

Biological Mechanisms and Management

Recent studies show that persistent pain can produce changes in the nervous system pathways responsible for the transmission and perception of pain messages, and thereby affect future responses to pain. This form of neuroplasticity is supported by animal research showing that painful stimulation produces changes in nervous system functioning in the spinal cord, as well as higher nervous system sites involved in pain perception (Coderre, Katz, Vaccarino, & Melzack, 1993). Research with rats has shown that painful electrical stimulation applied to the hind paw can produce a state of spinal cord hyperexcitability (Wall & Woolf, 1984), and when this occurs, the spinal cord responds in an exaggerated way to subsequent painful stimulation (i.e., paw pinch). The key to managing hyperexcitability seems to be prevention through early intervention. Thus, although a large dose of morphine (5 mg/kg) is required to reverse spinal hyperexcitability once established, as little as 10% of this dose can prevent spinal hyperexcitability if administered prior to the electrical stimulation (Woolf & Wall, 1986).

Perhaps the most dramatic example of the benefits of early pain intervention in humans comes from the literature on the treatment of surgical pain. Studies have shown that delivering pain medication before surgery significantly reduces patients' pain and requests for pain medication in the days after surgery (Coderre et al., 1993). Premedication may work because it blocks the changes in central nervous system excitability that occur when the spinal cord is bombarded by impulses during the trauma of surgery (e.g., cutting of tissue, nerve, bone).

Is the phenomenon of neuroplasticity important to understanding chronic pain? People who have severe, acute pain in a limb shortly before it is amputated often reexperience a similar pain in their missing, or phantom, limb following amputation. Interestingly, recent research has found evidence of neuroplasticity in the brains of people with phantom limb pain (Flor et al., 1995). Specifically, using innovative brain-imaging technology, scientists have begun to map out how the brains of people with phantom pain respond to stimulation of various body surfaces (e.g., fingers, lips, chin). In people who have had an upper limb amputated, there is a significant reorganization of the way the brain maps (i.e., responds to stimulation of) the upper body. Specifically, the areas of the brain that used to represent the amputated hand and lower arm now respond to facial stimulation. (The brain's representation of the face is normally adjacent to that of the hands and arms.) More important, greater reorganization is associated with more intense phantom limb pain (Flor et al., 1995). These findings suggest that phantom limb pain may be associated with changes in the brain that result from a loss of normal sensory input from the missing limb (or possibly generation of abnormal input from the remaining nerves). Similar evidence of changes in brain maps has been obtained in individuals with chronic back pain (Flor, Braun, Elbert, & Birbaumer, 1997).

Psychological Mechanisms and Management

There is growing evidence that psychological factors play a role in the pain experience. Pain, when it persists over months and years, can influence one's coping efforts, beliefs about pain, and sense of confidence in one's own ability to control pain. Fortunately, evidence suggests that this dynamic process can also be reversed. Treatments aimed at teaching pain-coping skills can restore a sense of control and a willingness to persist, despite pain, that can lead to significant improvements in mood and quality of life.

People faced with the stress of persistent pain develop ways to cope and deal with their experience. These pain-coping strategies, for example, may include efforts to ignore pain, pace activities, or use calming self-statements (i.e., positive statements about one's ability to cope or manage the situation). In the early 1980s, we developed the Coping Strategies Questionnaire (CSQ) to assess pain-coping strategies (Rosenstiel & Keefe, 1983), and this questionnaire has been used to study coping in people having a variety of painful conditions, such as rheumatoid arthritis, low-back pain, and sickle cell disease. One of the most interesting findings emerging from these and related studies is that individuals who have the same physiological basis for pain often vary substantially in how active they are in coping and how effective they view their own coping efforts. These variations in coping are important in understanding pain and pain-related problems in daily living. For example, in a study of people suffering from degenerative arthritis (osteoarthritis) of the knees, we found that those who reported they were able to use their coping strategies to control and decrease pain and who avoided overly negative thinking when coping (catastrophizing) had significantly lower levels of pain, psychological disability, and physical disability (Keefe et al., 1987). These findings about coping are particularly interesting because they were found even after we controlled for factors that arthritis specialists know can affect pain and disability in this disease (disease severity, obesity).

Findings regarding pain coping have led to the development of systematic training programs to help people enhance the use and perceived effectiveness of their pain-coping skills. We found that one such program was effective in reducing pain and improving psychological functioning in osteoarthritis patients and that improvements in coping abilities over the course of this training were related to improvements in pain, physical disability, and pain-related behaviors (Keefe et al., 1990). Other studies have shown similar benefits of systematic training in pain-coping skills (Compas, Haaga, Keefe, Leitenberg, & Williams, 1998).

People vary not only in how they cope with pain, but also in their beliefs about the cause of pain, its future trajectory, and the degree to which they are to blame for their pain. Studies have shown these beliefs can have an important influence on the pain experience and also influence compliance with medical and psychological efforts to manage pain. Williams and Thorn (1989) found that people who were uncertain about the cause of their pain and viewed it as a mysterious phenomenon had low self-esteem, failed to comply with physical therapy and behavioral therapy, and had poor treatment outcomes.

Self-efficacy, that is, confidence in one's ability to perform certain behaviors to control pain or its effects on one's lifestyle, appears to be particularly important in the pain experience. One study compared osteoarthritis patients who scored high and low on a measure of self-efficacy for control of pain. Compared with patients with low self-efficacy scores, those with high scores not only reported less arthritis pain, but also rated intense heat pain applied to the skin as significantly less unpleasant (Keefe, Lefebvre, Maixner, Salley, & Caldwell, 1997). Can people's sense of self-efficacy be enhanced? Recent studies show that training in pain-coping skills can significantly increase self-efficacy and that improvements in self-efficacy over the course of training are related to short- and long-term outcomes (Keefe et al., 1996; Lorig, Mazonson, & Holman, 1993).

How do psychological factors such as coping or beliefs about pain alter the pain experience? Recent advances in theory and research suggest these factors may influence higher centers in the brain that can actually block or reduce the flow of pain signals from the spinal cord to the brain itself (Melzack & Wall, 1996). Changes in pain coping and beliefs might also produce changes in behavioral processes (e.g., increased exercise, better compliance with medication) and social processes (e.g., improved marital and social interactions) that, in turn, can modify pain.

Social Mechanisms and Management

Although pain is a private experience, it can influence and be influenced by the people around the individual who has pain. Living with someone who has pain can be stressful, and spouses of persons with persistent pain often have problems with emotional distress. A supportive spouse can help a partner having persistent pain cope more adaptively. An overly solicitous spouse, however, may unwittingly increase a person's attention to, and experience of, pain.

Can spouses assist their partners in learning to manage persistent pain? We recently tested the effectiveness of a spouse-assisted pain-coping skills intervention (Keefe et al., 1996). This intervention, delivered to groups of arthritis patients and their spouses, included conventional training in pain-coping skills (e.g., relaxation, pleasant imagery, and learning to avoid overdoing activities by alternating periods of activity and rest). In addition, to supplement and reinforce those skills, it included systematic training in couples skills (e.g., communication skills and role playing how to apply pain-coping skills in challenging situations). Overall, patients in the spouse-assisted training program had the best outcomes, those in a conventional coping-skills program (patients seen on their own without their spouses) had the next best outcomes, and a control group (patients and spouses seen in educational group sessions) had the poorest outcomes.

IMPLICATIONS AND FUTURE DIRECTIONS

The recent advances in pain research that we have discussed have a number of important implications for pain research, assessment, prevention, and treatment, as well as health care policy.

The biopsychosocial model has many strengths, but efforts to apply this model have been limited in several respects. First, pain researchers who have contributed to current knowledge about individual elements of the model often work within their own disciplines and research traditions (e.g., psychologists explore psychological influences on pain). As a result, research designs often do not address how individual elements of the biopsychosocial model interact with each other. If the biopsychosocial model is to realize its potential, future studies must be conducted to demonstrate that explanations of pain based on multiple elements of the model provide a more complete understanding of pain than explanations based on a single element. Second, although the biopsychosocial model emphasizes that responses to pain are learned and develop over time, little is known about the trajectory of these changes. Do changes in biological responses to pain (e.g., plasticity) precede changes in psychological responses, or do changes in psychological functioning (e.g., reductions in self-efficacy) precede and contribute to biological changes? Are there risk factors, either biological or psychosocial, that predispose certain individuals to develop maladaptive pain-related responses more quickly than others? Third, little is known about how the brain processes the multiple sources of biological, psychological, and social information that contribute to the pain experience. Models of pain have evolved over the past 50 years from focusing exclusively on biological factors to giving greater consideration to psychological and sociocultural factors (e.g., Melzack & Wall's, 1965, gate control theory). Recently, Melzack (1996) has proposed a neuromatrix theory of pain that may well represent the next stage in the evolution of pain concepts. This theory maintains that the pain experience is the result of a complex interchange of information from diverse areas of the brain. The major advantage of the neuromatrix theory is that it views the brain as producing an integrated and multidimensional pain experience, rather than as simply responding to competing biological, psychological, and social inputs.

Adequate assessment of pain requires a broad perspective. The emerging evidence clearly suggests that professionals who treat people with pain need to understand how biological, psychological, and social systems can interact. In particular, health care professionals need to be alert to changes in the patients they see because processes that unfold over time can promote pain or help attenuate pain. Early identification of pain-related problems is the key to effective prevention and treatment.

In some cases, persistent pain can be prevented if it is managed aggressively with early medications. Not only can this approach prevent biological changes that can promote pain, but it can also prevent psychological changes (e.g., reductions in self-efficacy, use of coping strategies) and social changes (e.g., isolation, family and work problems) that can follow and maintain persistent pain.

At present, coping-skills training is seen as a specialized intervention reserved for individuals disabled by persistent pain. However, patients who have just begun to experience problems in coping with pain should not be denied access to these treatments. Biopsychosocial approaches to pain management need to be offered in primary care settings where patients are first seen (e.g., the pediatrician or family doctor's office). These treatments may prove to be most effective when delivered early and to a broad range of people. Cost-effective methods for delivering psychosocial pain treatments, such as home-based or telephone-based training in pain-coping skills, are being developed and have shown promise for several kinds of persistent pain (e.g., arthritis pain, headache, and back pain).

One disturbing trend in health care policy is the reduction (and in some cases, denial) of payments for treatment of persistent pain. The human costs entailed by this policy are enormous; individuals who might otherwise be able to return to an active and satisfying lifestyle are left to experience needless suffering and pain. How should health care policy be changed? In addition to providing early, aggressive biomedical treatment, the health care system needs to help people pay for psychosocial pain assessment and treatment in primary care settings. Although this shift in health care coverage might entail some additional short-term costs, these costs would clearly be outweighed by long-term reductions in pain, suffering, and disability in the large population of people who suffer from persistent pain.

Recommended Reading

Coderre, T.J., Katz, J., Vaccarino, A.L., & Melzack, R. (1993). (See References)
Keefe, F.J., & Caldwell, D.S. (1997). Cognitive behavioral control of arthritis pain. *Medical Clinics of North America, 81,* 277–290.
Melzack, R. (1996). (See References)

Acknowledgments—Preparation of this manuscript was supported by grants from the National Institute of Arthritis and Musculoskeletal and Skin Diseases (AR66064, AR42261) and the Fetzer Institute to Francis J. Keefe and by a grant from the American Heart Association, Ohio-West Virginia Affiliate, Columbus, Ohio, to Christopher R. France.

Note

1. Address correspondence to Francis J. Keefe, Health Psychology Program, Department of Psychology, Porter Hall Room 229, Ohio University, Athens, OH 45701.

References

Coderre, T.J., Katz, J., Vaccarino, A.L., & Melzack, R. (1993). Contribution of central neuroplasticity to pathological pain: Review of clinical and experimental evidence. *Pain, 52,* 259–285.
Compas, B.E., Haaga, D.A.F., Keefe, F.J., Leitenberg, H., & Williams, D.A. (1998). A sampling of empirically supported psychological treatments from health psychology: Smoking, chronic pain, cancer, & bulimia nervosa. *Journal of Consulting and Clinical Psychology, 66,* 89–112.
Flor, H., Braun, C., Elbert, T., & Birbaumer, N. (1997). Extensive reorganization of primary somatosensory cortex in chronic back pain patients. *Neuroscience Letters, 224,* 5–8.
Flor, H., Elbert, T., Knecht, S., Wienbruch, C., Pantev, C., Birbaumer, N., Larbig, W., & Taub, E. (1995). Phantom-limb pain as a perceptual correlate of cortical reorganization following arm amputation. *Nature, 375,* 482–484.
Keefe, F.J., Caldwell, D.S., Baucom, D., Salley, A., Robinson, E., Timmons, K., Beaupre, P., Weisberg, J., & Helms, M. (1996). Spouse-assisted coping skills training in the management of osteoarthritis knee pain. *Arthritis Care and Research, 9,* 279–291.
Keefe, F.J., Caldwell, D.S., Queen, K.T., Gil, K.M., Martinez, S., Crisson, J.E., Ogden, W., & Nunley, J. (1987). Pain coping strategies in osteoarthritis patients. *Journal of Consulting and Clinical Psychology, 55,* 208–212.
Keefe, F.J., Caldwell, D.S., Williams, D.A., Gil, K.M., Mitchell, D., Robertson, C., Martinez, S., Nunley, J., Beckham, J.C., Crisson, J.E., & Helms, M. (1990). Pain coping skills training in the management of osteoarthritic knee pain: A comparative study. *Behavior Therapy, 21,* 49–62.
Keefe, F.J., Lefebvre, J.C., Maixner, W., Salley, A.N., & Caldwell, D.S. (1997). Self-efficacy for arthritis pain: Relationship to perception of thermal laboratory pain stimuli. *Arthritis Care and Research, 10,* 177–184.

Lorig, K.R., Mazonson, P.D., & Holman, H.R. (1993). Evidence suggesting that health education for self-management in patients with chronic arthritis has sustained health benefits while reducing health care costs. *Arthritis and Rheumatism, 36,* 439–446.

Melzack, R. (1996). Gate control theory: On the evolution of pain concepts. *Pain Forum, 5,* 128–138.

Melzack, R., & Wall, P.D. (1965). Pain mechanisms; A new theory. *Science, 150,* 971–979.

Melzack, R., & Wall, P.D. (1996). *The challenge of pain.* London: Penguin Books.

Rosenstiel, A.K., & Keefe, F.J. (1983). The use of coping strategies in chronic low back pain patients: Relationship to patient characteristics and current adjustment. *Pain, 17,* 33–44.

Wall, P.D., & Woolf, C.J. (1984). Muscle but not cutaneous C-afferent input produces prolonged increases in the excitability of the flexion reflex in the rat. *Journal of Physiology, 356,* 443–458.

Williams, D.A., & Thorn, B.E. (1989). An empirical assessment of pain beliefs. *Pain, 36,* 351–358.

Woolf, C.J., & Wall, P.D. (1986). Morphine-sensitive and morphine-insensitive actions of C-fiber input on the rat spinal cord. *Neuroscience Letters, 64,* 221–225.

Are Pets a Healthy Pleasure?
The Influence of Pets on Blood Pressure

Karen Allen[1]

Department of Oral Diagnostic Sciences, School of Dental Medicine, State University of New York at Buffalo, Buffalo, New York

Abstract

Pet owners often describe their pets as important and cherished family members who offer solace in times of stress. This article considers evidence suggesting that pets influence human blood pressure. Studies on this topic extend current research testing the hypothesis that having other people around in stressful times can buffer the negative consequences of stress. The existing data suggest that people perceive pets as important, supportive parts of their lives and that the presence of a pet is associated with significant cardiovascular benefits, among both people with normal blood pressure and those with high blood pressure. Studies about pets and blood pressure have examined both naturally occurring and randomly assigned pet ownership but are limited by their focus on responses to short-term, acute stress. Future prospective studies should explore the influence of pets on people at risk for cardiovascular disease and also consider explanatory mechanisms for the pet effect.

Keywords

pets; social support; blood pressure; stress

In recent years the popular media have publicized widely the idea of the "healing power of pets." Ubiquitous advertisements featuring winsome puppies and kittens suggest that having a pet can cure everything from loneliness and alienation to hypertension and heart disease. The phrase "pets lower your blood pressure" is stated as a commonly known fact and appears in television commercials and even in publicity for nursing homes and hospitals. In this article, I discuss the existing scientific evidence about the influence of pets on their owners' blood pressure, along with the limitations of the research in this area.

Today in the United States, there are more than 68 million pet dogs and at least 75 million pet cats. Considering the expense (Americans spend nearly $30 billion annually on their pets) and the responsibility a pet adds to a person's life, it is reasonable to question why people have pets. According to several nationwide surveys, about 90% of pet owners describe their pets as important, cherished family members. Further, they say that pets make them feel calm, happy, and able to handle stress in their lives. Inspired by the intuitive feelings of pet owners, the studies I summarize here have tested the ability of pets to diminish stress responses, investigating this possibility within the theoretical framework of ongoing research about social support and cardiovascular health.

BACKGROUND

Perhaps the most frequently cited publications about pets and health are two reports indicating that pet ownership is a significant predictor of 1-year survival after a heart attack (Friedmann, Katcher, Lynch, & Thomas, 1980; Friedmann & Thomas, 1995). Specifically, Friedmann and her colleagues showed that high social support and pet ownership were associated with better survival after heart attack, and that these effects were independent of the physiological severity of the heart attack, demographic characteristics of the patient, and psychosocial factors. This finding aroused curiosity among researchers in several fields and engendered considerable research about people and pets. This research has demonstrated, for example, that compared with their counterparts without pets, elderly people with pets appear to be buffered from the impact of stressful life events and make fewer visits to physicians (Siegel, 1990). In addition, among people with AIDS, pet owners have a lower incidence of depression than do people without pets (Siegel, Angulo, Detels, Wesch, & Mullen, 1999). Just talking to pets, compared with talking to people, is associated with lower cardiovascular responses (Lynch, 1985), and the presence of pets reduces blood pressure of children reading aloud (Friedmann, Katcher, Thomas, Lynch, & Messent, 1983). Pet ownership also has been shown to be associated with lower lipid levels and reduced levels of other cardiovascular risk factors (Anderson, Reid, & Jennings, 1992).

THEORETICAL FRAMEWORK

Given that pet owners readily describe their dogs and cats as friends, studying the cardiovascular influence of pets within the framework of existing research on social support and blood pressure is a logical choice. Typically in such research, investigators assess cardiovascular measures while study participants experience various psychological stressors (e.g., performing mental arithmetic or giving a speech) and compare the participants' cardiovascular changes in different social environments. Numerous laboratory and community-based studies have focused on the role of supportive friends and friendly strangers in buffering responses to stress. Researchers who have reviewed this literature (Lepore, 1998; Uchino, Cacioppo, & Kiecolt-Glaser, 1996) have concluded that when friends are perceived as totally nonjudgmental, they can indeed buffer stress responses. In this literature, of course, the "others" who buffer stress are other people. This body of research is based on the idea that individuals who experience pronounced, frequent, or enduring blood pressure and heart rate responses to stress may be at risk for the development of heart disease (Gullette et al., 1997).

BLOOD PRESSURE AND PETS: SOME RESEARCH FINDINGS

The main research question addressed in studies about pets and social support is the degree to which a pet can ameliorate a person's response to stress. Such studies mirror the standard research I have just cited, with the exception that they take place in participants' homes rather than laboratories. The investigators who have conducted these studies consider an emotional bond between the person and animal to be important (just as it is between human friends), so the animals used always belong to the participants.

Beginning with a desire to learn more about the potential role of pets in providing social support, my colleagues and I first conducted a study about women, measuring their blood pressure when they performed mental arithmetic while alone or in the presence of their best (female) friends or their dogs (Allen, Blascovich, Tomaka, & Kelsey, 1991). Although we hypothesized that dogs would calm their owners to the same degree as their human friends, we found that participants perceived their friends as judgmental, but their dogs as totally friendly. That is, the friends produced large increases in blood pressure (relative to the control condition in which the women were alone), whereas the dogs did not.

Inspired to learn more about social factors and blood pressure, we went on to consider the differential effects of the presence of friends, spouses, and pet cats and dogs (Allen, Blascovich, & Mendes, 2002). Marriage involves the closest of relationships, and we reasoned that a person's soul mate would be perceived positively and have a calming effect. We wondered about the relative influence of a pet. Once again, however, people experiencing a stressor in the presence of other people (however supportive and friendly they tried to appear) exhibited dramatically large increases in blood pressure. For example, the blood pressure of people asked to work on mental arithmetic in the presence of their spouses increased on average from 120/80 to 155/100. In contrast, when our participants had only their pets present, their blood pressure increased slightly, to 125/83. From both clinical and research perspectives, these are significant differences that warrant consideration and explanation.

EXPLAINING THE PET EFFECT

One explanation might be that the pets served merely as an entertaining distraction, eliminating the source of stress because people gave up on the difficult arithmetic task. We found, however, that the opposite had happened. That is, study participants did not abandon the task, but actually performed better and faster when their pets were present than when their spouses were present. It also appears that pets can have a social facilitation effect; that is, perhaps pets allow people to relax and bring out the best in their owners, much as a cheering crowd helps an athlete perform well.

It is also possible that the buffering effect of social support depends on the relationship between the type of support needed (in the case of a mental arithmetic task, someone who thinks you are wonderful even if you cannot do it!) and the ability of the available supporters to fill that need. From this perspective, it appears that when people need complete positive regard, pets clearly are a preferred source of social support.

A valid criticism of the studies I have summarized is that it is possible that the pets had no effect at all and that people who choose to acquire pets are healthier than those who choose not to have a pet; that is, there might be some characteristic of pet owners that makes it unlikely they will ever experience large cardiovascular responses to stress. Clearly, the only way to determine the validity of this criticism is to conduct studies in which some participants are randomly selected to own pets and the others remain non-pet owners.

A CLINICAL RANDOMIZED TRIAL: PET ADOPTION

To test if a pet effect would occur among people who had not acquired pets on their own, we conducted a study in which half the participants were randomly selected to adopt a pet cat or dog from an animal shelter (Allen, Shykoff, & Izzo, 2001). The study participants were all stockbrokers who lived alone and described their work as extremely stressful. None had owned pets for at least the previous 5 years. In addition, they all had high blood pressure (greater than 160/100) and were scheduled to begin drug therapy with Lisinopril (part of a class of drugs called angiotensin converting enzyme inhibitors). Although Lisinopril is quite successful in reducing resting blood pressure, previous studies had demonstrated that it is not capable of blunting responses to stress. In this experiment, then, it was possible to consider two important issues: (a) the influence of random assignment to pet ownership and (b) the degree to which the combination of a pet and Lisinopril may produce effects different from those derived from drug therapy alone.

Results of the study provide strong evidence for the role of pets in providing social support. As predicted, Lisinopril lowered the resting blood pressure of all participants. While under stress, however, the individuals who acquired pets had blood pressure increases that were less than half the increases of their counterparts without pets. Interestingly, we also found that people who reported the fewest social contacts and friends benefited the most from the companionship of their pets. In addition, we demonstrated that resting blood pressure and blood pressure reactions to stress are influenced by independent mechanisms. That is, resting blood pressure can be influenced by a drug, but adding a pet to the social environment can alter stress responses.

LIMITATIONS AND FUTURE DIRECTIONS

Although existing research about pets and health demonstrates a supportive role for pets, there are also several important limitations to consider. For example, the studies of response to acute stress have been conducted independently from the epidemiological research that has followed people after heart attack. Consequently, although research indicates that pets can reduce blood pressure responses to short-term stress among people with normal and high blood pressure, it remains to be determined if such responses contribute to survival among individuals who have heart attacks, or if they could be factors that help prevent heart attack. In addition, most research about pets and blood pressure has not explored how explanatory mechanisms may be influenced by other physiological factors, such as endocrine function. One recent study provides an example of just such an innovative approach and demonstrates an association between a pet's influence on blood pressure responses to stress and the endocrine hormone oxytocin, which is associated with human attachment and bonding (Odendaal, 2000). In this study, as blood pressure decreased, levels of oxytocin increased, suggesting a relationship between social affiliation and blood pressure responses to stress.

Another shortcoming of the existing research is that it addresses only potentially positive physiological responses to having a pet. Because most researchers in this area are pet enthusiasts, experiments have not been designed to examine how the presence of pets may add stress to the lives of some people. Similarly, researchers do not know the degree to which the strong bonds people build with their pets have physiological consequences when their pets die. In addition, little is known about the potential benefits of species other than cats and dogs. Finally, additional research needs to focus on the degree to which health benefits from the presence of a pet may be related to personal, cultural, and demographic characteristics.

CONCLUSIONS

Several epidemiological and experimental studies have demonstrated that having a pet cat or dog can have significant cardiovascular benefits. Although the idea that a pet serves as social support may appear peculiar to some people, pet owners talk to and confide in their pets and describe them as important friends. Because pets, unlike human friends, are perceived as nonjudgmental, they are ideal candidates for psychological interventions aimed at increasing individuals' social support. An important consideration, however, is that media reports of the ability of pets to lower blood pressure are often highly inflated and misrepresent actual research. Although pets can be an important adjunct to drug therapy, a person with high blood pressure should never consider a pet as a replacement for a prescribed medication. So, although a pet can enhance a person's ability to handle stress, it is not accurate to say simply that "pets lower blood pressure."

In conclusion, existing evidence about how pets influence people's blood pressure suggests that for people who enjoy animals, and especially for those with few social contacts, pets can be a healthy pleasure.

Recommended Reading

Allen, K., Shykoff, B.E., & Izzo, J.L., Jr. (2001). (See References)
Fine, A.H. (2000). *Handbook on animal-assisted therapy.* San Diego, CA: Academic Press.
Friedmann, E., & Thomas, S.A. (1995). (See References)
Wilson, C.C., & Turner, D.C. (1998). *Companion animals in human health.* Thousand Oaks, CA: Sage Publications.

Note

1. Address correspondence to Karen Allen, Department of Oral Diagnostic Sciences, School of Dental Medicine, 355 Squire Hall, State University of New York at Buffalo, Buffalo, NY 14214; e-mail: kmallen@acsu.buffalo.edu.

References

Allen, K., Blascovich, J., & Mendes, W.B. (2002). Cardiovascular reactivity and the presence of pets, friends, and spouses: The truth about cats and dogs. *Psychosomatic Medicine, 64,* 727–739.
Allen, K., Blascovich, J., Tomaka, J., & Kelsey, R.M. (1991). Presence of human friends and pet dogs as moderators of autonomic responses to stress in women. *Journal of Personality and Social Psychology, 61,* 582–589.

Allen, K., Shykoff, B.E., & Izzo, J.L., Jr. (2001). Pet ownership, but not ACE inhibitor therapy, blunts home blood pressure responses to mental stress. *Hypertension, 38*, 815–820.

Anderson, W.P., Reid, C.M., & Jennings, G.L. (1992). Pet ownership and risk factors for cardio-vascular disease. *Medical Journal of Australia, 157*, 298–301.

Friedmann, E., Katcher, A.H., Lynch, J.J., & Thomas, S.A. (1980). Animal companions and one-year survival after discharge from a coronary care unit. *Public Health Reports, 95*, 307–312.

Friedmann, E., Katcher, A.H., Thomas, S.A., Lynch, J.J., & Messent, P.R. (1983). Social interaction and blood pressure: Influence of companion animals. *Journal of Nervous and Mental Disease, 171*, 461–465.

Friedmann, E., & Thomas, S.A. (1995). Pet ownership, social support, and one-year survival after acute myocardial infarction in the Cardiac Arrhythmia Suppression Trial (CAST). *American Journal of Cardiology, 76*, 1213–1217.

Gullette, E.C., Blumenthal, J.A., Babyak, M., Jiang, W., Waugh, R.A., Frid, D.J., O'Connor, C.M., Morris, J.J., & Krantz, D.S. (1997). Effects of mental stress on myocardial ischemia during daily life. *Journal of the American Medical Association, 277*, 1521–1526.

Lepore, S.J. (1998). Problems and prospects for the social support reactivity hypothesis. *Annals of Behavioral Medicine, 20*, 257–269.

Lynch, J.J. (1985). *The language of the heart.* New York: Basic Books.

Odendaal, J.S. (2000). Animal-assisted therapy: Magic or medicine? *Journal of Psychosomatic Research, 49*, 275–280.

Siegel, J.M. (1990). Stressful life events and use of physician services among the elderly: The moderating role of pet ownership. *Journal of Personality and Social Psychology, 58*, 1081–1086.

Siegel, J.M., Angulo, F.J., Detels, R., Wesch, J., & Mullen, A. (1999). AIDS diagnosis and depression in the multicenter AIDS cohort study: The ameliorating impact of pet ownership. *AIDS Care, 11*, 157–169.

Uchino, B., Cacioppo, J.T., & Kiecolt-Glaser, J.K. (1996). The relationship between social support and physiological processes: A review with emphasis on underlying mechanisms and implications for health. *Psychological Bulletin, 119*, 488–531.

Critical Thinking Questions

1. Lewis-Claar and Blumenthal show that psychosocial interventions improve quality of life, but do not bolster disease vulnerability or prolong patient survival. With these data in mind, what role is there for psychosocial interventions in the medical care of patients with chronic illness? Should these interventions be routinely delivered to patients, even if they don't influence the course of illness? If so, who should pay for these services? In an era of spiraling medical costs and tight budgets, can we expect insurers to pay, or should patients have to cover this expense themselves?

2. How would you integrate Christensen's patient by treatment approach, Schwarzer's social-cognitive model, and Nell's evolutionary perspective into an overall model of health practices?

3. Most of the articles in this section outline interventions that reduce stress or improve behavior. Given the readings you have done throughout this book, are there other psychosocial characteristics that you would attempt to manipulate in intervention studies and, if so, what are they and why?

4. Drawing on the social-cognitive model presented by Schwarzer, outline an intervention you would use to reduce cigarette smoking and sedentary behavior. What topics would you cover? What strategies would you use to get a person to change his/her behavior?

5. Interventions that can be delivered at higher-levels of organization—that is, to a workplace or an entire community—are likely to have a more profound impact on public health than one-on-one treatments. How can we transform Nell's ideas into a community-level intervention that could diminish risk-taking behavior in young men? What sorts of media could we use to deliver such an intervention, and what kinds of messages would we want to get across to the audience? Lastly, how would you go about evaluating the efficacy of such an intervention?